T0211836

# Communications in Computer and Information Science     1111

*Commenced Publication in 2007*
Founding and Former Series Editors:
Phoebe Chen, Alfredo Cuzzocrea, Xiaoyong Du, Orhun Kara, Ting Liu,
Krishna M. Sivalingam, Dominik Ślęzak, Takashi Washio, Xiaokang Yang,
and Junsong Yuan

More information about this series at http://www.springer.com/series/7899

Sokratis Katsikas · Vasilios Zorkadis (Eds.)

# E-Democracy – Safeguarding Democracy and Human Rights in the Digital Age

8th International Conference, e-Democracy 2019
Athens, Greece, December 12–13, 2019
Proceedings

 Springer

*Editors*
Sokratis Katsikas (iD)
Open University of Cyprus
Nicosia, Cyprus

Norwegian University
of Science and Technology
Gjøvik, Norway

Vasilios Zorkadis (iD)
Hellenic Data Protection Authority
Athens, Greece

ISSN 1865-0929         ISSN 1865-0937   (electronic)
Communications in Computer and Information Science
ISBN 978-3-030-37544-7         ISBN 978-3-030-37545-4   (eBook)
https://doi.org/10.1007/978-3-030-37545-4

This Springer imprint is published by the registered company Springer Nature Switzerland AG
The registered company address is: Gewerbestrasse 11, 6330 Cham, Switzerland

# Preface

This volume contains the papers presented at e-Democracy 2019: the 8th e-Democracy International Conference on Safeguarding Democracy and Human Rights in the Digital Age, held during December 12–13, 2019, in Athens, Greece. The conference was organized by the Scientific Council for the Information Society, in co-operation with the Hellenic Data Protection Authority. It was intended, as in previous occasions, to provide a forum for presenting and debating the latest developments in the field, from a technical, political, legal, and regulatory point of view. The conference continues from previous events that have always been held in Athens, the cradle of democracy, initially every three years starting in 2003 and every two years since 2009.

The ever-evolving digital age is becoming more intelligent and the future internet is shaping up. Technologies supporting the digital transformation, such as artificial intelligence, the Internet of Things, blockchain technologies, and robotics are developing in unprecedented rhythms. A new digital environment emerges, promising a lot, but also raising concerns about democracy itself and individual rights and freedoms.

The relatively recent Cambridge Analytica scandal has profoundly influenced public opinion and – as written by many – has changed the world and the way citizens see their digital future. The effects of fake news and targeted political campaigns enabled by data misuse on democratic processes raise serious concerns. There are also fears of affecting the outcome of a democratic election itself. Moreover, the rapid development of technologies supporting the digital transformation, which is largely driven by significant economic benefits, raises concerns about the impact on privacy and, in general, on individual rights and freedoms. The questions and the focus of this occasion of the conference were:

- How can we safeguard our democracy against such threats?
- How can we create an intelligent digital world while ensuring individual rights and freedoms?
- Will our future digital world be privacy-friendly and secure to withstand attacks and malicious activities?
- Which ethical principles should govern the evolution of our digital future?
- Will this fast moving and intelligent digital world be trustworthy and embraced by the citizens?

The conference attracted 27 high quality submissions. Each submission was reviewed by at least 2, and on the average 2.8, Program Committee members. The review process resulted in accepting 15 papers to be included in the conference proceedings.

e-Democracy 2019 brought together academic researchers, industry developers, and policy makers. We thank the attendees for coming to Athens to participate and debate the new emerging advances in the field of e-Democracy.

We would like to express our thanks to all those who assisted us in organizing the event and putting together the program. We are very grateful to the Program Committee members for their timely and rigorous reviews of the papers. Thanks are also due to the Organizing Committee for the event. Last but by no means least, we would like to thank all the authors who submitted their work to the conference and contributed to an interesting set of conference proceedings.

December 2019                                          Sokratis Katsikas
                                                       Vasilios Zorkadis

# Organization

## Program Committee

| | |
|---|---|
| Isaac Agudo | University of Malaga, Spain |
| Evgenia Alexandropoulou | The University of Macedonia, Greece |
| Leonidas Anthopoulos | University of Applied Science (TEI) of Larissa, Greece |
| Maria Bottis | Ionian University, Greece |
| Christos Bouras | University of Patras, Greece |
| Athena Bourka | ENISA, Greece |
| David Chadwick | University of Kent, UK |
| Nathan Clarke | University of Plymouth, UK |
| Sabrina De Capitani di Vimercati | Universita' degli Studi di Milano, Italy |
| Prokopios Drogkaris | ENISA, Greece |
| Nicola Fabiano | Studio Legale Fabiano, Italy |
| Carmen Fernández-Gago | University of Malaga, Spain |
| Steven Furnell | University of Plymouth, UK |
| Jürgen Fuß | University of Applied Sciences Upper Austria, Austria |
| Dimitris Geneiatakis | Joint Research Centre, European Commission, Italy |
| Christos Georgiadis | The University of Macedonia, Greece |
| Dimitris Gouscos | University of Athens, Greece |
| Stefanos Gritzalis | University of Piraeus, Greece |
| Mp Gupta | Indian Institute of Technology Delhi, India |
| Christos Kalloniatis | University of the Aegean, Greece |
| Ioanna Kantzavelou | University of West Attica, Greece |
| Zoe Kardasiadou | European Data Protection Board, Belgium |
| Maria Karyda | University of the Aegean, Greece |
| Sokratis Katsikas | Norwegian University of Science and Technology, Norway, and Open University of Cyprus, Cyprus |
| Eleni Kosta | Tilburg University, The Netherlands |
| Panayiotis Kotzanikolaou | University of Piraeus, Greece |
| Stewart Kowalski | Norwegian University of Science and Technology, Norway |
| Costas Lambrinoudakis | University of Piraeus, Greece |
| Georgios Lappas | Technological Educational Institute of Western Macedonia, Greece |
| Konstantinos Limniotis | Hellenic Data Protection Authority, Greece |
| Georgios Lioudakis | ICT abovo P.C., Greece |
| George Loukas | University of Greenwich, UK |
| Euripidis Loukis | University of the Aegean, Greece |

| Vojtech Merunka | Czech Technical University in Prague and Czech University of Life Sciences in Prague, Czech Republic |
|---|---|
| Martin Molhanec | Czech Technical University in Prague, Czech Republic |
| Haralambos Mouratidis | University of Brighton, UK |
| Maria Ntaliani | Agricultural University of Athens, Greece |
| Christoforos Ntantogian | University of Piraeus, Greece |
| Martin Olivier | University of Pretoria, South Africa |
| Rolf Oppliger | eSECURITY Technologies, Switzerland |
| Grammati Pantziou | University of West Attica, Greece |
| Andreas Pashalidis | BSI, Germany |
| Charalampos Patrikakis | University of West Attica, Greece |
| Elias Pimenidis | University of the West of England, UK |
| Panagiotis Rizomiliotis | Harokopio University of Athens, Greece |
| Evangelos Sakkopoulos | University of Piraeus, Greece |
| Pierangela Samarati | Universita' degli Studi di Milano, Italy |
| Yucel Saygin | Sabanci University, Turkey |
| Mak Sharma | Birmingham City University, UK |
| Alexander B. Sideridis | Agricultural University of Athens, Greece |
| Antonis Stasis | Hellenic Ministry of Interior and Administrative Reconstruction, Greece |
| Stephanie Teufel | University of Fribourg, Switzerland |
| Stergios Tsiafoulis | Hellenic Ministry of Administrative Reconstruction, Greece |
| Aggeliki Tsohou | Ionian University, Greece |
| Vassilios Verykios | Hellenic Open University, Greece |
| Vasileios Vlachos | University of Thessaly, Greece |
| Edgar Weippl | SBA Research, Austria |
| Christos Xenakis | University of Piraeus, Greece |
| Constantine Yialouris | Agricultural University of Athens, Greece |
| Thomas Zacharias | The University of Edinburgh, UK |
| Vasilios Zorkadis | Hellenic Data Protection Authority, Greece |

## Additional Reviewers

Athanasiadis, Elias
Bolgouras, Vaios
Diamantopoulou, Vasiliki
Katsadouros, Evaggelos
Mavriki, Paola Viola
Mohammadi, Farnaz
Toumanidis, Lazaros
Vemou, Konstantina

# Contents

## Online Social Networks and "Fake News"

# Privacy and Data Protection

# Big Data Analytics: From Threatening Privacy to Challenging Democracy

Paola Mavriki$^{(\boxtimes)}$ and Maria Karyda$^{(\boxtimes)}$

Department of Information and Communication Systems Engineering,
University of the Aegean, 83200 Karlovassi, Samos, Greece
{pmavriki,mka}@aegean.gr

**Abstract.** The vast amount of accumulated information and the technologies that store, process and disseminate it are producing deep changes in society. The amount of data generated by Internet users poses great opportunities and significant challenges for political scientists. Having a positive effect in many fields, business intelligence and analytics tools are used increasingly for political purposes. Pervasive digital tracking and profiling, in combination with personalization, have become a powerful toolset for systematically influencing user behaviour. When used in political campaigns or in other efforts to shape public policy, privacy issues intertwine with electoral outcomes. The practice of targeting voters with personalized messages adapted to their personality and political views, has already raised debates about political manipulation; however, studies focusing on privacy are still scarce. Focusing on the democracy aspects and identifying the threats to privacy stemming from the use of big data technologies for political purposes, this paper identifies long-term privacy implications which may undermine fundamental features of democracy such as fair elections and political equality of all citizens. Furthermore, this paper argues that big data analytics raises the need to develop alternative narratives to the concept of privacy.

**Keywords:** Big data analytics · Democracy · Privacy

## 1 Introduction

Today information is being produced at an unprecedented rate. People express their feelings on Facebook accounts, tweet opinions, call friends on cell phones, post photographs on Instagram and log locations with GPS on phones [28]. Moreover, businesses, administrations, industrial sectors, scientific research are continuously generating vast amounts of structured or unstructured textual data and multimedia content on various platforms such as social media sites, sensors networks, machine to machine communication etc. [66].

Big data's potential value is unlocked when it is processed in meaningful insights and leveraged to drive decision making [24]. Analytics is a term that refers to techniques used to analyze and acquire intelligence from big data, the process of researching massive amounts of complex data in order to reveal hidden patterns or identify secret correlations [24, 32]. Big data analytics attracts the attention of

© Springer Nature Switzerland AG 2020
S. Katsikas and V. Zorkadis (Eds.): e-Democracy 2019, CCIS 1111, pp. 3–17, 2020.
https://doi.org/10.1007/978-3-030-37545-4_1

academia, industry and governments around the world [35] transforming the way businesses and organizations work, having a positive effect in many fields.

The vast amount of information and the technologies that store, process and disseminate it are producing deep changes in society. Data has become a social and political issue not only because it concerns anyone who is connected to the Internet but also because it reconfigures relationships between states and citizens. There has never been a state, kingdom, government, or corporation in history 'that has had command over such granular, immediate, varied, and detailed data about subjects and objects that concern them' [63].

Business intelligence and analytics tools are used for opinion mining, social network analysis, for supporting online political participation, e-democracy etc. [9]. In recent years, there has been a rising interest not just in campaign messages, traditional news coverage or online attention, but also in understanding the relationship among the three [57]. Modern social media provides a unique technological means to extend the reach of political communication by candidates and parties. During the 2014 European elections for example, new media technologies became integral parts of electoral campaigning providing new avenues for communication between candidates and citizens [56].

On one hand Internet is considered as promoting innovation, freedom, egalitarianism, openness and facilitating new opportunities for citizen deliberation and direct decision-making. On the other hand though, individuals are constantly being monitored while consuming products, services and content [82] while contemporary ubiquitous systems collect massive amounts of information about them accumulating a large amount of personal information [75]. The current round of disputes over privacy are fueled by data science and several authors argue for a new approach to privacy research and practical design focused on the development of conceptual analytics that facilitate dissecting privacy's multiple uses across multiple contexts [50]. The study on big data privacy is still at a very early stage [81] and at the moment there is not a clear view of the best strategies to protect privacy in big data [70].

Pervasive digital tracking and profiling, in combination with personalization, advanced customer management technologies, and testing, have become a powerful toolset for systematically influencing behaviour. In previous work [45] we argue that the use of personalization tools in the political area results beside the implications with direct impact on individuals, long term implications related to society such as manipulation of the results in ways that might impact financially, socially or politically. When used in political campaigns or in other efforts to shape public policy, big data analytics may undermine democracy at large and there is a need to be examined as a political process involving questions of power, transparency and surveillance [76]. Furthermore, the practice of targeting voters with personalized messages adapted to their personality and political views on certain issues has already raised debates about the potential for political manipulation [11]. However, studies focusing on related privacy issues are still scarce. It seems that privacy issues intertwine with electoral outcomes, but research is needed to clarify the mechanisms of these processes. There is a need to improve existing privacy protection methods to meet the unprecedented requirements of big data and new privacy frameworks and mechanisms are highly expected [81]. Furthermore, there is need 'to rethink the relations between media institutions, society, and democracy in ways that are more explicit about the profound, if indirect, consequences of the advertising industries' self-transformation for the whole public media environment' [14].

This paper addresses this gap, investigating privacy threats stemming from the use of big data for political purposes. Highlighting the democratic value of privacy and focusing on the European political landscape, this paper explores the long-term implications of privacy threats on democracy.

The remaining paper is structured as follows: the next Section analyses the European digital political landscape related literature. Section 3 examines the political value of big data and the democratic value of privacy while Sect. 4 identifies new privacy threats stemming from big data analysis. Section 5 investigates the long-term implications of the new privacy threats for society and democracy. The paper concludes in Sect. 6 with a discussion on open issues and further research.

## 2 Background: The Professionalization of Political Communication in European Democracies

Prompted among others by the transformations of the media landscape, election campaigning has moved through a series of phases [42]. The key element of the latest phase is the adoption of new technologies which allow a more targeted approach to voter contact [25].

Recent years have seen a growing interest in the role of data in election campaigns [25, 40, 76]. Authors suggest that data are now shaping the way campaigners communicate with voters facilitating the efficient allocation of scarce resources [2]. The 2008 and 2012 Obama campaign created a wave of interest in how communications technologies were reshaping elections [25, 36]. In the case of the 2016 campaign, social media may have been the most visible digital element, but there was also a much larger digital campaign infrastructure [36].

Evidence on data-driven campaigns are coming mainly from the US. Literature in the political area, however, discusses the continuity between emerging data-driven campaigning and older forms of electoral political communication: authors [2, 7], suggest that the European digital campaigning is following the American example. Despite the differences between the European countries and US, there are according to Lisi in [43], common trends changing the nature and character of political campaigns communication in contemporary western democracies. One of these trends refers to the adoption of marketing techniques such as voters' segmentation and targeting using different combinations of communication tools. Many authors [31, 43, 53, 59] refer to this shift through terms such as 'postmodern', 'Americanized', 'hi-tech' campaigns. Whichever term they are using though, they address among others the intensive use of new ICTs and a marketing-oriented strategy of campaigns [43].

In comparison to the US, European political parties have far less access to the types of data required to target voters and much stronger data protection laws. In spite of this there are several examples proving the professionalization of campaigns in Europe and the integration of the Internet in the political communication [2]. In the 2007 Finnish general election for instance, political marketing procedures have been used for targeting young voters [41]. Also, in the 2003, 2006, 2010 and 2012 Catalan elections technological advances were used by the political parties [60]. In addition, related to the 2014 election for the European Parliament, many political parties have made the new media technologies, especially social networking sites and micro-blogs an integral parts of their electoral campaigning [56]. Moreover, related to the 2015 General elections in the UK, conservatives seem to have adopted the US model of microtargeting while Labour has engaged in data-driven campaigning calling a considerable number of activists through segment-based targeting [2]. Even more, authors [27, 83] argue that one of the principal components to Trump's digital campaign operation, the microtargeting firm Cambridge Analytica had worked on the Brexit campaign as well.

Concluding, research evidence shows that parties, politicians, political movements in Europe are using increasingly the digital environment for communicating they political messages. As political campaigners need to use the most effective advertising techniques available, they have begun to use data-driven marketing approaches as well. According to their level of professionalism and the local conditions [2] political parties, organizations, politicians etc. may use big data analysis seeking to influence individuals or groups politically. Through new technologies meaningless big data may acquire a political value while at the same time privacy laws and restrictions may be potentially overpassed challenging the related to democracy features of privacy, issues which the paper explores in the next section.

## 3 The Political Value of Big Data and the Democratic Value of Privacy

As already mentioned, access to consumer data is more restrictive in Europe than in the US. Yet, there may be ways to approach the big data model through other methods [18]. The unprecedented availability of social media data for example, provides insights on a range of phenomena and influence processes from personality traits to political behaviors and from public opinion to relationship formation [34, 65]. Social media data is particularly valuable to political scientists because it provides information about peoples' opinions regarding politics, their choices of information sources, the nature of their associations, and their strategic choices in specific political situations [51].

Through conducting social media analytics, governments and political parties may gain valuable insights such as those which will allow them to derive useful strategies for the next period of elections [72]. Some of the most fertile fields of research involve analyses of Twitter, Facebook, and social media postings. Identifying patterns of conduct or activities out of unconsciously left (meta)data on social network sites increasingly serves to predict future behavior. Information scientists claim that Twitter is ready to become "a substitute and supplement for traditional polling" [18, 19].

In addition, big data technology also has the potential to help political science by scaling up conventional approaches to data collection. One approach to scaling up expensive, small scale procedures (e.g. surveys, experiments) is to use statistical learning techniques to replicate human judgment and behaviors. Thus, a small amount of human-generated data may be turned in a large amount. Another approach is to design the data generation task so that people provide data at much lower cost, even for free, through crowd sourcing for example [49].

Privacy has been defined in many ways over the last few hundred years while the meaning of it has been much disputed throughout its history in response to new technological capabilities and social configurations [50]. For instance, Westin's [78] concept explains how people protect themselves by temporarily limiting access of others to themselves. Altman's [1] analysis of privacy focuses on individual and group privacy and behavior operating as a coherent system. Petronio's [58] Communication Privacy Management concept addresses privacy in the digital environment by understanding interpersonal computer mediated communication, such as blogging and social networking.

Depending on its political philosophy, every society sets a distinctive balance between the private sphere and the public order. In broad terms, privacy norms are set in two alternative societal models, in authoritarian and democratic societies. Democracies value and institutionalize privacy while at the same time, officials have to engage in surveillance of properly identified antisocial activity to control illegal or violent acts [79]. For Westin [78], at the sociopolitical level, in political democracies, 'privacy provides opportunities for political expression and criticism, political choice, and freedom from unreasonable police interference; it provides opportunities for people and organizations to prepare and discuss matters "in private"; it allows non-political participation in family, religion, and in other forms of association'. For Janssen and van den Hoven in [33], privacy is a fundament of democracy, because without privacy people might exercise power to influence others. According to Voice in [77], privacy also allows us to form our political, democratic selves. The same way an individual reveal or hide information in order to manage personal and social relations, the individual hide and reveal information to build its political self. Moreover, the ideal of full deliberative democracy is that citizens encounter one another as political equals and have respect for each other opinions. A right to privacy is essential to the vision of full deliberative democracy, because it enables the existence of a distinct political self. The right to shelter information about oneself makes authentic democratic citizenship possible. 'We are therefore free to be citizens only in so far as we are also free to fashion our political selves, and this freedom rests on a robust right to privacy.'

Furthermore, as Regan claims in [62], privacy is essential to the maintenance of democracy because it ensures that citizens are able to hold elected governments to account and place limits on the expansion of the state. Privacy's public value also stems from its importance to the exercise of political rights. Individuals need to be free to share those thoughts with others without being subject to the watchful, possibly critical, eye of the state [26].

After years of consultation and debate, the privacy principles now form the basis of numerous countries' personal data or information privacy laws, as well as the organizing framework for much institutional and professional work across the public and private sectors [50]. Today, the salient theoretical justification for information privacy (especially in Europe) is the theory of control [82] but the information privacy landscape is rapidly evolving and the digital age brings with it novel forms of data flow. As a result, the accepted and established so far privacy principles are getting less useful.

Concluding, big data analytics is changing how data is collected, stored, shared, analyzed, and disseminated potentially bypassing privacy laws and restrictions. Advanced and sophisticated technologies make possible the political exploitation of users' personal data challenging the related to democracy aspects of privacy raising this way new types of threats which we examine next.

## 4   Privacy Harms Stemming from the Use of Big Data

The recent revelations about Cambridge Analytica [27] and the breach that allowed the harvesting of the personal information of millions of Facebook users it pushed once again the power of platforms and privacy protection, along with their political implications, onto front pages around the world [4].

The difficulty with big data analysis is that privacy breaches are hard to make specific while misdiagnosing a problem makes it hard to fix [8]. According to Calo in [8], 'privacy harm is conceptualized, if at all, as the negative consequence of a privacy violation. ... a privacy harm must be "cognizable," "actual," "specific," "material," "fundamental," or "special" before a court will consider awarding compensation'. But there are harms without privacy violations involved such as unwelcome mental state such as anxiety, embarrassment, fear that stem from the belief that one is being watched or monitored. Furthermore, there is difficult to convincingly arguing today that individuals must be provided with a right to control their personal data. According to Zarsky in [82], 'recognizing and enforcing the control claim calls for creating normative rights in a society in which a broad majority of the population signal their disinterest in control'. Moreover, privacy harms need not occur in the moment; many feelings of violation have a delayed effect ...a 'hidden microphone, for instance—will be backward looking insofar as the offending observation has already ended at the time of discovery (or because of it)' [8].

We have underlined in the previous section the essential role of privacy in preserving freedom and democracy. Focusing on this aspect, the "object" of privacy in this case, seeks to secure a zone of freedom and action for citizens. Privacy as a zone of freedom is justified because it is intrinsic to human dignity, or instrumental for realizing self-development. The "subject" of privacy as agents whom privacy protects might be a single individual, a distinctive social class (e.g. young Greeks or citizens of Athens) or a distinctive social role (e.g. voters). The "actions" against privacy refer to actions which constitute or initiate privacy harms [8, 50].

One of the most debated category of privacy threats stemming from big data analysis is related to surveillance. Nowadays, in the public arena, people have become targets of surveillance at just about every turn of their lives [55]. Social network data may be used by campaigns to create profiles that can be used to show users targeted adverts. Governments may conduct surveillance by analyzing and exchanging ever greater quantities of information on their citizens, using data mining tools to identify individuals "of interest" [6].

For the observed, surveillance can lead to self-censorship and inhibition. According to Julie Cohen in [69], surveillance 'threatens not only to chill the expression of eccentric individuality, but also, gradually, to dampen the force of our aspirations to it.'

Surveillance inhibits freedom of choice, impinging upon self-determination. It also creates a trail of information about a person. Surveillance's inhibitory effects are especially potent when people are engaging in political protest or dissent. People can face persecution, public sanction, and blacklisting for their unpopular political beliefs [22, 69].

Another new category of privacy harms is stemming from the use of big data to predict user's behavior. Big data technologies allow practitioners, researchers, policy analysts, and others to predict the spread of opinions, political trends, etc. [21]. Campaigns need accurate predictions about the preferences of voters, their expected behaviors, and their responses to campaign outreach. In addition, campaigns may use data to construct predictive models to make targeting communication more efficient [54]. Based on existing publicly available information, big data analysis tools can generate a predictive model of what has a high probability of being PII, essentially imagining an individual's data [13]. Kosinski et al. [38] method for instance is able to predict political party affiliation about 85% using only Facebook "likes". Personal harms emerge from the inappropriate inclusion and predictive analysis of an individual's personal data without their knowledge or consent.

Solove in [68], refers to deducing extensive information from 'clues' as the "aggregation effect" and claims that the kinds of predictions that can be made from this type of data are 'far too vast and complex, and are evolving too quickly, for people to fully assess the risks...involved'. Once released to the public, data cannot be taken back [52]. A person may leave behind in several years thousands of pieces of data which does not affect her/him negatively. As time passes, data analytic techniques improve, and a newly created algorithm may process the previously harmless digital footprints deducing potentially harmful information [52, 68]. Predictions also 'risks limiting individuals' human rights and freedoms, insofar as people self-regulate, being aware of 'a state of conscious and permanent visibility' [46].

One more stream of privacy threats stem from automated profiling techniques. Profiling with big data analytics may raise new problems. The relations found using data mining are not necessarily causal or they may be causal without being understood. In this way, the scope of profiles that are discovered may be much broader with unexpected profiles in unexpected areas [16]. In addition, fragments of data regarding an individual user may be linked peace by peace until an individual profile is entirely exposed [74]. According to Solove in [67], aggregation can cause dignitary harms because of how it unsettles expectations. Aggregation can also lead to power asymmetries, as it can increase the power that others have over individuals. Moreover, data compilations may be both telling and incomplete. Aggregated data may reveal facets of people's lives, but the data is often reductive and disconnected from the original context in which it was gathered, and this leads to distortion. Privacy harms may arise for which individual control offers no protection, for instance, in the case of the based on group classifications decisions [30, 50, 80], or in the case of inferring through big data techniques sensitive personal data from digital footprints or from data that individuals have intentionally disclosed [38, 74]. In the case decisions are taken based on data mining and profiling, undesirable discrimination may occur [80].

Threats coming from the poor execution of big data methods may create additional harms by constructing inaccurate profiles that nonetheless impact an individual's life and livelihood [15]. In a political context, a person may be profiled inaccurately as an extremist movement or party adherent or supporter. Also, a party could target particular voters with tailored information that maximizes, or minimizes, voter engagement [83].

In a pervasive data collection environment, privacy discussions are complicated by the difficulty of defining harm from privacy violations at the individual level [3].

New technologies and powerful analytics make it possible to collect and analyse large amounts of data in order to identify patterns in the behaviour of groups, communities and even entire countries [44]. A new aspect of privacy has been recently recognized: several authors [23, 48, 73] argue that, since most people are not targeted by profiling as individuals, but as members of specific groups, the privacy of these groups needs also to be explored. Supporters of the idea of group rights claim that there are some kinds of rights that belong to a group as a group such as the political rights [23]. Since Snowden leaked classified cyber intelligence documents in the United Kingdom (UK), France, Germany, the Netherlands and the United States of America (US), human rights organisations (Euro Parliament 2013; Free Snowden 2015) are trying to hold intelligence and/or security agencies accountable for their mass surveillance programs [20]. Some are concerned about the privacy of specific groups such as non-governmental organisations (NGOs) or journalists. They argue that activists are not just individual targets, but, because of their work, they have been targeted as a group [20].

According to Raymond in [61], demographically identifiable information (DII) comprises all forms of data in which the identification, classification, and tracking of demographic groups; this includes personal identifiable information, online data, geographic and geospatial data, environmental data, survey data, census data. In the case of the release of DII, group privacy risks may occur. In western democracies group privacy violations may result in unwanted targeted ads and other inconveniences.

Concluding, new privacy threats stemming from processing data with big data tools are related to surveillance, predictions, the inferred new knowledge and groupings (profiling). Research evidence shows that in the case that big data tools are used for political goals the occurring privacy threats may have beside the implications for the individual, long-term implications for society, for democracy itself. Next, we explore this issue.

## 5   Long - Term Implications for Democracy and Society

A democratic functioning public sphere may be understood as aggregation of communicative spaces in society that permit the free circulation of information, ideas, debates and the formation of political will [17]. These spaces also serve to facilitate communicative links between citizens and the power holders of society. But the way modern mass media and social media function today obstruct this flow by becoming increasingly personalized and creating "filter bubbles." Media's capacity to circulate material that builds connections between otherwise diverse groups is undermined, by the pressures toward personalization [14]. Consequently, the own opinion is reinforced, while the ability to handle different points of view is reduced facilitating in this way the polarization of society.

In addition, the representational dimension of the public sphere refers to the out-put of the media that target specific small groups via, for example, newsletters or campaign promotion materials [17]. In this terms, questions and criteria may be raised about media output for political communication, including fairness, accuracy, completeness, pluralism of views, etc. - characteristics of a democracy which may be undermined through personalization. Content is selected for citizens on the basis of criteria unknown to them and is calibrated not to their proximate selection decisions, but to big data–generated assumptions about where those citizens would want to focus their attention or where marketers need those citizens' attention to be focused [14]. The "filter bubbles" and financial means of potent influencers facilitates the spread of inaccurate, misleading or even wrong information becoming increasingly personalized, manipulative, and deceptive, spreading oversimplified messages or misinformation [29].

Platforms' algorithms highlight popular information, especially if it has been shared by friends, surrounding us with content from relatively homogenous groups [10]. For citizens it is increasingly hard to judge, which information can be trusted and why [29]. Digital impersonation for example, is increasingly realistic and convincing potentially may harm society in a variety of ways. The damage may extend to, among other things, distortion of democratic discourse on important policy questions, manipulation of elections etc. [10].

Politicians may use microtargeting to manipulate voters. Gorton in [83], warns that microtargeting 'turns citizens into objects of manipulation and undermines the public sphere by thwarting public deliberation, aggravating political polarization, and facilitating the spread of misinformation'. The targeted information does not even need to be true to maximize its impact. Political parties could also use microtargeting to suppress voter turnout for their opponents. Such messages can remain hidden for people who are not targeted. A political party could also misleadingly present itself as a one-issue party to each individual. A party may highlight a different issue for each voter, so each voter sees a different one-issue party. In this way, microtargeting could lead to a biased perception regarding the priorities of that party. Moreover, online political microtargeting could lead to a lack of transparency about the party's promises. Voters may not even know a party's views on many topics [83].

The structural dimension of the public sphere includes among others the legal frameworks of classic democratic issues [17]. Political rights of participation are preconditions for elections while they are embodied in the unlimited validity of the right to freedom of speech and opinion and among others the freedom of speech, expression, of association, etc. [47]. Surveillance may disrupt this structural dimension while one of the greatest harms is the potential chilling effect on political discourse, on the ability of both individuals and groups to express their views and on the possibilities for whistle-blowing and democratic activism [6, 26]. Also, harms may occur from unsophisticated algorithms and faulty data generate high rates of false positives that might serve as a basis for baseless, stigmatizing criminal investigations [12].

The minimal requirement for a state to be listed as democratic is that of so-called electoral democracy. In a democracy, the electoral regime has the function of making the access to public power positions of the state dependent on the results of open, competitive, fair elections [47]. But the current ecosystem around big data creates a new kind of digital divide: the big data rich and the big data poor [5]. This environment favours incumbents who already are in the possession of valuable data, also entrenched and moneyed candidates within parties, as well as the data–rich among existing parties [76]. Also, the institutional core of political rights is the right to political communication and organization, which are vital parts of a complete democratic regime [47]. However, the current big data ecosystem undermines those political rights which have the function both of enabling organized democratic elections and of furthering the unorganized pluralistic interests of complex societies. Data-driven campaigning might even be a form of cartelization [37] where large parties erect barriers to protect their dominance from new entrants. The high expense of new campaigning techniques is a significant disadvantage for smaller and newer parties [2].

Concluding, research evidence indicates that there are plenty reasons for concerns involving the data and analysis practices of campaigns. While strategic and tailored political communication can increase turnout and electoral participation, the sophisticated data gathering and analysis techniques of contemporary campaigns both catalyze political participation and undermine important democratic norms [39]. As Zarsky in [82] claims, much of the justification for voting in a democratic state is premised on the expectation of autonomous voters but it seems that voters' personal data may be a fuel of the manipulation. Accepting the notion that individuals could be systematically and easily manipulated shakes many of the foundational assumptions related to democracy.

## 6   Discussion and Conclusions

Big data analytics has given rise to a variety of concerns, which are most often framed using "privacy" and "data protection"-related paradigms while the enforcement of privacy rights is meeting substantial challenges on both a theoretical and a doctrinal level. Beside the situations (surveillance of private communications, gathering health data etc.) in which the core values of individual autonomy and protection from scrutinizing gazes and data collection are and remain highly important, it seems that big data analytics poses the need to alternative narratives to the privacy concepts [82].

Through data-driven technologies, companies, political parties, interests groups and other institutions have the means to effectively influence behavior at scale [11]. Each element of the offer—policy, party, and person—can be the subject of marketing communication designed to either reinforce or change voters' perceptions [71]. Manipulation in a political context, potentially undermine a basic feature of democracy: the electoral fairness. Research evidence indicates that big data technologies facilitate this procedure: the algorithms used by Google, Twitter and other sites are proved to be selective and manipulative [19] while citizens increasingly rely on news disseminated by Internet intermediaries such as Facebook, Twitter or Google for making political decisions. Moreover, the variables induced by the newly shaped digital landscape are highly complex and some authors [29] suggest that voters cannot handle this complexity. Thus, they would be easily manipulable and lean towards populist and inadequate solutions.

Furthermore, there are today even more new long-term threats for democracy which similarly to manipulation are "fueled" by data such as misinformation, disinformation, discrimination etc. The automation generates unforeseen problems for the adjudication of important individual rights. In the past, computer systems helped humans apply rules to individual cases. 'Today, voters are purged from the rolls without notice' [12].

We identify in this paper three categories of privacy threats (related to surveillance, users' behavior predictions and automated profiling) stemming from the use of big data in political context. We argue that there are privacy harms stemming from information which are not addressed by strategies centered on individual control over information. Data used for manipulation and discrimination may be inferred through algorithms so it may be sensitive personal data which is used without the individual's consent. Consequently, in our opinion, considering Calo,'s [8], conception of subjective privacy harms, discrimination and manipulation could be comprised in a broader notion of data protection. However, there is a need for further research related to this issue. Similarly, as parties, interests groups, politicians are rather interested in discovering influenceable groups of people than individuals, the privacy on group level has to be also further investigated.

Moreover, it is crucial that humanities scholars tackle questions about how quantification affects forms of social interaction and organization, political developments, and our understanding of democracy [64]. Highlighting the related to democracy aspects and identifying the threats to this specific feature of privacy stemming from the use of big data technologies for political purposes, this paper contributes to this issue indicating several long-term privacy implications which may undermine fundamental features of democracy such as fair elections and political equality of all citizens for example.

Finally, for about two decades now, researchers have been asking whether the Internet will have an impact on the public sphere and, if so, the attributes of this impact [17]. The newly shaped digital landscape is highly complex, and it needs a multidisciplinary approach in order to be investigated. This paper highlights some of the mechanisms through which privacy issues intertwine with fundamental features of democracy. It indicates that the use of big data analysis in political context may have a deep impact on democracy. There is a need however to further research related to the new privacy threats stemming from big data and to find ways to digitally support/protect democracy.

# References

1. Altman, I.: Privacy regulation: culturally universal or culturally specific? J. Soc. Issues **33**(3), 66–84 (1977). https://doi.org/10.1111/j.1540-4560.1977.tb01883.x
2. Anstead, N.: Data-driven campaigning in the 2015 United Kingdom general election. Int. J. Press./Polit. **22**(3), 294–313 (2017). https://doi.org/10.1177/1940161217706163
3. Baruh, L., Popescu, M.: Big data analytics and the limits of privacy self-management. New Media Soc. **19**(4), 579–596 (2017)
4. Bennett, C.J.: The European general data protection regulation: an instrument for the globalization of privacy standards? Inf. Polity **23**(2), 239–246 (2018)
5. Boyd, D., Crawford, K.: Six Provocations for Big Data. Social Science Research Network, Rochester (2011)

6. Brown, I.: Social media surveillance. In: The International Encyclopedia of Digital Communication and Society, pp. 1–7. American Cancer Society (2014). https://doi.org/10. 1002/9781118767771.wbiedcs122
7. Cadwalladr, C.: The great British Brexit robbery: how our democracy was hijacked. Guardian **7** (2017)
8. Calo, R.: The boundaries of privacy harm. Ind. LJ. **86**, 1131 (2011)
9. Chen, H., et al.: Business intelligence and analytics: from big data to big impact. MIS Q. **36** (4), 1165–1188 (2012)
10. Chesney, R., Citron, D.K.: Deep Fakes: A Looming Challenge for Privacy, Democracy, and National Security. Social Science Research Network, Rochester (2018)
11. Christl, W.: How companies use personal data against people. In: Automated Disadvantage, Personalized Persuasion, and the Societal Ramifications of the Commercial Use of Personal Information. Cracked Labs (2017)
12. Citron, D.K.: Technological due process. Wash. UL Rev. **85**, 1249 (2007)
13. Citron, D.K., Pasquale, F.: The scored society: due process for automated predictions. Wash. L. Rev. **89**, 1 (2014)
14. Couldry, N., Turow, J.: Advertising, big data and the clearance of the public realm: marketers' new approaches to the content subsidy. Int. J. Commun. **8**, 1710–1726 (2014)
15. Crawford, K., Schultz, J.: Big data and due process: toward a framework to redress predictive privacy harms. BCL Rev. **55**, 93 (2014)
16. Custers, B.: Data dilemmas in the information society: introduction and overview. In: Custers, B., Calders, T., Schermer, B., Zarsky, T. (eds.) Discrimination and Privacy in the Information Society, vol. 3, pp. 3–26. Springer, Heidelberg (2013). https://doi.org/10.1007/ 978-3-642-30487-3_1
17. Dahlgren, P.: The Political Web: Media, Participation and Alternative Democracy. Springer, Heidelberg (2013). https://doi.org/10.1057/9781137326386
18. Dalton, R.J.: The potential of big data for the cross-national study of political behavior. Int. J. Sociol. **46**(1), 8–20 (2016). https://doi.org/10.1080/00207659.2016.1130410
19. van Dijck, J.: Datafication, dataism and dataveillance: big data between scientific paradigm and ideology. Surveill. Soc. **12**(2), 197–208 (2014)
20. Eijkman, Q.: Indiscriminate bulk data interception and group privacy: do human rights organisations retaliate through strategic litigation? In: Taylor, L., Floridi, L., van der Sloot, B. (eds.) Group Privacy. PSS, vol. 126, pp. 123–138. Springer, Cham (2017). https://doi.org/ 10.1007/978-3-319-46608-8_7
21. Ekbia, H., et al.: Big data, bigger dilemmas: a critical review. J. Assoc. Inf. Sci. Technol. **66** (8), 1523–1545 (2015). https://doi.org/10.1002/asi.23294
22. Fisher, L.E.: Guilt by expressive association: political profiling, surveillance and the privacy of groups. Ariz. L. Rev. **46**, 621 (2004)
23. Floridi, L.: Group privacy: a defence and an interpretation. In: Taylor, L., Floridi, L., van der Sloot, B. (eds.) Group Privacy. PSS, vol. 126, pp. 83–100. Springer, Cham (2017). https:// doi.org/10.1007/978-3-319-46608-8_5
24. Gandomi, A., Haider, M.: Beyond the hype: big data concepts, methods, and analytics. Int. J. Inf. Manag. **35**(2), 137–144 (2015). https://doi.org/10.1016/j.ijinfomgt.2014.10.007
25. Gibson, R.K.: Party change, social media and the rise of 'citizen-initiated' campaigning. Party Polit. **21**(2), 183–197 (2015). https://doi.org/10.1177/1354068812472575
26. Goold, B.J.: How Much Surveillance is Too Much? Some Thoughts on Surveillance, Democracy, and the Political Value of Privacy. Social Science Research Network, Rochester (2010)
27. Grassegger, H., Krogerus, M.: The data that turned the world upside down. Luettavissa, 28 (2017): http://motherboard.vice.com/read/big-data-cambridge-analytica-brexit-trump.Luettu

28. Grimmer, J.: We are all social scientists now: how big data, machine learning, and causal inference work together. PS: Polit. Sci. Polit. **48**(1), 80–83 (2015). https://doi.org/10.1017/S1049096514001784
29. Helbing, D., Klauser, S.: How to make democracy work in the digital age. In: Helbing, D. (ed.) Towards Digital Enlightenment, pp. 157–162. Springer, Cham (2019). https://doi.org/10.1007/978-3-319-90869-4_12
30. Hildebrandt, M.: The Dawn of a Critical Transparency Right for the Profiling Era (2012)
31. Holtz-Bacha, D.C.: Professionalization of political communication. J. Polit. Mark. **1**(4), 23–37 (2002). https://doi.org/10.1300/J199v01n04_02
32. Jain, P., et al.: Big data privacy: a technological perspective and review. J. Big Data **3**(1), 25 (2016). https://doi.org/10.1186/s40537-016-0059-y
33. Janssen, M., van den Hoven, J.: Big and Open Linked Data (BOLD) in government: a challenge to transparency and privacy? Gov. Inf. Q. **32**(4), 363–368 (2015). https://doi.org/10.1016/j.giq.2015.11.007
34. Jenkins, J.C., et al.: Political behavior and big data. Int. J. Sociol. **46**(1), 1–7 (2016). https://doi.org/10.1080/00207659.2016.1130409
35. Jin, X., et al.: Significance and challenges of big data research. Big Data Res. **2**(2), 59–64 (2015). https://doi.org/10.1016/j.bdr.2015.01.006
36. Karpf, D.: Digital politics after Trump. Ann. Int. Commun. Assoc. **41**(2), 198–207 (2017). https://doi.org/10.1080/23808985.2017.1316675
37. Katz, R.S., Mair, P.: Changing models of party organization and party democracy: the emergence of the cartel party. Party Polit. **1**(1), 5–28 (1995). https://doi.org/10.1177/1354068895001001001
38. Kosinski, M., et al.: Private traits and attributes are predictable from digital records of human behavior. Proc. Natl. Acad. Sci. **110**(15), 5802–5805 (2013)
39. Kreiss, D., Howard, P.: New challenges to political privacy: lessons from the first US Presidential race in the Web 2.0 era. Int. J. Commun. **4**, 1032–1050 (2010)
40. Kreiss, D., Jasinski, C.: The tech industry meets presidential politics: explaining the democratic party's technological advantage in electoral campaigning, 2004–2012. Polit. Commun. **33**(4), 544–562 (2016). https://doi.org/10.1080/10584609.2015.1121941
41. Leppäniemi, M., et al.: Targeting young voters in a political campaign: empirical insights into an interactive digital marketing campaign in the 2007 finnish general election. J. Nonprofit Public Sect. Mark. **22**(1), 14–37 (2010). https://doi.org/10.1080/10495140903190374
42. Lilleker, D.G.: Interactivity and branding: public political communication as a marketing tool. J. Polit. Mark. **14**(1–2), 111–128 (2015)
43. Lisi, M.: The professionalization of campaigns in recent democracies: the Portuguese case. Eur. J. Commun. **28**(3), 259–276 (2013). https://doi.org/10.1177/0267323113475463
44. Mantelero, A.: Personal data for decisional purposes in the age of analytics: from an individual to a collective dimension of data protection. Comput. Law Secur. Rev. **32**(2), 238–255 (2016)
45. Mavriki, P., Karyda, M.: Using personalization technologies for political purposes: privacy implications. In: Katsikas, Sokratis K., Zorkadis, V. (eds.) e-Democracy 2017. CCIS, vol. 792, pp. 33–46. Springer, Cham (2017). https://doi.org/10.1007/978-3-319-71117-1_3
46. McDermott, Y.: Conceptualising the right to data protection in an era of big data. Big Data Soc. **4**(1), 1–7 (2017). https://doi.org/10.1177/2053951716686994
47. Merkel, W.: Embedded and defective democracies. Democratization **11**(5), 33–58 (2004). https://doi.org/10.1080/13510340412331304598
48. Mittelstadt, B.: From individual to group privacy in big data analytics. Philos. Technol. **30**(4), 475–494 (2017). https://doi.org/10.1007/s13347-017-0253-7

49. Monroe, B.L.: The five Vs of big data political science introduction to the virtual issue on big data in political science political analysis. Polit. Anal. **21**(V5), 1–9 (2013)

50. Mulligan, D.K., et al.: Privacy is an essentially contested concept: a multi-dimensional analytic for mapping privacy. Philos. Trans. R. Soc. A: Math. Phys. Eng. Sci. **374**(2083), 20160118 (2016)

51. Nagler, J., Tucker, J.A.: Drawing inferences and testing theories with big data. PS: Polit. Sci. Polit. **48**(1), 84–88 (2015). https://doi.org/10.1017/S1049096514001796

52. Narayanan, A., Huey, J., Felten, E.W.: A precautionary approach to big data privacy. In: Gutwirth, S., Leenes, R., De Hert, P. (eds.) Data Protection on the Move. LGTS, vol. 24, pp. 357–385. Springer, Dordrecht (2016). https://doi.org/10.1007/978-94-017-7376-8_13

53. Negrine, R., Papathanassopoulos, S.: The "Americanization" of political communication: a critique. Harv. Int. J. Press./Polit. **1**(2), 45–62 (1996)

54. Nickerson, D.W., Rogers, T.: Political campaigns and big data. J. Econ. Perspect. **28**(2), 51–73 (2014)

55. Nissenbaum, H.: Protecting privacy in an information age: the problem of privacy in public. Law Philos. **17**(5), 559–596 (1998). https://doi.org/10.1023/A:1006184504201

56. Nulty, P., et al.: Social media and political communication in the 2014 elections to the European Parliament. Electoral. Stud. **44**, 429–444 (2016)

57. Oates, S., Moe, W.W.: Donald Trump and the "Oxygen of Publicity": Branding, Social Media, and Mass Media in the 2016 Presidential Primary Elections. Social Science Research Network, Rochester (2016)

58. Petronio, S.: Communication privacy management theory: what do we know about family privacy regulation? J. Fam. Theory Rev. **2**(3), 175–196 (2010). https://doi.org/10.1111/j.1756-2589.2010.00052.x

59. Plasser, F.: Assessing the Americanization of Austrian politics and politicians. In: The Americanization/Westernization of Austria, pp. 235–254. Routledge (2017)

60. Pont-Sorribes, C., et al.: Is there Americanization in catalan election campaigns? A decade of electoral communication strategies from postmodernist perspective. Am. Behav. Sci. **62**, 375–390 (2017). https://doi.org/10.1177/0002764217707625

61. Raymond, Nathaniel A.: Beyond "do no harm" and individual consent: reckoning with the emerging ethical challenges of civil society's use of data. In: Taylor, L., Floridi, L., van der Sloot, B. (eds.) Group Privacy. PSS, vol. 126, pp. 67–82. Springer, Cham (2017). https://doi.org/10.1007/978-3-319-46608-8_4

62. Regan, P.M.: Legislating Privacy: Technology, Social Values, and Public Policy. University of North Carolina Press, Chapel Hill (1995)

63. Ruppert, E., et al.: Data politics. Big Data Soc. **4**(2), 1–7 (2017). https://doi.org/10.1177/2053951717717749

64. Schäfer, M.T., Van Es, K.: The Datafied Society: Studying Culture Through Data. Amsterdam University Press, Amsterdam (2017)

65. Shah, D.V., et al.: Big data, digital media, and computational social science: possibilities and perils. ANNALS Am. Acad. Polit. Soc. Sci. **659**(1), 6–13 (2015). https://doi.org/10.1177/0002716215572084

66. Sivarajah, U., et al.: Critical analysis of big data challenges and analytical methods. J. Bus. Res. **70**, 263–286 (2017). https://doi.org/10.1016/j.jbusres.2016.08.001

67. Solove, D.J.: A Taxonomy of Privacy. Social Science Research Network, Rochester (2005)

68. Solove, D.J.: Introduction: privacy self-management and the consent dilemma. Harv. L. Rev. **126**, 1880 (2012)

69. Solove, D.J.: Reconstructing electronic surveillance law. Geo. Wash. L. Rev. **72**, 1264 (2003)

70. Soria-Comas, J., Domingo-Ferrer, J.: Big data privacy: challenges to privacy principles and models. Data Sci. Eng. **1**(1), 21–28 (2016). https://doi.org/10.1007/s41019-015-0001-x
71. Speed, R., et al.: Human branding in political marketing: applying contemporary branding thought to political parties and their leaders. J. Polit. Mark. **14**(1–2), 129–151 (2015). https://doi.org/10.1080/15377857.2014.990833
72. Stieglitz, S., et al.: Social media analytics – challenges in topic discovery, data collection, and data preparation. Int. J. Inf. Manag. **39**, 156–168 (2018). https://doi.org/10.1016/j.ijinfomgt.2017.12.002
73. Taylor, L.: Safety in numbers? Group privacy and big data analytics in the developing world. In: Taylor, L., Floridi, L., van der Sloot, B. (eds.) Group Privacy. PSS, vol. 126, pp. 13–36. Springer, Cham (2017). https://doi.org/10.1007/978-3-319-46608-8_2
74. Tene, O., Polonetsky, J.: Big data for all: privacy and user control in the age of analytics. Nw. J. Tech. Intell. Prop. **11**, xxvii (2012)
75. Toch, E., Birman, Y.: Towards behavioral privacy: how to understand AI's privacy threats in ubiquitous computing. In: Proceedings of the 2018 ACM International Joint Conference and 2018 International Symposium on Pervasive and Ubiquitous Computing and Wearable Computers, pp. 931–936. ACM, New York (2018). https://doi.org/10.1145/3267305.3274155
76. Tufekci, Z.: Engineering the public: big data, surveillance and computational politics. First Monday **19**, 7 (2014)
77. Voice, P.: Privacy and democracy. S. Afr. J. Philos. **35**(3), 272–280 (2016). https://doi.org/10.1080/02580136.2016.1204843
78. Westin, A.F.: Privacy and Freedom, p. 7. Atheneum, New York (1967)
79. Westin, A.F.: Social and political dimensions of privacy. J. Soc. Issues **59**(2), 431–453 (2003). https://doi.org/10.1111/1540-4560.00072
80. Winter, J.: Algorithmic discrimination: big data analytics and the future of the internet. In: Winter, J., Ono, R. (eds.) The Future Internet. PAIT, vol. 17, pp. 125–140. Springer, Cham (2015). https://doi.org/10.1007/978-3-319-22994-2_8
81. Yu, S.: Big privacy: challenges and opportunities of privacy study in the age of big data. IEEE Access **4**, 2751–2763 (2016). https://doi.org/10.1109/ACCESS.2016.2577036
82. Zarsky, T.: Privacy and Manipulation in the Digital Age. Social Science Research Network, Rochester (2019)
83. Zuiderveen Borgesius, F., et al.: Online Political Microtargeting: Promises and Threats for Democracy. Social Science Research Network, Rochester (2018)

# What Do We Know About Our Rights to Data Protection? A Greek Case Study

Maria Sideri[1(✉)], Athanasios Fontaras[2], and Stefanos Gritzalis[3]

[1] Privacy Engineering and Social Informatics Laboratory,
Department of Cultural Technology and Communication,
University of the Aegean, 81100 Lesvos, Greece
msid@aegean.gr
[2] e-Governance Department, National Centre for Scientific Research
"Demokritos", 15310 Athens, Greece
a.fontaras@egov.demokritos.gr
[3] Laboratory of Systems Security, Department of Digital Systems,
University of Piraeus, 18534 Piraeus, Greece
sgritz@unipi.gr

**Abstract.** Technological developments have led to tools for collecting personal data in a volume and form that in the past would have been difficult to gather. This creates new opportunities for public and private sector agencies to store and process personal data for a variety of purposes, while it also produces risks for data subjects regarding data protection and privacy. In this frame, the General Data Protection Regulation (GDPR) focuses on enhancing data subjects' rights in order to increase their control over personal data, establishing at the same time stricter obligations for data controllers and compliance monitoring procedures. This research explores a group of Greek data subjects' knowledge about their rights and the rights-related behavior showing that, one year after the implementation of GDPR, they are not yet fully aware of all their rights and in some cases they do not know how to exercise these rights.

**Keywords:** General Data Protection Regulation (GDPR) · Data subjects' rights · Rights' knowledge · Rights' exercise

## 1 Introduction

The usage of mobile devices, social media platforms and cloud services by citizens as well as crowdsourcing models used by governments or companies have led to the creation of a big volume of personal data transmitted and exchanged between different actors, agencies and states worldwide. As data is nowadays the most valuable source of the global economy, incidents of personal data breach or leakage are constantly increasing. In this context, the European Parliament, responding to the challenges of the digital era, voted on April 2016 the General Data Protection Regulation (GDPR) [1] which is applicable to all Member-States of the European Union (EU) since May 25, 2018. Comparing to the replaced Directive 95/46/EC, GDPR focuses on enhancing data subjects' rights, introducing a stricter framework regarding the obligations of data

© Springer Nature Switzerland AG 2020
S. Katsikas and V. Zorkadis (Eds.): e-Democracy 2019, CCIS 1111, pp. 18–33, 2020.
https://doi.org/10.1007/978-3-030-37545-4_2

controllers and the control measures for compliance with legislation, while it broadens its scope since it is addressed to any company or organization offering goods or services to citizens in Europe irrespective of its location.

Although the concerns for personal data protection and privacy grow worldwide and legal measures are taken, citizens aren't always fully aware of the legislation, their rights and the actions they should take in case of personal data protection problems [2, 3]. Moreover, in some cases they express confidence to service providers considering that they abide the law or to governments believing that they protect their data.

In this context, this paper refers to an exploratory research investigating a group of Greek adult data subjects' knowledge regarding their rights as set in GDPR and the provisions of the Regulation for the collection and processing of personal data by organizations or companies. The paper is organized as follows. Section 2 refers to data subjects' rights in GDPR and Sect. 3 to the research framework focusing on the role of legislation and rights' knowledge for data subjects' protection. Research methodology issues are presented in Sect. 4. Section 5 records and discusses the results of the research, while Sect. 6 concludes the paper raising future research directions.

## 2 Data Subjects' Rights in GDPR

Referring to data safeguarding, the strengthening of legislation is considered over time very important in order for the technological planning of data collection and the control of data to be regulated [4]. Although legislation has defined the general principles for personal data protection and several legal documents have been produced at EU level since 1980 s, states differentiate regarding their legal culture [5]; states use different definitions for personal data and apply different rules throughout data collection and process. In this frame, GDPR is expected to impact positively since it aims to achieve an equivalent level of data protection by ensuring *"coherent and uniform application of the rules on the protection of fundamental rights and of the freedoms of natural persons with regard to the processing of personal data throughout the Union"* (recital 10) [1]. In GDPR, personal data collection and process is based on the principles of: (a) legality, objectivity and transparency, (b) limitation of purpose, (c) minimization of data, (d) accuracy, (e) limitation of the storage period, (f) integrity and confidentiality and (g) accountability (Article 5) [1].

Data subjects' rights are an important part in Regulation's provisions (Articles 12–23) [1]. GDPR strengthens existing rights, while introducing new ones, such as data portability. Data subjects' right to be informed is essential. Controllers, when collecting data, have the obligation to inform, within a reasonable period of time, the data subject in a clear and easily accessible way for the processing in which his/her data is going to be submitted, his/her rights, the purposes of the processing, the recipients of the data - if any-, the period of time that data will be retained and the criteria affecting that period. Information should be also provided in case of data transfer to third parties or of data breach. GDPR émphasizes on subject's consent for personal data usage. Consent should be provided by a positive action constituting a free, specific, explicit and fully informed indication of the subject's agreement and can be withdrawn at any time. Moreover, data subjects have the right to access their personal data and demand to be corrected, altered or deleted if inaccurate, incomplete or obsolete. They also have the right to oppose at any time to the processing of personal data and the controller is obliged to cease processing, unless he/she claims imperative and legitimate reasons for it (e.g. reasons of public interest). In GDPR, data subjects are protected towards 'profiling' and have the right to oppose to a decision evaluating personal aspects, which is taken solely on the basis of automated processing and produces legal effects or affects them substantially. In order to enhance data subjects' rights and increase their control over personal data, GDPR also imposes several obligations to data controllers and processors (Articles 24–43) [1], while it emphasizes on regulatory compliance monitoring too.

Within this new legal frame formed by GDPR, data subjects' role regarding their data protection and their rights exercise is crucial, considering the risks that daily come up for the control, management and security of personal data and the preservation of privacy. The rights to privacy and to personal data protection are closely linked, since they protect similar human values (e.g. individual autonomy, human dignity).

## 3    Research Framework

Although users often think they can control the data they share, [3, 6] point out that nowadays data are not under the control of individuals but of organizations, governmental agencies and companies. This provokes a series of events that data subjects experience or are informed about, ranging from personal data breach cases to personalized advertisements, which increase data subjects' concerns regarding their protection, as they acknowledge that others are invading in their life and have access to their personal data. Despite these concerns, data subjects disclose their data, intentionally or unintentionally, consciously or unconsciously, failing thus, as [7] argues, to ultimately translate their privacy concerns into protective behavior.

Beyond legislation that aims to protect data subjects, the knowledge that individuals have about their rights and the legislation for data and privacy protection is extremely important. According to [8], literacy privacy is the combination on one hand of data subjects' knowledge regarding the technical aspects of data protection, the relevant laws and directives, and on the other hand of their ability to use strategies to regulate their privacy and protect their data. Indeed, [8] have included into the Online Privacy Literacy Scale (OPLIS) the dimension of knowledge about the practices of organizations and service providers (dimension 1) arguing that since data subjects daily use a number of services (platforms, sites, digital communities), they have to know how providers handle and exploit their data. According to [9] the knowledge of technical aspects and of data collection practices can help individuals take appropriate actions. As a fourth dimension in the OPLIS, [8] integrated knowledge about legislation, legal aspects of data protection and protection policies, noting that only if data subjects know their personal rights and the legal constraints imposed on companies can make informed decisions to control their data or optimize their privacy. In a data-driven world, the effective control over personal data is important considering that data subjects daily disclose vast amounts of personal data in order to have access to services or goods.

The issue of data subjects' knowledge about their rights and the legislation has been studied. The work of [8] is an example referring to Germans, while [10] during their survey focused on the role of legislation and public authorities. The research of [11] showed that people feel protected by the law anyway (so they don't read privacy policies for example), while the work of [12] showed that individuals are convinced that companies abide the law taking care of their customers' safety. With reference to GDPR, although data about individuals' complaints handled by Data Protection Authorities are available[1], to the best of our knowledge there is insufficient research up to the date that the current research was completed exploring data subjects' knowledge on their rights as set in GDPR. Special Eurobarometer 487a is the first official survey to explore awareness of GDPR and the rights it guarantees, published in June 2019 [13].

In this context, this exploratory research is based on [8] and [9] thesis that if data subjects are aware of their rights, the legal aspects of data protection, the data collection practices and the constraints imposed on public or private sector entities, they can make informed decisions to control their data or optimize their privacy. So, the main hypothesis is that the high degree of data subjects' knowledge about their rights as set in GDPR is expected to have a positive effect on their behavior related to these rights.

## 4   Methodology

Beginning a research, researchers decide on issues concerning the sample, its selection and the research tool [14]. Considering that the number of Greek potential research population (adults using digital services) is big, a sample was selected using availability sampling [15]. In other words, the sample was recruited according to individuals' willingness to participate in the research. Although this method doesn't allow the generalization of the research results, findings can highlight trends for future research.

A structured questionnaire was used for the purposes of the research[2] carried out from 18 March to 18 April 2019. This form of questionnaire contributes to the standardization of analysis and makes conclusions' drawing easier. Questionnaire's design followed the rules set by [16]; (a) a title was given at the beginning, (b) the questionnaire was organized into sections including similar questions, (c) questions were numbered per section/subsection, (d) emphasis was given so as questions don't dictate the answer. The participants were clearly informed about the research purpose in the introductory note [17], being asserted about the anonymity of their responses which ensures the protection of research confidentiality. The four-section questionnaire described below included close-ended questions (in yes-no form, Likert scale or multiple-choice option).

*Section A: General Data Protection Regulation.* The 4 questions explore general issues regarding respondents' source of information about GDPR and their knowledge on GDPR objectives.

---

[1] https://ec.europa.eu/commission/sites/beta-political/files/190125_gdpr_infographics_v4.pdf.

[2] https://drive.google.com/file/d/1BXlxqMMxqOUc3gindABJf2cqNYflCY9b/view?usp=sharing.

*Section B: The Rights of the Data Subjects.* This section includes 14 questions exploring respondents' extent of knowledge regarding the rights described in GDPR. The questions were selected in order to cover the most important legal provisions in GDPR excluding special cases that would probably confuse the participants.

*Section C: Risks to Personal Data and Ways of Protection.* It is divided into two (2) sub-sections. The first (*Personal Data Control and Risks*) (10 questions) focuses on respondents' perceived control over personal data, privacy concerns and perceived risks. High privacy concerns and the perception of online risks are assumed to motivate data subjects to be better informed about their rights. The second sub-section (*Personal Data Protection*) (7 questions) explores respondents' rights-related behavior aiming to identify the relation between the extent of subjects' knowledge about their rights as set in GDPR and the exercise of these. Several questions in sub-Section C1 (2–5 and 8–10) and C2 (1–6) as well as question A.4 have been drawn from a previous survey [11].

*Section D: Personal Information.* The 4 questions record respondents' demographic and social characteristics (gender, age, education level, occupation) that may impact on GDPR awareness.

The questionnaire was checked for its language, clarity, difficulty and reliability in a pilot survey addressed to 10 participants. This stage is important as it aims to detect (a) if the questions are understood, (b) if they ensure the information for which they were designed, (c) the interest and cooperation of the respondents [18]. After its pilot implementation, the questionnaire was corrected and received its final form using Google forms tool. Data collected were analyzed using IBM SPSS Statistics 21.

## 5    Results and Discussion

This section records and discusses the descriptive findings regarding data subjects' extent of knowledge about their rights and their behavior relevant to these rights. Other findings such as those referring to perceived data risks or privacy concerns are included briefly, due to space limitation. 101 people participated in the research; 49 men and 51 women (one didn't respond). Half of them are of the age group of 36–45 (49.5%), while 25.7% of 26–35. Regarding education level, 42.6% of the respondents hold a Master and 38.6% a graduate degree.

### 5.1    Section A: General Data Protection Regulation

Although the majority of respondents (82.2%) recognized that GDPR enforcement is a responsibility at EU level, almost 10% didn't know who had this responsibility. A high percentage (41.6%) didn't also know the Greek Supervisory Authority that is responsible for protecting their rights regarding personal data.

In order to evaluate respondents' knowledge about GDPR objectives, question A.3 was posed. Respondents could choose one or more answers: (a) data subjects' rights strengthening, (b) obligations increase of entities collecting and managing data, (c) stricter delimitation of data collection and processing procedures, (d) tighter regulatory compliance control measures. Article 1, par. 2 of GDPR clarifies that *"This*

*Regulation protects fundamental rights and freedoms of natural persons and in particular their right to the protection of personal data*" [1]. According to answers, 17.8% of the participants stated that GDPR is about "stricter delimitation of data collection and processing procedures", while options (a), (b) and (d) were selected by 5%, 2% and 5% respectively. All the above options were selected by 21.8% which implies that approximately only 1/5 of participants acknowledge both the objective of GDPR and the ways to be achieved. Combinations of answers were also recorded in lower rates (from 1% to 9.9%).

## 5.2    Section B: The Rights of Data Subjects

Respondents were asked to answer questions regarding the extent of knowledge about their rights using a 5-point scale, from 1 "not at all" (absence of knowledge) to 5 "very well" (excellent knowledge). This scale was used in all questions with the exception of the last two (B.13 and B.14) where multiple choice option was given. Findings regarding the knowledge of right to be informed are recorded in Table 1.

**Table 1.** Extent of knowledge regarding the right to be informed

|  |  | Right to be informed for data processing (B.1) | Right to be informed for data transmission (B.8) | Right to be informed for data breach (B.9) |
|---|---|---|---|---|
| Valid | not at all | 9.7 | 18.4 | 18.4 |
|  | little | 10.7 | 19.4 | 20.4 |
|  | moderate | 23.3 | 17.5 | 19.4 |
|  | well | 28.2 | 20.4 | 18.4 |
|  | very well | 25.2 | 21.4 | 21.4 |
|  | Total | 97.1 | 97.1 | 98.1 |
| Missing system |  | 2.9 | 2.9 | 1.9 |
| Total |  | 100.0 | 100.0 | 100.0 |

Replies in question B.1 reveal that 53.4% of the respondents knew "very well" and "well" the right to be informed by data controller within a reasonable time for the processing their data will be submitted and for their rights. GDPR defines controller's obligation to inform data subjects for the transmission of their data to third parties after the first transmission the latest. In this frame, question B.8 investigates data subjects' knowledge extent in relation to this obligation. The results showed a rather equal distribution of answers. This is worrying as data subjects were expected to be aware of the specific obligation, due to often expressed concerns regarding to whom their data be can transferred. A similar responses distribution appeared in question B.9 that refers to data subjects being informed by the controller about high-risk personal data breach, consequences and measures taken. Finding in this question are interesting too, considering that although data subjects worry about data breaches and potential consequences, they don't seem sufficiently aware of the controller's obligation to inform them.

Question B.2 focuses on data subjects' right to require data controller to amend incorrect personal data without undue delay. Findings showed that 19.2% of the respondents stated they know this right "very well", 27.3% "well" and 31.3% "moderate". Only 22.2% stated "little" or "not at all" equally distributed.

The results in questions B.3 to B.6 that refer to subject's consent are shown in Table 2 below. Specifically, the findings of B.3 question regarding respondents' extent of knowledge about their consent as a prerequisite for data processing showed that 46.5% of them knew this "very well", while 27.7% stated "well". Moreover, as it is apparent from replies to question B.4 concerning the form of consent, a total 60.4% of the respondents know "very well" (23.8%) and "well" (36.6%) that consent must be free, specific and explicit. Although the percentage of respondents who knew "very well" and "well" that consent is required for personal data processing is high (74.2%), the corresponding percentage regarding the extent of knowledge about the right to withdraw consent at any time is much lower (44.5%), as findings in question B.5 reveal. Considering that 18.8% of the respondents didn't know they have the right to withdraw consent, 11.9% knew this "little" and 21.8% "moderate", it is rather possible that respondents believe that once they have given their consent, they have little or no ability to withdraw it. Users often think that their consent is a prerequisite for services provision, although [19] notes that consent is a false precondition for specific social needs such as Internet access or search engines and social networks usage. The results of question B.6 that refers to the extent of knowledge that consent is not a prerequisite for services provision unless the use of data is necessary for their provision, showed that 33.6% of the respondents -equally distributed- stated that they did not know this at all or knew it "little". On the contrary, 28.7% stated "moderate", 20.8% "well" and 15.8% "very well". These results are rather encouraging revealing a trend about users gradually acknowledging that their consent is not a prerequisite for using a service.

**Table 2.** Extent of knowledge regarding subject's consent

| | | Consent required for data processing (B.3) | Consent form (B.4) | Consent recalled (B.5) | Consent not required for service usage (B.6) |
|---|---|---|---|---|---|
| Valid | not at all | 5.0 | 7.9 | 18.8 | 16.8 |
| | little | 9.9 | 7.9 | 11.9 | 16.8 |
| | moderate | 9.9 | 23.8 | 21.8 | 28.7 |
| | well | 27.7 | 36.6 | 17.8 | 20.8 |
| | very well | 46.5 | 23.8 | 26.7 | 15.8 |
| | Total | 99.0 | 100.0 | 97.0 | 99.0 |
| Missing system | | 1.0 | 0 | 3.0 | 1.0 |
| Total | | 100.0 | 100.0 | 100.0 | 100.0 |

The issue of profiling is recorded several times in GDPR. The results of question B.7 concerning the extent to which data subjects know that if their data are used for profiling they should be informed for the process and its consequences, showed that 14.6% of respondents were unaware of this, while 38.8% stated "moderate" and "little" knowledge. The "very well" and "well" options were selected by 29.1% and 14.6% respectively. These findings show partial knowledge regarding profiling.

**Table 3.** Extent of knowledge regarding subject's right to oppose

|  |  | Right to oppose to data processing (B.10) | Right to oppose to automated decision (B.11) |
|---|---|---|---|
| Valid | not at all | 13.6 | 17.5 |
|  | little | 25.2 | 28.2 |
|  | moderate | 21.4 | 25.2 |
|  | well | 23.3 | 15.5 |
|  | very well | 13.6 | 10.7 |
|  | Total | 97.1 | 97.1 |
| Missing system | | 2.9 | 2.9 |
| Total | | 100.0 | 100.0 |

The right to data portability, introduced in GDPR, is considered to increase data subjects' control over their data constituting also an opportunity for the interoperability of services and increased competition between digital services [20]. Question B.12 refers to data subjects' extent of knowledge about the right to receive their personal data delivered to a controller and transfer them to another. Findings show that 30% of the respondents didn't know this right and 24% knew it "little". The options "well" and "moderate" were selected by 23% and 15% respectively, while only 8% stated "very well".

Comparing the means (Table 4) of data subjects' knowledge extent in relation to the rights explored (B.1–B.12), it can be concluded that users have a higher degree of knowledge about the requirement of consent and its form. Relatively satisfactory is the knowledge extent regarding the right to be informed about data processing and the right to demand the correction of inaccurate data. On the contrary, the knowledge extent about the right to data portability and the right not to be subjected to a decision taken exclusively on the basis of automated processing appear to be much lower.

Moreover, according to Table 5 the minimum and maximum knowledge values for all rights were 12 and 60 respectively, with a mean value of 37.75 which shows that data subjects' knowledge extent regarding their rights is rather moderate in general.

Question B.13 investigates the knowledge regarding the conditions for the exercise of the right to data erasure (right to be forgotten). This right is important as the possibility of uncontrolled digital reproduction of personal data is effectively eliminated and subjects' control over the flow of their data increases [21]. Participants were asked to state in which of the three cases (a. if data are no longer necessary, b. if

**Table 4.** Mean value of data subjects' knowledge per right

|  |  | Mean |
|---|---|---|
| Right to be informed | for data processing (B.1) | 3.5 |
|  | for profiling (B.7) | 3.10 |
|  | for data transmission (B.8) | 3.07 |
|  | for data breach (B.9) | 3.04 |
| Consent | required for data processing (B.3) | 4.02 |
|  | form (B.4) | 3.6 |
|  | recalled (B.5) | 3.22 |
|  | not required for service usage (B.6) | 3.02 |
| Right to oppose | to data processing (B.10) | 2.98 |
|  | to automated decision (B.11) | 2.73 |
| Right to demand amendment of incorrect personal data (B.2) |  | 3.32 |
| Right to data portability (B.12) |  | 2.55 |

**Table 5.** Total scores for data subjects' rights

| N | Valid | 101 |
|---|---|---|
| Mean |  | 37,7525 |
| Mode |  | 36,00 |
| Minimum |  | 12,00 |
| Maximum |  | 60,00 |

consent has been withdrawn, c. if there is no legal basis for data processing) could ask data controller to erase their personal data, being able to choose more than one answer. Only 14.9% knew they had this right in all three cases, while 22.8% stated they didn't know. The case of consent withdrawal appeared with a higher response rate (21.8%), while a combination of responses with lower percentages was also recorded.

Similarly, participants were asked (question B.14) to identify in which of the following cases they have the right to request the restriction of data processing: (a). when data accuracy is disputed, (b). when processing is illegal, (c). when data controller no longer needs personal data for the purposes of the processing, but data are required by the subject for the foundation, exercise or support of legal claims and (d). when data subject has objections to the processing, pending verification that the legitimate reasons of the controller prevail all those of the data subject. In this case too, more than one answer could be selected. Almost 1/3 of the respondents (29.7%) didn't know when they had this right, while only 9.9% selected all four cases. This is the highest rate that appeared compared to other responses, cases combination included. Cases (a) and (c) were selected by 2% of the respondents each, case (b) by 7.9% and case (d) by 6.9%.

### 5.3   Section C-Subsection 1: Personal Data Control and Risks

Beyond rights' knowledge, data subjects' awareness about the way that others manage their data and the risks potentially arising from this management is significant. Due to space limitation, this paper focuses on rights' knowledge extent and data subjects' rights-related behavior, so the findings of this sub-section are presented briefly.

The perception of control is crucial as it may lead either to a sense of security and thus greater disclosure of information or to high concerns for privacy and thus reduced willingness to disclose, even in cases when the risks from the disclosure are lesser [22]. In this frame, respondents were asked to state (C.1.1) whether they control the personal data they provide online. Findings show that 12.9% were "absolutely sure", 39.6% "quite sure", 33.7% "not really sure" and 13.9% "not sure at all". However, replying to question C.1.2 "How much control do you feel you have over the information you provide online?" only 3% of the respondents stated "complete control", 56% "partial control" and 20% "no control at all". This differentiation reveals that respondents can distinguish between the process of data release and that of others' access to their data, recognizing that after data provision these are no longer under their control as already supported by [6]. The findings of question C.1.2 are verified by those of C.1.3 that refers to concerns about others controlling the information data subjects provide online. Only 2% stated "not at all concerned" and 14.9% "no particularly concerned".

Questions C.1.4–C.1.7 explored respondents concerns on specific issues revealing high rates of concerns; "very concerned" or "quite concerned" stated 70.3% regarding governments collecting data (C.1.4), 89.1% regarding data use for different reasons than those originally collected (C.1.6), 83.1% regarding search engines recording history of navigation (C.1.7), while 89.1% stated "no particularly comfortable" or "not at all comfortable" about personal information usage by companies' websites (C.1.5).

Half of the respondents (51.5%) stated equally concerned about the loss or theft of data stored on PCs, mobile devices and online/cloud (question C.1.9). Answers to question C.1.10 regarding the risks when providing personal data online showed that respondents worry more about security issues ("personal safety being at risk" 74.3%) and personal data usage for fraud ("Becoming a victim of fraud" 76.2% and "Online identity used for fraudulent purposes" 77.2%). Personal data usage without data subjects having been informed (63.4%) and data transmission to third parties without subjects' consent (64.4%) were also stated as risks, while misunderstanding of views and behavior (37.6%) and personal data usage for sending data subjects unwanted advertising material (34.7%) were recorded at lower rates.

### 5.4   Section C-Subsection 2: Data Protection

Information regarding personal data collection and processing is important for subjects' data control in order to make informed decisions about their protection. Providers can supply this information through privacy policies. Literature has shown that data subjects often do not read privacy policies, and this is a risky behavior [23]. Participants were asked (question C.2.1) if they read privacy policies. Only 6.9% stated reading the whole text, 64.4% stated "partially" and 28.7% declared not reading at all. The low reading rate is due to the extent of the text (73.4%) and the unclear way text is written

(55.4%) as responses to question C.2.2 revealed, supporting previous researches [24, 25]. Moreover, 21.8% of respondents stated as a reason for not reading or partially reading privacy policies that "websites will not honor them anyway" showing thus lack of trust to providers. On the contrary, 13.9% stated that it is sufficient to see that websites have a privacy policy which implies confidence to the providers. Only 2% stated that they didn't know where to find privacy policy, 4% that they didn't think it is important to read them and 8.9% that law will protect them in any case.

Questions C.2.3–C.2.6 explore participants' rights-related behavior. In this frame participants were asked to indicate whom they will address to if they experience a problem regarding personal data protection (C.2.3) having the option of answers combination. The question aimed at exploring whether data subjects understand their right to legal remedies exercise. The results showed that 11.9% of the participants did not know where to address to and 1% stated that it would not address anyone. The national "Supervisory Authority" was stated by 28.7% and the "Independent Authority for Data Protection" by 10.9%. At lower rates "public or private actor managing my data", "Court" and "European Authority" (5.9%, 4% and 2% respectively) were chosen, while a combination of options was also recorded. Considering that the proposed answers which were retrieved from previous survey [11] are probably confusing, future research should also focus on scenarios in order to investigate whether people can identify the appropriate Authority to complain to in cases of personal data protection problems.

In order for data to be used, data subject's free and explicit consent is a prerequisite. Participants were asked to state (C.2.4) if they give their consent for the collection and processing of any kind of personal data explicitly. Results showed that 1/4 (25%) of the respondents were unsure of this. Not doing this was stated by 21%, while 19% declared providing consent explicitly in any case, the same percentage in the case when data is requested online and 16% in the case of sensitive data only.

Data subjects should be informed regarding how their personal data is going to be used in order to give their consent or opt out if consent is required for processing. Question C.2.5 focused on this issue. Findings showed that 5.9% of the respondents "didn't not know" if they had information about the conditions for data collection and processing when providing their data online. Only 4% answered "always" and 10.9% "never", while high rates were recorded for "sometimes" (37.6%) and "rarely" (39.6%).

The right to data portability is essential for enhancing data subjects' right of control and constitutes a first step towards the "preselected ownership" of personal data by subjects [20] (p. 201). Question C.2.6 explored respondents' attitude regarding the importance of this right. Most of the respondents considered the right "very important" (38.6%) or "quite important" (36.6%), despite the fact that, as recorded in B.12 question, half of the respondents (54%) did not know or knew this right "little". Data portability was considered "not important at all" by 2% of the respondents, "no particularly important" by 18.8%, while 4% stated "do not know".

The last question (C.2.7) includes 6 phrases with which respondents were asked to state their agreement/disagreement. Findings are shown in Table 6 below.

**Table 6.** Rates of agreement and disagreement regarding personal data protection

|  | Totally agree | Agree | Neither agree nor disagree | Disagree | Totally disagree |
|---|---|---|---|---|---|
| (a) I am confident that the personal data I provide will not be used by anyone else | 3% | 14.9% | 28.7% | 34.7% | 18.8% |
|  | **17.90%** |  |  | **53.50%** |  |
| (b) I am aware of data protection legislation to protect myself | 1% | 25.7% | 34.7% | 24.8% | 13.9% |
|  | **26.70%** |  |  | **38.70%** |  |
| (c) I trust service providers to protect my data | 2% | 14.9% | 30.7% | 36.6% | 15.8% |
|  | **16.90%** |  |  | **52.40%** |  |
| (d)Legislation and Supervisory Authorities fully protect my personal data | 3% | 16.8% | 39.6% | 35.6% | 5% |
|  | **19.80%** |  |  | **40.60%** |  |
| (e) To protect myself it is sufficient to be careful about the data I provide online | 9.9% | 22.8% | 32.7% | 25.7% | 8.9% |
|  | **32.70%** |  |  | **34.60%** |  |
| (f) Governments protect my data | 3% | 10.9% | 24.8% | 42.6% | 18.8% |
|  | **13.90%** |  |  | **61.40%** |  |

With none of the statements the rates of agreement/absolute agreement were higher than those of disagreement/absolute disagreement. The same was observed when comparing agreement/absolute agreement rates to "neither agree nor disagree" rates with the exception of statement (e). The higher percentages of disagreement/absolute disagreement were recorded for statements (f), (a) and (c), showing that data subjects trust neither governments nor providers, while being conscious that their data can be exploited by others. The latter may explain the rather equal distribution rates in the case of (e) revealing respondents' uncertainty whether their careful behavior when providing data is sufficient for their protection. Moreover, responses to statement (b) revealed that less than 1/3 of respondents were sure they know the law to protect their data. Distrust towards legislation and Supervisory Authorities was recorded in statement (d).

## 5.5  Discussion on Main Findings

Although significant progress has been made at European level for the protection of privacy and personal data since the implementation of EU 95/46 Directive, differences have been observed between Member States in terms of legislation and its implementation. In this context, the recently implemented GDPR is expected to contribute positively creating a homogenous legal landscape. Enhancing data subjects' rights in order to increase control over their data is undoubtedly GDPR's priority. As [21] note regarding GDPR *"the need for individual control seems to be addressed more explicitly and with greater prudence compared to earlier regulations"* (p. 92). Data subjects are better informed, their consent is a prerequisite for data processing, new rights emerge and stricter obligations for the controllers are imposed.

Laws and regulations enhance data subjects' rights, but data subjects have to be fully aware of their rights in order to exercise them and protect themselves. Both knowledge regarding the techniques and practices of organizations and service providers for the collection and process of subjects' data, as well as knowledge about laws and protection policies help data subjects to make informed decisions about the disclosure of personal data, to better control their data and optimize their privacy [8, 9]. In this context, this exploratory research aimed at investigating the knowledge of a sample of Greek data subjects regarding their rights and their rights-related behavior.

Respondents don't seem to have a clear view regarding GDPR objective. Only 5% acknowledge that GDPR addresses to data subjects' rights strengthening, 17.8% to the stricter delimitation of data collection and processing procedures and 21.8% to all the options given. These findings reveal that GDPR is considered more as a legal frame referring to data controllers, their obligations and the measures taken for data collection and management than to data subjects and their rights. A high percentage (41.6%) of the respondents doesn't know the Greek Supervisory Authority responsible for protecting their rights, which may explain the low percentage (28.7%) of those stated that they will address to national "Supervisory Authority" if they experience a problem regarding personal data protection. Considering that 11.9% of the respondents stated they did not know where to address to in order to be protected in case they encounter a problem with their personal data, and the plethora of answers given in the relevant question, it can be assumed data subjects' ignorance about the competences of each of the bodies proposed and, consequently, ignorance regarding legal remedies exercise.

Data subjects' responses regarding the extent of knowledge about their rights showed a higher degree of knowledge about consent being a requirement in order for personal data to be used, and the form of consent. Though, approximately 1/5 (18.8%) of respondents didn't know they could withdraw their consent at any time. Respondents seem to know quite well the rights to be informed for data processing and demand the correction of inaccurate data. On the contrary, low degree of knowledge was recorded for the data portability right and the right of not being subjected to a decision taken solely on the basis of automated processing. Moreover, 22.8% of respondents did not know when they could ask data controller to erase their personal data, which is important as it increases data subjects' control over data flow, while 29.7% did not know when the right to personal data processing limitation could be exercised.

Altogether more than half of the respondents (52.5%) were absolutely or quite sure they control personal data they provide online, though acknowledging that after data release they have partial (56%) or no control at all (20%). Participants expressed high concerns regarding a series of cases explored and stated risks when providing personal data focusing on security issues, data exploitation for fraud and data dissemination to third parties without their consent. Nevertheless, respondents show risky behavior considering that 64.4% read privacy policies partially and 28.7% do not read them.

The findings up to this point show on one hand that data subjects are more familiar with specific rights (their knowledge extent regarding all the rights they have been asked for is rather moderate) and on the other that they have high concerns and acknowledge that they encounter risks when providing data. Although these findings are rather encouraging and can lead to the assumption that data subjects would take up data protection measures, this doesn't seem to happen. Specifically, although respondents had shown a high level of knowledge regarding the requirement for consent and its form, only 19% provides consent explicitly in any case (online and offline) regardless the kind of data. This shows that the right is known, but not properly exercised. The same phenomenon appeared in the case of the right to be informed, the extent of which was high according to data subjects' self-assessment. However, respondents stated that they had "sometimes" (37.6%) or "rarely" (39.6%) information on the conditions for the collection and processing of their data. Only in the case of data portability right seems to be an inversion to data subjects' attitude. Although 54% of the participants had no or little knowledge of this right, the possibility of data portability is considered "very important" (38.6%) or "quite important" (36.6%). This may imply that participants think of the right as a way to increase control over their data.

Finally, participants were asked to declare their agreement/disagreement on 6 statements. Findings showed respondents' lack of trust regarding data protection to governments (61.4%), providers (52.4%), and legislation and Supervisory Authorities (40.6%). These results although encouraging with reference to data subjects view on providers' operation, indicate, in the frame of GDPR, lack of confidence towards legislation, governments' responsibility for its implementation, and Authorities' role. Respondents also acknowledged that their data could be exploited by others (53.5%) confirming results of other questions related to data control. This finding may also explain the distribution of responses to the statement "To protect myself it is sufficient to be careful regarding the data I provide online". It seems that individual data protection strategies are not considered to be sufficiently effective. Finally, replies to the statement that refers to knowledge regarding the laws for data protection reveal data subjects' doubts confirming the results regarding the extent of rights knowledge.

## 6 Conclusions

GDPR implementation is a complex process requiring a holistic approach with reference to people, processes and systems [26], since all these are involved, in a different way, in data processing. Within the new legal frame introduced by GDPR, data subjects new modus operandi is essential. This requires knowledge regarding data protection legislation, the rights that data subjects have and the conditions to exercise them, as well as knowledge about data collection and processing procedures and the legal constraints imposed on controllers, in order for data subjects to better control and protect their data, as already proposed by [8, 9].

One year after the implementation of GDPR, the results of this research are interesting showing fluctuations in data subjects' knowledge about their rights, while highlighting that data subjects are in some cases unaware of the conditions within which they can exercise their rights and in others they don't exercise these despite their knowledge. In a future extension of this paper inferential statistics will help to identify how privacy concerns, age or education level may contribute to the extent of rights' knowledge. Future research should also investigate other factors that may impact on rights' knowledge such as the way rights are being perceived at personal level, subjects' past experiences, or the emphasis given on specific rights from information sources. Obviously relevant surveys in other EU Member States are necessary too. Moreover, considering that people during a self-assessment process may tend to overestimate or underestimate their knowledge on legal or technical issues, future research should focus on verifying the actual knowledge using, in addition to the questions posed, others including specific scenarios. The discrepancy revealed between the knowledge of rights and subjects' behavior, in the case of consent for example, should be further investigated in order to clarify whether it constitutes a paradox, a contradiction between knowledge and behavior in this case, in accordance to the already recognized Privacy Paradox (contradiction between attitude and behavior) or whether behavior is not determined by knowledge but mostly by the habit of practice. Considering that personal data are also stored and processed offline, future research should focus on people who don't use digital services exploring their knowledge and behavior regarding their rights.

Although the results of this research cannot be generalized, they provide particularly strong indications that care must be given to enhance data subjects' knowledge in relation to the legislation, their rights and their data protection. Researches showed that enhancing awareness regarding the degree of knowledge in relation to data protection and privacy has a positive impact on users' taking up protective behavior [9, 27]. In this frame educational interventions and information campaigns are important. In fact, the inclusion of legislation in the context of educational interventions is crucial [28] for data subjects to understand their responsibility in the protection of personal data.

# References

1. European Council: Regulation (EU) 2016/679 of the European Parliament and of the Council of 27 April 2016 on the protection of natural persons with regard to the processing of personal data and on the free movement of such data, and repealing Directive 95/46/EC (General Data Protection Regulation) (2016). https://eur-lex.europa.eu/legal-content/EN/TXT/PDF/?uri=CELEX:32016R0679&from=EL
2. The Surveillance Project: The Globalization of Personal Data Project: An International Survey on Privacy and Surveillance, Summary of Findings. Queen's University, Kingston (2008). https://qspace.library.queensu.ca/bitstream/handle/1974/7660/2008_Surveillance_Project_International_Survey_Findings_Summary.pdf?sequence=1&isAllowed=y
3. Mantelero, A.: The future of consumer data protection in the EU Re-thinking the "notice and consent" paradigm in the new era of predictive analytics. Comput. Law Secur. Rev. 30(6), 643–660 (2014)
4. Buschel, I., Mehdi, R., Cammilleri, A., Marzouki, Y., Elger, B.: Protecting human health and security in digital Europe: how to deal with the "privacy paradox"? Sci. Eng. Ethics 20, 639–658 (2014)
5. Mitrou, L.: Law in the Information Society. Sakkoulas Publ., Athens (2002). (in Greek)
6. Conger, S., Pratt, J.H., Loch, K.D.: Personal information privacy and emerging technologies. Inf. Syst. J. 23(5), 401–417 (2013)
7. Baek, Y.M.: Solving the privacy paradox: a counter-argument experimental approach. Comput. Hum. Behav. 38, 33–42 (2014)

8. Trepte, S., et al.: Do people know about privacy and data protection strategies? Towards the "online privacy literacy scale" (OPLIS). In: Gutwirth, S., Leenes, R., de Hert, P. (eds.) Reforming European Data Protection Law. LGTS, vol. 20, pp. 333–365. Springer, Dordrecht (2015). https://doi.org/10.1007/978-94-017-9385-8_14

9. Park, Y.J.: Digital literacy and privacy behavior online. Commun. Res. **40**(2), 215–236 (2011)

10. Miltgen, C.L., Peyrat-Guillard, D.: Cultural and generational influences on privacy concerns: a qualitative study in seven European countries. Eur. J. Inf. Syst. **23**, 103–125 (2014)

11. European Commission: Special Eurobarometer 431. Data Protection Report (2015). http://ec.europa.eu/commfrontoffice/publicopinion/archives/ebs/ebs_431_en.pdf

12. Kelley, P.G., Cranor, L.F., Sadeh, N.: Privacy as part of the app decision-making process. In: Proceedings of the SIGCHI Conference on Human Factors in Computing Systems, pp. 3393–3402. ACM, Paris (2013)

13. European Commission: Special Eurobarometer 487a. The General Data Protection Regulation, Report (2019). file:///C:/Users/user/Downloads/ebs487a_en%20(2).pdf

14. Cohen, L., Manion, L.: Research Methods in Education. Metaichmio Publ., Athens (1994). (in Greek)

15. Zafeiropoulos, K.: How to Do a Scientific Research. Kritiki Publ., Athens (2015). (in Greek)

16. Javeau, C.: The Research Using Questionnaire. Tipothito Publ., Athens (1996). (in Greek)

17. Babbie, E.: Introduction to Social Research. Kritiki Publ., Athens (2011). (in Greek)

18. Oppenheim, A.: Questionnaire Design, Interviewing and Attitude Measurement. Pinter, London (1992)

19. Poullet, Y.: Is the general data protection regulation the solution? Comput. Law Secur. Rev. **34**(4), 773–778 (2018)

20. De Hert, P., Papakonstantinou, V., Malgieri, G., Beslay, L., Sanchez, I.: The right to data portability in the GDPR: towards user-centric interoperability of digital services. Comput. Law Secur. Rev. **34**(2), 193–203 (2018)

21. van Ooijen, I., Vrabec, H.U.: Does the GDPR enhance consumers' control over personal data? An analysis from a behavioral perspective. J. Consum. Policy **42**, 91–107 (2019)

22. Brandimarte, L., Acquisti, A., Loewenstein, G.: Misplaced confidences: privacy and the control paradox. Soc. Psychol. Pers. Sci. **4**(3), 340–347 (2012)

23. Marwick, A.E., Murgia-Diaz, D., Palfrey, J.G.: Youth, Privacy and Reputation (Literature Review). Social Science Research Network, Rochester (2010)

24. Cadogan, R.A.: An imbalance of power: the readability of internet privacy policies. J. Bus. Econ. Res. **2**(3), 49–62 (2011)

25. Proctor, R.W., Athar Ali, M., Vu, K.-P.L.: Examining usability of web privacy policies. Int. J. Hum.-Comput. Interact. **24**(3), 307–328 (2008)

26. Datoo, A.: Data in the post-GDPR world. Comput. Fraud Secur. **9**, 17–18 (2018)

27. Moll, R., Pieschl, St., Bromme, R.: Competent or clueless? Users' knowledge and misconceptions about their online privacy management. Comput. Hum. Behav, **41**, 212–219 (2014)

28. Sideri, M., Kitsiou, A., Tzortzaki, E., Kalloniatis, C., Gritzalis, S.: Enhancing university students' privacy literacy through an educational intervention. A Greek case-study. Int. J. Electron. Gov. (in press)

# A Case Study of Intra-library Privacy Issues on Android GPS Navigation Apps

Stylianos Monogios[1], Konstantinos Limniotis[1,2,3(✉)] ⓘD,
Nicholas Kolokotronis[3] ⓘD, and Stavros Shiaeles[4] ⓘD

[1] School of Pure and Applied Sciences,
Open University of Cyprus, 2220 Latsia, Cyprus
{stylianos.monogios,konstantinos.limniotis}@ouc.ac.cy
[2] Hellenic Data Protection Authority, Kifissias 1-3, 11523 Athens, Greece
klimniotis@dpa.gr
[3] Department of Informatics and Telecommunications,
University of Peloponnese, Akadimaikou G. K. Vlachou Street,
22131 Tripolis, Greece
{klimn,nkolok}@uop.gr
[4] Cyber Security Research Group, School of Computing,
University of Portsmouth, Portsmouth PO1 2UP, UK
sshiaeles@ieee.org

**Abstract.** The Android unrestricted application market, being of open source nature, has made it a popular platform for third-party applications reaching millions of smart devices in the world. This tremendous increase in applications with an extensive API that includes access to phone hardware, settings, and user data raises concerns regarding users privacy, as the information collected from the apps could be used for profiling purposes. In this respect, this paper focuses on the geolocation data and analyses five GPS applications to identify the privacy risks if no appropriate safeguards are present. Our results show that GPS navigation apps have access to several types of device data, while they may allow for personal data leakage towards third parties such as library providers or tracking services without providing adequate or precise information to the users. Moreover, as they are using third-party libraries, they suffer from the intra-library collusion issue, that could be exploited from advertising and analytics companies through apps and gather large amount of personal information without the explicit consent of the user.

**Keywords:** Android system · GPS navigation app · Geo-location · Privacy · Profiling · Third-party libraries

---

 This project has received funding from the European Union's Horizon 2020 research and innovation programme under grant agreement no. 786698. The work reflects only the authors' view and the Agency is not responsible for any use that may be made of the information it contains.

S. Katsikas and V. Zorkadis (Eds.): e-Democracy 2019, CCIS 1111, pp. 34–48, 2020.
https://doi.org/10.1007/978-3-030-37545-4_3

# 1    Introduction

Personal data protection in the mobile applications ecosystem constitutes an important challenge from both technical and legal aspects, due to the unprecedented growth in recent years of users carrying smart devices, whereas the corresponding smart applications may become highly intrusive in terms of users privacy (see, e.g., [11,23]). More than 7.6 billion mobile connections serving 4.7 billion unique mobile consumers globally [12], whilst it is expected that by 2020 the mobile subscriptions will cover almost the 75% of the global population; regarding the smart phones, about 5.8 billions are expected to be used by 2020. At the same time, smart applications may process large amounts of personal data, such as the users' location, friendships, habits and interests – thus profiling users. This information can be used for commercial purposes, including behavioural advertising, although it may go far beyond this purpose—e.g. to infer a user's socio-economic class, health status or political beliefs. Such privacy issues are further accentuated by the fact that Internet-of-Things (IoT) solutions (platforms and services) can also be accessed via mobile apps, as well as that the next generation of mobile networks technology will realise part of the IoT's connectivity.

**Privacy Issues of Smart Mobile Applications.** Towards implementing behavioral advertising, (efficient) tracking mechanisms is a prerequisite for the ad networks in order to create accurate profiles of the users. Generally, several tracking mechanisms of different forms exist [5,6]. Probably the most difficult one to be tackled towards protecting users' privacy rests with the generation of a so-called fingerprint of the user—that is, a unique identifier of a device, operating system, browser version, or other instance that can be read by a web service when the user browses, allowing the tracking of the user when he visits several websites belonging to different entities. Fingerprinting was first defined as *browser* fingerprinting in [8] and has been subsequently generalized to describe any unique instance that a device leaves based on, e.g., a specific software that is installed on the device or the particular device configurations [16]. The difficulty in dealing with fingerprinting rests with the fact that fingerprints are not based on any client-based storage (such as the case of cookies) and thus sophisticated *data protection by design* solutions are needed to alleviate the relevant privacy risks. Especially in the mobile applications ecosystem, behavioral advertising can be upgraded into ubiquitous advertising [15], that is advertisements will not only be personalised to users' online profiles, but also to their physical profiles—e.g., advertisements will be customised to users' locations, physical or intellectual activities, etc. [6].

The average smartphone has more than 25 apps installed [22], each having its own access rights to the device depending on the permissions that the user grants. The vast majority of the apps utilize third-party libraries—e.g. to provide integration with social networks or to facilitate the programming procedure via easily embedding complex functionalities. These libraries obtain the same access rights with the host app. However, the use of such libraries may pose some risks for the users' privacy, since they may, e.g. track the users [4,21]. Moreover, as it is analysed in [22], the use of several popular libraries by several different smart apps may result in the so-called *intra-library collusion*, that is the case that a single library embedded in several apps on a device may appropriately combine the set of permissions given by each host app so as to leverage the acquired privileges and gather (a possibly large amount of) personal information without the explicit consent of the user. More specifically, as also stated in [22], the current Android security model, which does not support the separation of privileges between apps and the embedded libraries, facilitates the following relative privacy threats without the user's consent:

– Libraries may abuse the privileges granted to the host applications.
– Libraries may track the users.
– Libraries may aggregate multiple signals for detailed user profiling.

Moreover, obtaining a valid user's consent according to corresponding legal provisions, as well as being able to demonstrate its validity, is not trivial in such a challenging environment (see, e.g., [14]).

More than half of the apps available on Google Play contain ad libraries linked to third party advertisers [3] and as being studied through analysis of many versions of popular Android apps studied in [18], the question whether privacy issues are being efficiently addressed over time reveal that there is an increased collection of personally identifiable information across app versions, a slow adoption of HTTPS to secure the information sent to other parties, and a large number of third parties being able to link user activity and locations across apps. Interestingly enough, in [13] it is shown that even in privacy enhancing technologies such as ad blockers (see, e.g., [10]) we may encounter privacy issues, since the analysis therein indicates that neither ad blockers are free of third-party tracking libraries and permissions to access critical resources on users' mobile devices.

**Our Contribution.** This paper focuses on the privacy issues that occur in applications providing Navigation through GPS component, motivated by the special nature of these apps which necessitate access to the current device's geolocation data. Our approach is based on analysing the user's personal data that such applications process and examining whether this process may pose some (hidden) risks for user's privacy. In this direction, we studied five popular GPS navigation apps on Android devices via performing dynamic analysis in order to id which personal data—including user's device identifiers— they process. The dynamic analysis was carried out by using known appropriate software tools that help monitor what mobile applications are doing at runtime. We particularly investigated whether such applications share the personal information they access with third-parties, due to the existence of third-party libraries. Moreover, we examined the Android permissions granted to these applications, with the aim to investigate whether such similar applications require the same permissions or not. In the process, we also examined the privacy policies of these apps, in terms of finding out whether the information provided to the users is satisfactory.

Our analysis shows that there is underlying data processing in place, which could possibly result in data protection risks, especially with respect to data leakage to third parties for tracking users, since the users are not fully aware of all these processes taking place at the background. Moreover, discrepancies occur with respect to the permissions that each application requires; again, since any such permission actually corresponds to a specific purpose of data processing, the relevant information provided to the users is not always adequate. Hence, this work further reveals the privacy challenges that span the entire mobile applications ecosystem.

It should be pointed out that the aim of the paper is not to make a comparative study between GPS applications, neither to perform a legal evaluation of the relevant personal data processing they perform; our aim is to examine, in a typical scenario of a GPS navigation, which type of personal data processing occurs, so as to subsequently yield useful information on potential data protection concerns that are in place.

The paper is organized as follows. First, a short discussion of the main legal provisions is given in Sect. 2, in conjunction with the presentation of device identifiers that should be considered as personal data. Section 3 provides a short overview on the permission model that Android adopts, focusing on the so-called high-risk permissions in terms of privacy. Section 4 constitutes the main part of this work, where the results of our dynamic analysis on the corresponding applications are presented. More precisely, we first describe our testing environment and the methodology that have been utilized for our dynamic analysis, whilst we next present the findings of the analysis, as well as a discussion on them. Finally, conclusion as well as some recommendations, are given in Sect. 5.

## 2   Preliminaries

The European Regulation (EU) 2016/679 (2016)—known as the *General Data Protection Regulation* or GDPR—that applies from May 25th, 2018, constitutes the main legal instrument for personal data protection in Europe. The GDPR, which has been adopted in 2016 replacing the previous Data Protection Directive 95/46/EC, results in a harmonization of relevant data processing rules across the European Union and aims to further protect and empower all EU citizens data privacy. Although the GDPR is a European Regulation, its territorial scope is not restricted within the European boundaries, since it applies to all organizations that process personal data of individuals residing in the European Union, regardless of the organizations' location, which can be outside European Union.

The term *personal data* refers to any information relating to an identified or identifiable natural person, that is a person who can be identified; as it is explicitly stated in the GDPR, an identifiable natural person is one who can be identified, directly or indirectly, in particular by reference to an identifier such as a name, an identification number, location data, an online identifier or to one or more factors specific to the physical, physiological, genetic, mental, economic, cultural or social identity of that natural person. *Personal data processing* means any operation that is performed on personal data, including the collection, recording, structuring, storage, adaptation or alteration, retrieval, use, disclosure by transmission, dissemination, combination and erasure.

The notion of the personal data is quite wide, since special attention needs to be given whenever some data are being characterized as *anonymous*, i.e. non–personal. Indeed, according to the GDPR, although the data should be considered as anonymous if the person is no longer identifiable, all the means reasonably likely to be used to identify the natural person directly or indirectly should be taken into account towards determining whether a natural person is identifiable (see also [7]).

In general, device identifiers should be considered as personal data since they may allow the identification of a user (if possibly combined with other information). The Android operating system, which is the case considered in this work, is associated with two identifiers (see, e.g., [20]):

– The Android ID, which is a permanent 64bit randomly generated number.
– The Google Advertising ID (GAID), which is a 32-digit alphanumeric identifier that can be reset at any time, according to the user's request.

Other device or network identifiers, such as the *medium access control* (MAC) and the *Internet protocol* (IP) addresses, should also be considered as personal data.

The GDPR codifies the basic principles that need to be guaranteed when personal data are collected or further processed and sets specific obligations to those that process personal data (data controllers/data processors). Any processing of personal data requires a lawful basis. In case that such a lawful basis is the individual's consent, then consent must meet certain requirements in order to be considered as being sufficient; more precisely, consent means any freely given, specific, informed and unambiguous indication of the data subject's agreement to the processing of his or her personal data must be given by a statement or a clear affirmative action (art. 4 of the GDPR). As stated in [9], since many smart apps will need to rely on users' consent for the processing of certain personal data, the requirement of consent deserves special attention, in particular as it relates to the issue of *permissions*. Unfortunately, users have limited understanding of the associated risks of enabling permissions (or access to) in certain apps, whilst app developers have difficulties in comprehending and appropriately handling permissions [9]. Moreover, this permissions model does not facilitate the provision of a legally valid consent for any third-party functionality that might be integrated into the app (since, in the Android platforms, third-party libraries inherit the privileges of the host app); hence, a major data protection risk occurs whenever a third-party library uses personal data for profiling and targeting, without the user's consent.

It should be pointed out that, depending on the techniques used, tracking of a mobile user may fall into the scope of the legal framework of the so-called cookie provision in the ePrivacy Directive (Directive 2002/58/EC); this applies only to the European Union. Again, this cookie provision requires informed consent for such app behaviour. In any case, the new Regulation that is currently being prepared in the EU to replace the ePrivacy Directive (the so-called ePrivacy Regulation), aims at being aligned with the GDPR, also covering new stakeholders and technologies in the field of electronic communications.

The GDPR sets new rules and obligations for each *data controller*, i.e. the entity that, alone or jointly with others, determines the purposes and means of the processing of personal data. Amongst them, the so-called *data protection by design* and *data protection by default* constitute important challenges involving various technological and organisational aspects [1]. According to the Recital 78 of the GDPR, appropriate measures that meet in particular the above two principles of data protection by design/default

> *(. . . ) could consist, inter alia, of minimising the processing of personal data, pseudonymising personal data as soon as possible, transparency with regard to the functions and processing of personal data, enabling the data subject to monitor the data processing, enabling the controller to create and improve security features.*

In the same Recital, there is also an explicit reference to the producers of the products, services and applications that are based on the processing of personal data or process personal data; namely, these stakeholders

> *(. . . ) should be encouraged to take into account the right to data protection when developing and designing such products, services and applications and (. . . ) to make sure that controllers and processors are able to fulfill their data protection obligations.*

This is the only reference within the GDPR to stakeholders others than the data controllers or data processors (which are the entities that process personal data on behalf of the controller). In the mobile ecosystem, application developers or library providers could lie in this category and thus, even in cases that these actors are neither data controllers nor data processors (hence, they may not be directly regulated under the GDPR), they are encouraged to make sure that controllers and processors are able to fulfill their data protection obligations [9].

## 3   Permissions of Applications

One of the Android system's core features is that applications are executed in their own private environment, referred to as a *sandbox*, being unable to access resources or perform operations outside of their sandbox that would adversely impact the system's security (e.g. by downloading malicious software) or user's privacy (e.g. by reading contacts, emails, or any other personal information). An application must explicitly request the permissions needed either at install-time, via its `AndroidManifest.xml` file, or at run-time. Our experimental environment, as it is discussed next, involved Android version 8.0 (API level 26), as well as Android Lollipop 5.0.1 (API level 21); therefore, for the first case the permissions granted to the GPS applications were requested at runtime, whilst for the second case they were requested at install-time.

The permissions granted to applications are classified to several protection levels, based on their ability to harm the system or the end-user, out which three levels affect third-party applications [2]:

1. *Normal permissions*: these cover areas where the application needs to access data or resources outside its sandbox, but where there's low risk to the user's privacy or the operation of other applications.
2. *Signature permissions*: these are granted only if the application that requests the permission is signed by the same certificate as the application that defines the permission.
3. *Dangerous permissions*: these cover areas where the application wants data or resources that involve the user's private information, or could potentially affect the user's stored data or the operation of other applications.

## 4    Dynamic Analysis of GPS Applications

This section provides the methodology that was followed, along with the results that have been obtained from the dynamic analysis performed on five popular GPS applications of the Android platform.

### 4.1    The Testing Environment

For our research experiments, we utilized an Android device (Android version Oreo 8) in which we installed five indicative popular GPS navigation apps which are available through the Google Play Store, namely: [1] the Google Maps (v. 10.12.1), [2] the Sygic GPS Navigation & Maps (v. 17.7.0), [3] the TomTom GPS Navigation - Traffic Alerts & Maps (v. 1.17.1), [4] the MAPS.ME (v. 9.0.7) and [5] the MapFactor GPS Navigation Maps (v. 4.0.109).

To be able to analyse these smart apps, via investigating whether they send personal data to third parties, as well as to obtain a direct information on potentially privacy–intrusive processes, we utilized the Lumen Privacy Monitor (Lumen)[1], which is a free, privacy–enhancing app with the ability to analyze network traffic on mobile devices in user space. The Lumen runs locally on the device and intercepts all network traffic since it inserts itself as a middleware between apps and the network interface ([17]). Lumen is able to identify personal data leaks that do not require explicit Android permissions, including software and hardware identifiers. Therefore, Lumen has been used in several cases by the research community for analysing potential personal data leakages from Android devices (see, e.g. [19]).

It should be noted that according to a communication we had with the team developing Lumen, it is possible that some leaks in our current version of Android (i.e. 8) may not be detectable, since several apps use obfuscation or encoding to upload the data, even for location, and not all such mechanisms are supported in the public version of the Lumen. Therefore, we additionally performed

---

[1] https://www.haystack.mobi/.

an analysis through an appropriate module of the Xposed framework[2], namely the Inspeckage Android packet inspector—that is an application with an internal HTTP server[3], which is useful for performing dynamic analysis of Android applications. Due to practical limitations, the Inspeckage Android packet inspector has been installed into a different device with an older version of the Android system, namely Android Lollipop 5.0.1; it should be pointed out though that, as of July 2019, the Lollipop versions have still about 14.5% share combined of all Android devices accessing Google Play store[4]. Since the same GPS applications, with the same embedded libraries, have been installed in both devices, it is expected that, for both scenarios we investigated, the same third-party domains collect data (differences may occur in which personal data the applications get access; for example, Android 8 does not allow applications getting access to the unique Android ID).

All the experiments took place during February and March 2019. The default settings were accepted during the installation of all GPS applications, whereas any permission that was required during their execution was also given.

## 4.2 Permission Analysis of GPS Applications

By using the Lumen tool, we observed the permissions that each of the application granted. We noticed that all applications asked for several access rights that are generally considered by the Lumen tool as high or medium risk with respect to user's privacy, such as the access to external storage and to the existing accounts on the device; all the permissions that are characterised as high-risk by Lumen are also considered as dangerous in [2]. We summarize our observations, focusing explicitly on the so-called high-risk permissions, in Table 1.

**Table 1.** Dangerous permissions (`android.permission.*`) obtained by GPS navigation apps

| Permissions | Google Maps | Sygic | TomTom | MAPS.ME | MapFactor |
|---|---|---|---|---|---|
| ACCESS_COARSE_LOCATION | × | × | | × | × |
| ACCESS_FINE_LOCATION | × | × | × | × | × |
| READ_EXTERNAL_STORAGE | × | × | × | × | × |
| WRITE_EXTERNAL_STORAGE | × | × | × | × | × |
| CAMERA | × | × | | | |
| GET_ACCOUNTS | | × | × | | |
| RECORD_AUDIO | × | × | | | |
| READ_CONTACTS | × | × | × | | |
| WRITE_CONTACTS | | | × | | |
| READ_PHONE_STATE | | × | | | × |

---

[2] https://repo.xposed.info.
[3] https://mobilesecuritywiki.com/.
[4] https://developer.android.com/about/dashboards.

It is of interest that, although all the applications provide similar services, there exist variations on the permissions that each of them requires. Therefore, the intra-library collusion privacy threat seems to be present; for example, if the same third-party library is being used by Google Maps and TomTom or Sygic and TomTom, then such a library will obtain all high-risk permissions that are shown in Table 1.

It should be explicitly pointed out that none of these permissions should be considered, by default, as unnecessary; for example, obviously, having location permission is prerequisite for GPS apps. Moreover, depending on the services provided, several other permissions may still be needed. However, it is questionable whether sufficient information is provided to the users regarding the necessity of these permissions, as well as whether third-party domains also get such permissions and have access to device data, as discussed next.

### 4.3   Data Traffic to Third-Party Domains

By using the Lumen monitoring tool, we noticed that, for all GPS applications studied, there exists data traffic to several domains. With respect to Advertising Tracking Services (ATS), there exists - based on Lumen's output - one ATS in Google Maps, four ATS in Sygic, two ATS in TomTom, six ATS in MAPS.ME and two ATS in MapFactor. Indicative screenshots from the Lumen tool are provided in Fig. 1.

**Fig. 1.** Data leakages to several domains for the Google Map app, the Sygic app, the TomTom app, the MAPS.ME app and the Map Factor app respectively.

By combining the outputs derived from both the Lumen and the Inspeckage tools, we summarize the results regarding the data leakages to several domains (either ATS or not) in Table 2; note that both first-party and third-party domains are shown. Based on these outputs, we conclude that, in most cases, the ATS that are associated with the apps are more than their number that was initially estimated by the Lumen tool.

We subsequently focused on the exact personal data, including device data, that are being transmitted to these domains. As explained previously, we utilized both the Lumen monitoring tool (for an Android 8) and the Inspeckage tool (for an Android Lollipop device). It should be pointed out that transmission

**Table 2.** Data leakages by GPS navigation apps to several domains (either first or third-party)

| Domains | Google Maps | Sygic | TomTom | MAPS.ME | MapFactor |
|---|---|---|---|---|---|
| app-measurement.com | X | | | | |
| google.com | X | | | | X |
| youtube.com | X | | | | |
| appsflyer.com | | X | | X | |
| crashlytics.com | | X | X | X | |
| facebook.com | | X | | X | |
| foursquare.com | | X | | | |
| infinario.com | | X | | | |
| sygic.com | | X | | | |
| uber.com | | X | | | |
| windows.net | | X | | | X |
| adjust.com | | | X | | |
| tomtom.com | | | X | | |
| flurry.com | | | | X | |
| maps.me | | | | X | |
| mopub.com | | | | X | |
| my.com | | | | X | |
| pushwoosh.com | | | | X | |
| mapswithme.com | | | | X | |
| mapfactor.com | | | | | X |
| google-analytics.com | X | X | | | X |
| googlesyndication.com | | | | | X |
| googleadservices.com | | | | | X |
| akamaized.net | | X | | | |
| twitter.com | | X | X | X | |
| doubleclick.net | | | | X | X |

FLURRY_SHARED_PREFERENCES.xml

```
<?xml version='1.0' encoding='utf-8' standalone='yes' ?>
<map>
    <string name="advertising_id">fafb64ce-33ca-4b62-8b96-f85d6046585e</string>
    <string name="com.flurry.sdk.api_key">FP4MRV3698TD7JYF684V</string>
    <boolean name="ad_tracking_enabled" value="false" ></boolean>
    <boolean name="com.flurry.sdk.previous_successful_report" value="true" ></boolean>
    <long name="com.flurry.sdk.initial_run_time" value="1551302313613" ></long>
</map>
```

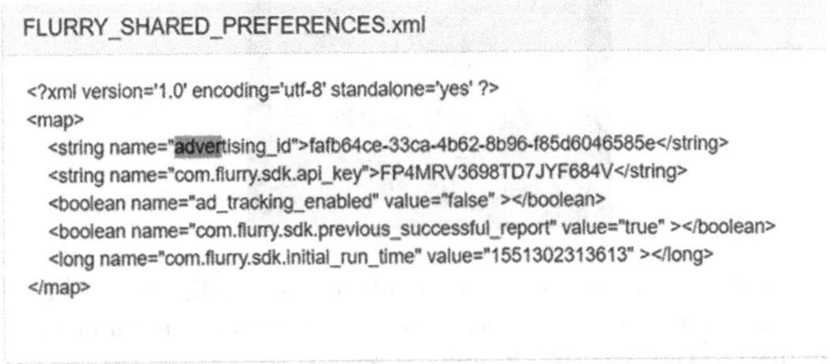

**Fig. 2.** Transmission of the GAID to the flurry.com, based on the analysis through the Inspeckage tool.

of the GAID to third-party domains has been captured only by the Inspeckage tool, due to the encryption that takes place on such transmissions. An indicative screenshot on the information obtained by the Inspeckage tool is shown in Fig. 2.

Our analysis illustrated that the GAID, as a unique device identifier, is being collected by several ATS services - namely by infinario.com (via the Sygic app), by appsflyer.com (via Sygic and MAPS.ME apps), by twitter.com (via Sygic, TomTom and MAPS.ME apps), by flurry.com (via the MAPS.ME app), by windows.net (via Sygic and MapFactor apps) and by crashlytics.com (via the MAPS.ME app).

Interestingly enough, we noticed that there exist domains which may collect a combination of personal data due to the fact that are being embedded into several different apps. For example, the domain crashlytics.com collects the Facebook ID via the app [2]. Hence, if both apps [2] and [4] are being installed into the same device, both the GAID and the Facebook ID are being transmitted to this domain, thus allowing this ATS service linking a device with a social network user. Ofcourse, it is also possible that such a pair - i.e. GAID and Facebook ID - are also being sent to an ATS service through a unique app; this is the case, e.g. of app [4] that sends these data to appsflyer.com. Moreover, it is highly probable that these domains may also collect user's information through other smart apps that are installed into the device, thus further increasing the privacy risks. For example, again for the Crashlytics tracking service, the Lumen tools informs us that several apps that are installed in our device also communicate with this domain; this is shown in Fig. 3.

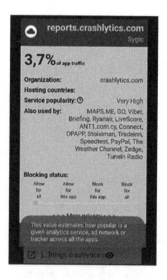

**Fig. 3.** The percentage of Sygic's outgoing traffic corresponding to the crashlytics service, as well as an enumeration of other apps in our device communicating with this service (including the two other GPS apps [2] and [3]).

Apart from the content of the information itself, it is of interest to investigate whether this information is being transmitted in a secure way - i.e. appropriately encrypted. To this end, we utilized the Lumen monitoring tool, which also provides information on the protocols that the applications use in order to transmit data to several domains. The output of Lumen indicates that the vast majority of the output traffic generated by these applications is indeed encrypted through the HTTPS protocol or the Quic protocol (in case of the Google Maps app). In two apps, the whole amount of outgoing data is encrypted, whereas in the remaining three apps the proportion of the encrypted outgoing traffic ranges from 57% to 68%; these are shown in Fig. 4. Therefore, although we may conclude that, generally, encryption is in place for protecting the personal data that are being transmitted, it seems that there is room for improvement in some cases.

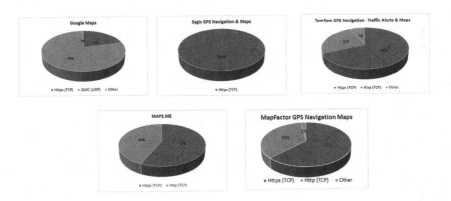

**Fig. 4.** Protocol usage by GPS navigation apps

## 4.4   Transparency of the Processing

With regard to the transparency of the underlying data processing, we studied the privacy policies of the GPS applications. As of July 2019, the main conclusion is that the information provided therein does not suffice to clarify all the processes that have been noticed by our above dynamic analysis. For example, in one case, the privacy policy of the app states (where the name of the organisation providing the app is being mentioned as *Company*):

> *When using the software on certain mobile devices, the Company may need to access and collect certain details and data from your mobile device including details of your location (shall include, but not be limited to country, state, city/town/locality, street). The company collects and stores such information:*
> *– to inform you about your location;*
> *– to send you notifications or content according to your location;*
> *– to show you content (e.g. images) according to your location;*

- *to inform you about your goal course;*
- *to inform you about certain points of interest (e.g. museums, stores, restaurants, hotels, gasoline stations etc.);*
- *to inform you about other user's comments on certain points of interest;*
- *to improve Services.*

*(...) The Company's Services may contain features, functionalities and/or third party offerings that may link you or provide you with certain reference, functionality or products of third parties ("Other Services"). These Other Services are provided by the Company only as a convenience. The Other Services are not controlled by the Company in any way and the Company is not responsible for the content of any such Other Services, any link contained therein or for the performance, availability, or quality, of any Other Service.*

Similar statements generally occur in all applications; even in cases that more details on the data process are given, there is still room for improvement with respect to the transparency of the processing.

## 5 Conclusions

In this work we focused on five popular GPS navigation applications for Android platforms, with the aim to examine whether they suffer from known privacy issues that are present in the mobile applications ecosystem, taking into account relevant legal provisions. The main findings of our preliminary analysis can be summarized as follows:

- It is possible that some GPS applications, taking into account their access rights, process some personal data in a way that it is questionable if the data protection by design and by default principles are being met.
- The known privacy threat that rests with the so-called intra-library collusion seems to exist in GPS applications we tested.
- The information that is provided to the users regarding the relevant underlying personal data processing is not always complete or clear; this in turn weakens the validity of the user's consent.
- In some cases it is possible that outgoing data generated by these applications are not encrypted.

The above validates the data protection issues that are present in the mobile applications ecosystem. Although such issues are known to exist for several types of smart apps (see, e.g. [7,13,18]), the fact that they are also present in applications processing user's location has significant importance as it may result higher privacy violations. Moreover, it should be pointed out that the above findings do not necessarily constitute an exhaustive list; there is still room for further analysis of these apps (e.g. via performing static analysis on their source code) in conjunction with other popular apps that are expected to be present into a smart device.

From this research, it becomes prominent that much effort should be put on promoting the data protection by design and by default principles in smart applications such as privilege separation strategies for apps and their embedded libraries, proper pseudonymisation techniques, as well as improvement on personal data policies (both on their content/clarity but on their ease on readability). This way we are taking the right steps to mitigate intra-library collusion and protect users privacy.

**Acknowledgment.** The authors would like to thank Narseo Vallina-Rodriguez from the International Computer Science Institute (ICSI) in Berkeley for providing useful explanation on the Lumen tool's monitoring process, as well as the anonymous reviewers for their useful comments and suggestions.

# References

1. Alshammari, M., Simpson, A.: Towards a principled approach for engineering privacy by design. In: Schweighofer, E., Leitold, H., Mitrakas, A., Rannenberg, K. (eds.) APF 2017. LNCS, vol. 10518, pp. 161–177. Springer, Cham (2017). https://doi.org/10.1007/978-3-319-67280-9_9

2. Android Developers, Permissions Overview. https://goo.gl/A7QG1J. Accessed 22 Jan 2019

3. Athanasopoulos, E., Kemerlis, V.P., Portokalidis, G., Keromytis, A.D.: NaClDroid: native code isolation for android applications. In: Askoxylakis, I., Ioannidis, S., Katsikas, S., Meadows, C. (eds.) ESORICS 2016. LNCS, vol. 9878, pp. 422–439. Springer, Cham (2016). https://doi.org/10.1007/978-3-319-45744-4_21

4. Binns, R., Lyngs, U., Van Kleek, M., Zhao, J., Libert, T., Shadbolt, N.: Third Party Tracking in the Mobile Ecosystem. arXiv:1804.03603v3 [cs.CY] (2018)

5. Bujlow, T., Carela-Español, V., Solé-Pareta, J., Barlet-Ros, P.: A survey on web tracking: mechanisms, implications, and defenses. Proc. IEEE **105**, 1476–1510 (2017). https://doi.org/10.1109/jproc.2016.2637878

6. Castelluccia, C.: Behavioural tracking on the internet: a technical perspective. In: Gutwirth, S., Leenes, R., De Hert, P., Poullet, Y. (eds.) European Data Protection: In Good Health, pp. 21–33. Springer, Heidelberg (2012). https://doi.org/10.1007/978-94-007-2903-2_2

7. Chatzistefanou, V., Limniotis, K.: On the (non-)anonymity of anonymous social networks. In: Katsikas, S.K., Zorkadis, V. (eds.) e-Democracy 2017. CCIS, vol. 792, pp. 153–168. Springer, Cham (2017). https://doi.org/10.1007/978-3-319-71117-1_11

8. Eckersley, P.: How unique is your web browser? In: Atallah, M.J., Hopper, N.J. (eds.) PETS 2010. LNCS, vol. 6205, pp. 1–18. Springer, Heidelberg (2010). https://doi.org/10.1007/978-3-642-14527-8_1

9. European Union Agency for Network and Information Security: Privacy and data protection in mobile applications - A study on the app development ecosystem and the technical implementation of GDPR (2017). https://doi.org/10.2824/114584

10. Gervais, A., Filios, A., Lenders, V., Capkun, S.: Quantifying web adblocker privacy. In: Foley, S.N., Gollmann, D., Snekkenes, E. (eds.) ESORICS 2017. LNCS, vol. 10493, pp. 21–42. Springer, Cham (2017). https://doi.org/10.1007/978-3-319-66399-9_2

11. Grammatikakis, K.-P., Ioannou, A., Shiaeles, S., Kolokotronis, N.: Are cracked applications really free? An empirical analysis on Android devices. In: 16th IEEE International Conference on Dependable, Autonomic and Secure Computing (DASC), pp. 730–735 (2018). https://doi.org/10.1109/DASC/PiCom/DataCom/CyberSciTec.2018.00127

12. GSM Association: Safety, privacy and security across the mobile ecosystem - Key issues and policy implications. https://www.gsma.com/publicpolicy/wp-content/uploads/2017/02/GSMA_Safety-privacy-and-security-across-the-mobile-ecosystem.pdf (2017). Accessed 23 Dec 2018

13. Ikram, M., Kaafar, M. A.: A first look at mobile Ad-Blocking apps. In IEEE 16th International Symposium on Network Computing and Applications (NCA), pp. 1–8 (2017). https://doi.org/10.1109/NCA.2017.8171376

14. Jesus, V., Mustare, S.: I did not accept that: demonstrating consent in online collection of personal data. In: Gritzalis, S., Weippl, E.R., Katsikas, S.K., Anderst-Kotsis, G., Tjoa, A.M., Khalil, I. (eds.) TrustBus 2019. LNCS, vol. 11711, pp. 33–45. Springer, Cham (2019). https://doi.org/10.1007/978-3-030-27813-7_3

15. Krumm, J.: Ubiquitous advertising: the killer application for the 21st century. IEEE Pervasive Comput. **10**, 66–73 (2010). https://doi.org/10.1109/mprv.2010.21

16. Kurtz, A., Gascon, H., Becker, T., Rieck, K., Freiling. F.: Fingerprinting mobile devices using personalized configurations. In: Proceedings on Privacy Enhancing Technologies (PoPETs), vol. 1, pp. 4–19 (2016). https://doi.org/10.1515/popets-2015-0027

17. Razaghpanah, A., et al.: Apps, trackers, privacy, and regulators: a global study of the mobile tracking ecosystem. In: Network and Distributed System Security Symposium (2018)

18. Ren, J., Lindorfer, M., Dubois, D.J., Rao, A., Choffnes, D., Vallina-Rodriguez, N.: Bug fixes, improvements, ... and privacy leaks - a longitudinal study of PII leaks across android app versions. In: Network and Distributed System Security Symposium (2018). https://doi.org/10.14722/ndss.2018.23159

19. Reyes, I., et al.: Is our children's apps learning? Automatically detecting coppa violations. In: IEEE Workshop on Technology and Consumer Protection (ConPro) (2017)

20. Son, S., Kim, D., Shmatikov, V.: What mobile ads know about mobile users. In: Network and Distributed System Security Symposium (2016). https://doi.org/10.14722/ndss.2016.23407

21. Stevens, R., Gibler, C., Crussell, J., Erickson, J., Chen, H.: Investigating user privacy in Android ad libraries. In: Workshop on Mobile Security Technologies (MoST), p. 10 (2012)

22. Taylor, V.F., Beresford, A.R., Martinovic, I.: Intra-Library Collusion: A Potential Privacy Nightmare on Smartphones. arXiv:1708.03520v1 [cs.CR] (2017)

23. Wang, W., Wang, X., Feng, W., Liu, J., Han, Z., Zhang, X.: Exploring permission-induced risk in android applications for malicious application detection. IEEE Trans. Inf. Forensics Secur. **9**, 1869–1882 (2014). https://doi.org/10.1109/TIFS.2014.2353996

# A Constraint-Based Model
# for the Frequent Itemset Hiding Problem

Vassilios S. Verykios[1], Elias C. Stavropoulos[2]([⊠]), Vasilis Zorkadis[3],
and Ahmed K. Elmagarmid[4]

[1] Big Data Analytics and Anonymization Laboratory,
School of Science and Technology, Hellenic Open University, Patras, Greece
verykios@eap.gr
[2] Educational Content, Methodology and Technology Laboratory,
Hellenic Open University, Patras, Greece
estavrop@eap.gr
[3] Hellenic Data Protection Authority, Athens, Greece
zorkadis@doa.gr
[4] Qatar Computing Research Institute, HBKU, Doha, Qatar
aelmagarmid@hbku.edu.qa

**Abstract.** This paper introduces a novel constraint-based hiding model
to drastically reduce the preprocessing overhead that is incurred by
border-based techniques in the hiding of sensitive frequent itemsets. The
proposed model is solved by an efficient constraint-based mining algorithm that pushes a conjunction of antimonotone constraints into an
Apriori-like algorithm, for inducing the support theory of non-sensitive
frequent itemsets along with its negative border. The patterns induced by
the constraint-based mining algorithm can be used in border-based hiding algorithms to construct a sanitized version of the original database,
where the sensitive knowledge is concealed. The efficiency of the constraint-based mining algorithm is evaluated on real and synthetic datasets.

**Keywords:** Privacy Preserving Data Mining · Knowledge hiding ·
Frequent itemset hiding · Constraint-based data mining · Linear
programming

## 1 Introduction

Privacy Preserving Data Mining [2,4] has received a lot of attention from
researchers in the last fifteen years or so. In the meantime, a lot of techniques
have been introduced in order to deal with issues related to the privacy of the
input data known as input privacy techniques [18,36], as well as with the privacy
of the induced knowledge in a data mining setting, known as output privacy techniques [14,15,28]. The input privacy techniques are specialized in approaching
the problem of how to guarantee the privacy of the input data during its publication by ensuring the maximum utility of the data for data mining purposes.

© Springer Nature Switzerland AG 2020
S. Katsikas and V. Zorkadis (Eds.): e-Democracy 2019, CCIS 1111, pp. 49–64, 2020.
https://doi.org/10.1007/978-3-030-37545-4_4

Developed techniques in this category include various randomization, perturbation and anonymization algorithms. Cryptographic approaches [27,30] are also used for maintaining the anonymity of the data in a distributed environment.

The latter approaches take into consideration issues that touch upon the privacy of the induced patterns, and they aim at protecting the disclosure of sensitive patterns from the data in such a way that other non-sensitive patterns can be routinely produced from the so-called *sanitized data* (data from which sensitive knowledge has been removed). Because of the specific methodology that is used by these approaches to protect the sensitive patterns, they are collectively known as *knowledge hiding* techniques [9]. There is a large body of knowledge hiding techniques pertaining to different data mining tasks, such as frequent itemset and association rule mining [24], classification [17], sequence, sequential, temporal and spatial data mining [11], stream mining, and graph mining [1]. While both input and output privacy approaches focus on sharing data, a subarea of knowledge hiding investigates approaches for sharing knowledge [6] considering issues related to the inference channels among published patterns, the detection and blocking of these channels, and the anonymization of the shared patterns.

This paper focuses on the *frequent itemset hiding* problem, a specific subdomain of knowledge hiding, where the goal is to sanitize a database from a set of sensitive frequent itemsets, in such a way that (a) those sensitive itemsets cannot be mined from the sanitized database, (b) the quality of the sanitized data is maximized, and (c) the non-sensitive itemsets remain as close as possible to those that are mined from the original database. The frequent itemset hiding problem, which was introduced in 1999 by Atallah et al. [5], has been shown to be NP-Hard, and has been steadily investigated thereafter, producing a large array of solution approaches [21]. A large part of these approaches rely on the application of the Apriori algorithm [3] – as a preprocessing step – for the mining of the frequent itemsets.[1] A data curator should look into the results of the Apriori algorithm and should decide upon the sensitivity of the induced frequent itemsets, based on certain confidentiality rules and security regulations. A set of frequent itemsets, characterized as sensitive by the curator, is then provided as input to a frequent itemset hiding algorithm that tries to sanitize the data from these itemsets, by reducing their support in the data. The reduction in the support of a certain itemset can take place by taking out items (by changing 1-values for 0-values) of this itemset from transactions supporting it.

A major bottleneck in the hiding process is the tradeoff between the hiding of sensitive knowledge and the utility of the sanitized data. The techniques initially proposed were heuristic in nature and greedy in achieving the best possible result, and as such they could not satisfactorily minimize the so-called *hiding side-effects*, or else the undesirable effects of the hiding. The work of Sun and Yu [40,

---

[1] The algorithm processes the itemsets levelwise: it firstly determines the frequent itemsets of size 1, then generates all itemesets of size 2 and determines which of these are frequent, etc. At the n-th level, all frequent itemsets of size n-1 are known and an itemset of size n is frequent if all its subsets of size n-1 are frequent (*the Apriory property*).

41] was a cornerstone in addressing this problem, by focusing on the consequences that the hiding of the sensitive itemsets will have on the "ideal" positive border of the non-sensitive frequent itemsets alone. In doing so, their proposal was instrumental in guiding the hiding process to select items for hiding, so that the side-effects were minimized. A number of techniques was proposed thereafter, by delivering a considerable improvement over the older hiding heuristics as well as over other more recent approaches.

The drawback of the border idea is its high complexity, since the Apriori algorithm needs to run first –in exponential time to the number of items of the database– in order to produce the frequent itemsets along with their negative border. Secondly, the sensitive patterns have to be selected and finally the initial border has to be revised –also another time demanding procedure– before the hiding algorithm can start running. Moreover, the correlation between the positive border of the non-sensitive frequent itemsets a corresponding hypergraph shown in [39], reveals that the hiding process is at least as hard as the transversal hypergraph generation problem, solvable in *incremental output-subexponential time* [25] by calling as an oracle the algorithm of Fredman and Khachiyan [19]. Given that the datasets, on which these techniques should be applied, are massive in length, we realize that the complexity issue is insurmountable.

In this paper we propose a new model for the frequent itemset hiding problem that builds on the constraint-based frequent itemset mining [13] and minimizes the preprocessing overhead incurred by border-based techniques. We also adopt a level-wise algorithm for solving the constraint-based model formulation, by directly computing the revised border in one minimal phase, given that the sensitive itemsets are known beforehand (which is usually the case), without going back and forth traversing the itemset lattice. Additionally, an application of the proposed hiding model is presented. More specifically, we build a new exact approach for the frequent itemset hiding problem, by formulating a linear program based on the extension of the original database. Our approach outdoes all the existing approaches in complexity, in attained utility and in quality of the sanitized database. Experimental results indicate the superiority of our framework compared to all the other existing approaches.

## 2   Related Work

The hiding methodology proposed here, builds on the inaugural work of Atallah et al. [5] which presents a best effort greedy algorithm that turns 1's into 0's in the database in order to hide the sensitive frequent itemsets without offering any guarantees on the quality of the solution. Dasseni et al. [16] and Verykios et al. [42] extended the initial work by proposing algorithms for hiding not only frequent itemsets but also association rules, and by evaluating these approaches according to different performance and data quality metrics.

Saygin et al. [37] and Verykios et al. [43] propose a different approach by turning either 1's or 0's to question marks (implying unknown values), so that the hiding is achieved without falsifying the data. The works proposed by Oliveira and Zaiane [34,35] focus on hiding multiple rules simultaneously and on minimizing the database scans required for hiding. Menon et al. [31,32] were the first to propose an integer programming formulation of the frequent itemset hiding problem. The solution of the integer program determines the number of transactions that need to be sanitized. The selection of those items that will sanitize a transaction is addressed independently of the solution of the linear program, in a heuristic way and thus suboptimally.

Sun and Yu [41] develop a two phase border-based solution in which two minimal sets of itemsets need to be identified first. One of these sets should be hidden and the other one should be preserved. In the second phase, itemsets from the former set are hidden while as many as possible itemsets from the latter set have to be maintained. At the same time Sun and Yu propose a heuristic algorithm that takes advantage of the housekeeping between maximally non-sensitive and minimally sensitive itemsets to deliver an accurate and efficient hiding solution. Moustakides and Verykios [33] relied on the border idea of [41] to build an algorithm that implements the "maxmin" criterion and is similar in accuracy but much more efficient than the border-based algorithm.

Gkoulalas-Dinanis and Verykios [24] applied the border-based principle too, in order to develop two linear programming techniques for optimally solving the hiding problem. The first technique [22], the so called *inline* approach, was introducing binary variables into the original database while the second one [23], known as *hybrid*, was extending the original database with synthetically generated transactions. In both approaches the goal was to fix the contents of specific items in the database, or in its extension thereof, so that to control the support of sensitive and non-sensitive itemsets.

The work proposed in this paper relies also on the constraint-based data mining area apart from the frequent itemset hiding area which was previously presented. By being able to apply a constraint-based frequent itemset mining algorithm, like those presented in [38], we can speed up the process of identifying the expected borders by orders of magnitude compared to the approach proposed by Sun and Yu. The work by Bonchi and Lucchese [10] was also instrumental in helping us formalize our ideas about the border of constraint theories.

## 3    Background and Problem Formulation

Let $\mathcal{I} = \{i_1, i_2, i_3, \ldots, i_n\}$ be a set of distinct literals called *items*. An *itemset* $X$ is a nonempty subset of $\mathcal{I}$, and a $k$-itemset is an itemset of length $k$ (i.e., $|X| = k$). A transaction $T$ over $\mathcal{I}$ is a 2-tuple $T = <tid, t>$ where tid is the identifier of transaction $T$ and $t$ is an itemset such that $t \in 2^{\mathcal{I}}$. We say that a transaction $T = <tid, t>$ supports an itemset $X$ iff $X \subseteq t$. A transaction database $\mathcal{D}$ is a collection of transactions. The *support count* of an itemset $X$ in database $\mathcal{D}$, denoted by $\text{supc}_{\mathcal{D}}(X)$, is the cardinality of the set of transactions supporting $X$. Equivalently, we define the *support* of an itemset $X$, denoted by $\text{sup}_{\mathcal{D}}(X)$, as the fraction of the support count of transactions supporting $X$, over the total count of transactions in the database $\mathcal{D}$.

Given a user-specified support threshold $\sigma$, we call an itemset $X$ $\sigma$-*frequent* or, simply *frequent*, in $\mathcal{D}$ iff $\sup_{\mathcal{D}}(X) \geq \sigma$. Given a support threshold $\sigma$, and a database $\mathcal{D}$, let $\mathcal{F}_{\mathcal{D}}^{\sigma}$ be the collection of $\sigma$-frequent itemsets in $\mathcal{D}$, where $\mathcal{F}_{\mathcal{D}}^{\sigma} \subseteq \mathcal{P}(\mathcal{I})$ and $\mathcal{P}(\mathcal{I})$ is the powerset of $\mathcal{I}$. The positive border of the collection $\mathcal{F}_{\mathcal{D}}^{\sigma}$ denoted as $\mathcal{B}d^{+}(\mathcal{F}_{\mathcal{D}}^{\sigma})$ is given by $\mathcal{B}d^{+}(\mathcal{F}_{\mathcal{D}}^{\sigma}) = \{X \in \mathcal{F}_{\mathcal{D}}^{\sigma} \mid X \subset Y \text{ implies } Y \notin \mathcal{F}_{\mathcal{D}}^{\sigma}\}$, while the negative border is given by $\mathcal{B}d^{-}(\mathcal{F}_{\mathcal{D}}^{\sigma}) = \{X \in \mathcal{P}(\mathcal{I}) - \mathcal{F}_{\mathcal{D}}^{\sigma} \mid Y \subset X \text{ implies } Y \in \mathcal{F}_{\mathcal{D}}^{\sigma}\}$.

Let $\mathcal{S}_{\mathcal{D}}^{\sigma} \subseteq \mathcal{F}_{\mathcal{D}}^{\sigma}$ be the set of sensitive (frequent) itemsets that need to be hidden. Note here that $\mathcal{F}_{\mathcal{D}}^{\sigma}$ and $\mathcal{S}_{\mathcal{D}}^{\sigma}$ determine the ideal set $\widetilde{\mathcal{F}}_{\mathcal{D}}^{\sigma}$ of non-sensitive frequent itemsets based on the Apriori property. For example, if $ab$ and $abc$ belong to $\mathcal{S}_{\mathcal{D}}^{\sigma}$, then it suffices that $ab$ is hidden, since based on the antimonotonicity property of the Apriori, $abc$ will also be hidden in the process. In order to ensure the minimum impact on the quality of the original database, the set $\mathcal{B}d^{-}(\mathcal{S}_{\mathcal{D}}^{\sigma})$ of the *minimal*, with respect of the above property, itemsets of $\mathcal{S}_{\mathcal{D}}^{\sigma}$ should be transferred to the ideal negative border. Our goal then is to *transform $\mathcal{D}$ to $\mathcal{D}'$ by selectively removing some items from the transactions of $\mathcal{D}$* in such a way that we minimize (a) $|\mathcal{F}_{\mathcal{D}'}^{\sigma} - \widetilde{\mathcal{F}}_{\mathcal{D}}^{\sigma}|$ representing the number of the sensitive itemsets that are not hidden and (b) $|\widetilde{\mathcal{F}}_{\mathcal{D}}^{\sigma} - \mathcal{F}_{\mathcal{D}'}^{\sigma}|$ representing the number of hidden non-sensitive itemsets.[2] We give a formal definition of the problem in the sequel.

**Definition 1.** *[Frequent Itemset Hiding Problem] Given a transaction database $\mathcal{D}$ over a set of items $\mathcal{I} = \{i_1, i_2, i_3, \ldots, i_n\}$, a support threshold $\sigma$, and a set of sensitive frequent itemsets $\mathcal{S}_{\mathcal{D}}^{\sigma}$, transform $\mathcal{D}$ into $\mathcal{D}'$ such that:*

1. *$\sup_{\mathcal{D}'}(X) < \sigma$, for every $X \in \mathcal{S}_{\mathcal{D}}^{\sigma}$,*
2. *$|\mathcal{F}_{\mathcal{D}'}^{\sigma} - \widetilde{\mathcal{F}}_{\mathcal{D}}^{\sigma}|$ is minimized, and*
3. *$|\widetilde{\mathcal{F}}_{\mathcal{D}}^{\sigma} - \mathcal{F}_{\mathcal{D}'}^{\sigma}|$ is minimized.*

The problem has been shown to be NP-Hard in Atallah et al. [5] and for this reason a number of heuristics have been proposed to address the hiding while the quality of the sanitized database $\mathcal{D}'$ is preserved. Due to the large number of frequent itemsets in $\widetilde{\mathcal{F}}_{\mathcal{D}}^{\sigma}$, it is computationally inefficient to keep track of all these itemsets during the selective removal of items for the hiding of the itemsets in $\mathcal{S}_{\mathcal{D}}^{\sigma}$. We can instead focus on the positive border of $\widetilde{\mathcal{F}}_{\mathcal{D}}^{\sigma}$, which consists of the set of maximal non-sensitive frequent itemsets in $\widetilde{\mathcal{F}}_{\mathcal{D}}^{\sigma}$. At the same time we make sure that we hide the *minimal set of sensitive itemsets* from $\mathcal{S}_{\mathcal{D}}^{\sigma}$. This minimal set comprises the negative border $\mathcal{B}d^{-}(\mathcal{S}_{\mathcal{D}}^{\sigma})$ of the sensitive itemsets in $\mathcal{S}_{\mathcal{D}}^{\sigma}$.

**Definition 2.** *Given a transaction database $\mathcal{D}$ over a set of items $\mathcal{I}$, a support threshold $\sigma$, and a set of sensitive frequent itemsets $\mathcal{S}_{\mathcal{D}}^{\sigma}$ of $\mathcal{D}$, the negative border $\mathcal{B}d^{-}(\mathcal{S}_{\mathcal{D}}^{\sigma})$ of $\mathcal{S}_{\mathcal{D}}^{\sigma}$ is the set of minimal itemsets in $\mathcal{S}_{\mathcal{D}}^{\sigma}$ with respect to set inclusion.*

---

[2] Non-sensitive itemsets are indifferent to our problem and there is to need to be specified explicitly.

**Table 1.** A sample transaction database for our running example

| Tid | Itemsets |
|-----|----------|
| 1   | $abcd$   |
| 2   | $abc$    |
| 3   | $abd$    |
| 4   | $acd$    |
| 5   | $cd$     |
| 6   | $ac$     |

Let us continue with an example in order to demonstrate the semantics of this process. We consider the sample database shown in Table 1. For completeness purposes, on the left side of Fig. 1 we give the lattice of the itemsets corresponding to the mining of the sample database with $\sigma = 1/3$. The original positive border $\mathcal{B}d^+(\mathcal{F}_\mathcal{D}^\sigma) = \{abc, abd, acd\}$ and the negative border $\mathcal{B}d^-(\mathcal{F}_\mathcal{D}^\sigma) = \{bcd\}$ of the frequent itemsets are also shown on the right side of Fig. 1. Let also be $\mathcal{S}_\mathcal{D}^\sigma = \{ac, bd, abc, acd\}$. As it is shown in Fig. 1, for the ideal case we have that $\mathcal{B}d^+(\widetilde{\mathcal{F}}_\mathcal{D}^\sigma) = \{ab, ad, bc, cd\}$ and $\mathcal{B}d^-(\widetilde{\mathcal{F}}_\mathcal{D}^\sigma) = \{ac, bd\}$. Please note that in this example $\mathcal{B}d^-(\mathcal{S}_\mathcal{D}^\sigma) = \mathcal{B}d^-(\widetilde{\mathcal{F}}_\mathcal{D}^\sigma)$, even though in general it holds that $\mathcal{B}d^-(\mathcal{S}_\mathcal{D}^\sigma) \subseteq \mathcal{B}d^-(\widetilde{\mathcal{F}}_\mathcal{D}^\sigma)$. Sun and Yu [41] provide a sketch of an algorithm of high time and space complexity for computing $\mathcal{B}d^+(\widetilde{\mathcal{F}}_\mathcal{D}^\sigma)$ and $\mathcal{B}d^-(\widetilde{\mathcal{F}}_\mathcal{D}^\sigma)$, since the lattice of frequent itemsets $\mathcal{F}_\mathcal{D}^\sigma$ should be created first before other expensive set-oriented computations will take place on the lattice for determining the ideal positive and negative borders. In the next section we propose a theory for computing the borders of the sanitized database and then experimentally evaluate it to show its efficiency.

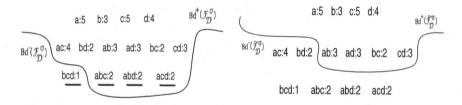

**Fig. 1.** The lattice of itemsets in the sample database with their original borders (left) and the lattice of itemsets and the expected ideal borders, after hiding (right).

## 4   A Constraint-Based Hiding Model

### 4.1   A Boolean Formula for Representing Sensitive Itemsets

At first, our approach relies on modeling the set of sensitive itemsets $\mathcal{S}_\mathcal{D}^\sigma$ presented in the previous discussion, as a *Boolean formula* defined over a set of variables that correspond to the items of $\mathcal{D}$. In this way we can take advantage of the simplification of this formula by using rules from the Boolean Algebra. In addition, we can easily get rid of the supersets of sensitive itemsets, that need to be neglected upon the computation of the borders.

Given a set of sensitive frequent itemsets $\mathcal{S}_\mathcal{D}^\sigma$ of a transaction database $\mathcal{D}$ over a set of items $\mathcal{I}$, we construct a Boolean formula $\mathcal{B}_\mathcal{D}^\sigma$ over a set of variables $\mathcal{V}$ as follows: every item in $\mathcal{I}$ is mapped to a variable in $\mathcal{V}$ and every itemset of $\mathcal{S}_\mathcal{D}^\sigma$ is mapped to a positive term, i.e. a conjunction of positive variables corresponding to the items of the itemset. The disjunction of all these terms comprises a Boolean formula $\mathcal{B}_\mathcal{D}^\sigma$ in Disjunctive Normal Form (DNF) with positive terms.

Continuing with our example database, the set of sensitive frequent itemsets $\mathcal{S}_\mathcal{D}^\sigma = \{ac, bd, abc, acd\}$ is mapped to $\mathcal{B}_\mathcal{D}^\sigma = a \cdot c + b \cdot d + a \cdot b \cdot c + a \cdot c \cdot d$. By the absorption law, we can remove redundancies and simplify the original formula as $\mathcal{B}_\mathcal{D}^\sigma = a \cdot c + b \cdot d$ (the rest of the terms are removed since they are subsumed by the term $a \cdot c$). This irredundant positive DNF Boolean formula corresponds to the set of sensitive frequent itemsets $\mathcal{S}_\mathcal{D}^\sigma$.

**Definition 3.** *The irredundant positive DNF Boolean formula $\mathcal{B}_\mathcal{D}^\sigma = C_1 + C_2 + \cdots + C_m$, where the i-th term is of the form $C_i = a_{i_1} \cdot a_{i_2} \cdot \ldots \cdot a_{i_{|C_i|}}$, is the Boolean formula obtained by the set of sensitive frequent itemsets $\mathcal{S}_\mathcal{D}^\sigma$ when every item of $\mathcal{D}$ is mapped to a variable of $\mathcal{B}_\mathcal{D}^\sigma$ and every itemset of $\mathcal{S}_\mathcal{D}^\sigma$ is mapped to a positive term of $\mathcal{B}_\mathcal{D}^\sigma$, after removing redundancies.*

At this point, the only requirement regarding $\mathcal{S}_\mathcal{D}^\sigma$ is the fact that the association among the items in the itemsets of $\mathcal{S}_\mathcal{D}^\sigma$ should be protected. No prior assumptions on support or on other related metrics are made. This is a legitimate knowledge in the hands of a data curator that tries to block out knowledge from the data. Also notice that, by removing redundancies, every term $C_j$ of $\mathcal{B}_\mathcal{D}^\sigma$ is minimal (it is not subsumed by no other term of $\mathcal{B}_\mathcal{D}^\sigma$), and maps a minimal sensitive itemset, say $S_j$, in $\mathcal{B}d^-(\mathcal{S}_\mathcal{D}^\sigma)$.

**Lemma 1.** *The DNF Boolean formula $\mathcal{B}_\mathcal{D}^\sigma$ corresponds to $\mathcal{B}d^-(\mathcal{S}_\mathcal{D}^\sigma)$ in the border-based theory.*

*Proof.* By construction, for every itemset in $\mathcal{B}d^-(\mathcal{S}_\mathcal{D}^\sigma)$ there exist a term in $\mathcal{B}_\mathcal{D}^\sigma$. These terms cannot be subsumed since they are minimal. Moreover, no other term corresponding to a non-minimal itemset of $\mathcal{S}_\mathcal{D}^\sigma$ appears in $\mathcal{B}_\mathcal{D}^\sigma$, since $\mathcal{B}_\mathcal{D}^\sigma$ is irredundand. Hence, the terms in $\mathcal{B}_\mathcal{D}^\sigma$ are exactly the terms corresponding to the itemsets in $\mathcal{B}d^-(\mathcal{S}_\mathcal{D}^\sigma)$. $\qquad\square$

To satisfy $\mathcal{B}d^-(\mathcal{S}_\mathcal{D}^\sigma)$, it suffices to assign 1 (true) to the variables of a term. Thus, every term (sensitive itemset) defines a pattern of truth assignments that makes $\mathcal{B}d^-(\mathcal{S}_\mathcal{D}^\sigma)$ true. For instance, the patterns $t_{ac} = 11$ and $t_{bd} = 11$ define the satisfying truth assignments of $\mathcal{B}d^-(\mathcal{S}_\mathcal{D}^\sigma)$ of our example. The semantics of a sensitive frequent itemset requires that this itemset is hidden, through the hiding process, by reducing its support just below the support threshold used for mining. This implies that no frequent itemset in the sanitized database should contain a sensitive itemset as its subset. If this does not hold, the pattern defined by this frequent itemset would satisfy $\mathcal{B}d^-(\mathcal{S}_\mathcal{D}^\sigma)$. Thus, we want for the non-frequent itemsets, their corresponding patterns of truth assignments not to satisfy $\mathcal{B}d^-(\mathcal{S}_\mathcal{D}^\sigma)$ or, equivalently their negated patterns (where every "1" is replaced with "0") to satisfy $\overline{\mathcal{B}_\mathcal{D}^\sigma}$.

**Theorem 1.** *If X is a non-sensitive frequent itemset of the ideal sanitized database, it corresponds to a negated pattern (a truth assignment with zero values) that satisfies $\overline{\mathcal{B}_\mathcal{D}^\sigma}$.*

*Proof.* Let $t_X$ be the pattern of X that assigns zero values to the variables that correspond to the items of X. Since X is not sensitive, it does not contain (is superset of) any sensitive itemset of $\mathcal{B}d^-(\mathcal{S}_\mathcal{D}^\sigma)$. Thus, its negated pattern $\overline{t}_X$ (containing only true values) does not satisfy none of the corresponding terms of $\mathcal{B}_\mathcal{D}^\sigma$, i.e. $t_X$ satisfies $\overline{\mathcal{B}_\mathcal{D}^\sigma}$. □

The following proposition states a trivial but important property of the Boolean formula $\overline{\mathcal{B}_\mathcal{D}^\sigma}$ that is related to a constraint defined in the next section.

**Lemma 2.** *The Boolean formula $\overline{\mathcal{B}_\mathcal{D}^\sigma}$ is equivalent to an irredundant negative DNF Boolean formula $\mathcal{B}$.*

*Proof.* $\mathcal{B}$ is produced by applying De Morgan's and distributive laws to $\mathcal{B}_\mathcal{D}^\sigma$. By applying these laws we can convert $\mathcal{B}$ to DNF. By construction, $\mathcal{B} = \widetilde{C}_1 + \widetilde{C}_2 + \cdots + \widetilde{C}_\mathcal{M}$ where the $i$-th term is of the form $\widetilde{C}_i = \overline{b}_{i_1} \cdot \overline{b}_{i_2} \cdot \ldots \cdot \overline{b}_{i_{m_i}}$. □

The maximum number of terms in $\mathcal{B}$ is $\prod_{i=1}^\mathcal{M} |C_i|$ where $C_i \in \mathcal{B}_\mathcal{D}^\sigma$ and $|C_i|$ is the number of literals in $C_i$, while the maximum number of literals in a term in $\mathcal{B}$, say $\mathcal{K}$, does not exceed the number of terms in $\mathcal{B}_\mathcal{D}^\sigma$.

Back to our example database, in order to verify the information in the proof of the previous lemma, we have that $\mathcal{B} = \overline{\mathcal{B}_\mathcal{D}^\sigma} = \overline{a \cdot c + b \cdot d} = (\overline{a} + \overline{c}) \cdot (\overline{b} + \overline{d}) = \overline{a} \cdot \overline{b} + \overline{a} \cdot \overline{d} + \overline{b} \cdot \overline{c} + \overline{c} \cdot \overline{d}$. The number of conjunctions in $\mathcal{B}$ is $|a \cdot c| \cdot |b \cdot d| = 2 \cdot 2 = 4$ while the maximum number of literals in a conjunction is $\mathcal{K} = 2$, which is the number of conjunctions in $\mathcal{B}_\mathcal{D}^\sigma$. Additionally, consider the sensitive itemset $abc$ that defines a pattern of truth assignments $t_{abc} = 111$ that satisfies $\mathcal{B}_\mathcal{D}^\sigma$ while its negation $\overline{t}_{abc} = 000$ and does not satisfy $\overline{\mathcal{B}_\mathcal{D}^\sigma}$. According to Theorem 2, this itemset is sensitive and it should be excluded from the itemsets that can be mined from the sanitized database $\mathcal{D}'$. On the contrary, itemset $ab$ is not sensitive (its pattern does not satisfy $\mathcal{B}_\mathcal{D}^\sigma$ and thus its negation satisfies $\overline{\mathcal{B}_\mathcal{D}^\sigma}$, and hence it can be mined from $\mathcal{D}'$. Based on the previous discussion, we can formalize the exclusion of sensitive patterns from the mining of the sanitized database by requiring that $\overline{\mathcal{B}_\mathcal{D}^\sigma} = \overline{a \cdot c + b \cdot d}$ should hold for all the frequent patterns that can be induced from the sanitized database $\mathcal{D}'$.

## 4.2   A Constraint-Based Theory for Mining of Borders

The next problem to deal with is how we can use the $\overline{\mathcal{B}_{\mathcal{D}}^{\sigma}}$ in order to efficiently compute the required, by the hiding algorithm, borders $\mathcal{B}d^{+}(\widetilde{\mathcal{F}_{\mathcal{D}}^{\sigma}})$ and $\mathcal{B}d^{-}(\mathcal{S}_{\mathcal{D}}^{\sigma})$. We address this problem by considering the computation of these borders as a constraint-based mining problem. It is well known that constraint-based mining allows the unearthing of interesting knowledge (a) by reducing the number of extracted patterns to only those of interest and (b) by pushing constraints inside the mining algorithm in order to achieve better performance. A constraint on itemsets is a function $\mathcal{C} : 2^{\mathcal{I}} \longrightarrow \{\text{true,false}\}$. We say that an itemset $X$ satisfies a constraint $\mathcal{C}$ iff $\mathcal{C}(X) = \text{true}$. We define the theory of a constraint $\mathcal{C}$, as the set of itemsets that satisfies the constraint $\mathcal{C}$, and we denote this theory by $\text{Th}(\mathcal{C}) = \{X \in 2^{\mathcal{I}} \mid \mathcal{C}(X) = \text{true}\}$. Fortunately, as we will show soon enough, the constraints that we have to deal with in our hiding problem formulation, are antimonotone constraints.

**Definition 4.** *For every pair of itemsets $X$ and $Y$, a constraint $\mathcal{C}$ is antimonotone if $Y \subseteq X : \mathcal{C}(X) \Rightarrow \mathcal{C}(Y)$.*

The first constraint in our problem formulation is the support constraint $\mathcal{C}_{\text{sup}}$ which is satisfied by itemsets having support greater than, or equal, to the support threshold $\sigma$. The support constraint is well known to be an antimonotone constraint [10]. The second constraint, which is related to itemsets that are non-sensitive denoted as $\mathcal{C}_{\overline{sen}}$, should also hold for all the induced itemsets from the sanitized database. This constraint specifies that an interesting itemset for our hiding problem can be a proper subset of any sensitive itemset, but not a sensitive itemset or a superset of a sensitive itemset. The next proposition associates $\mathcal{B}$ to $\mathcal{C}_{\overline{sen}}$.

**Proposition 1.** *The constraint $\mathcal{C}_{\overline{sen}}$ holds for an itemset $X$ if $X$ satisfies $\mathcal{B}$.*

We can now prove the antimonotonicity property of the $\mathcal{C}_{\overline{sen}}$ constraint.

**Theorem 2.** *The $\mathcal{C}_{\overline{sen}}$ constraint is an antimonotone constraint.*

*Proof.* According to Proposition 1, to prove that $\mathcal{C}_{\overline{sen}}$ is antimonotone, we have to show that for any pair of itemsets $X$ and $Y$ with $Y \subseteq X$, if $X$ satisfies the constraint, then $Y$ does too, i.e. $\mathcal{C}_{\overline{sen}}(X) \Rightarrow \mathcal{C}_{\overline{sen}}(Y)$. If $\mathcal{C}_{\overline{sen}}(X)$ holds, then the truth assignment corresponding to the items in $X$ satisfy $\mathcal{B}$. If $\mathcal{B}$ is true, then at least one of the conjunctions $\widetilde{C}_i$ in $\mathcal{B}$ is true. Based on Lemma 2, $\widetilde{C}_i$ contains only negated literals. In order for itemset X to satisfy $\widetilde{C}_i$, it should not contain any of the items listed in negated form in $\widetilde{C}_i$. Any subset Y of X will also not contain any of the items found in negated form in $\widetilde{C}_i$. Thus $\mathcal{C}_{\overline{sen}}(Y)$ also holds. $\square$

If, for example, $\mathcal{I} = \{a, b, c, d, e\}$, $\widetilde{C}_i = \overline{a} \cdot \overline{b}$, and $X = cde$, then $X$ satisfies $\widetilde{C}_i$ because it contains neither $a$ nor $b$. Any subset of $X$, let us say $Y = ce$, will also not contain both $a$ and $b$ and so it will satisfy $\widetilde{C}_i$, too. Having proved that both constraints $\mathcal{C}_{\text{sup}}$ and $\mathcal{C}_{\overline{\text{sen}}}$ in our hiding model are antimonotone constraints, we can easily push those constraints into the frequent itemset mining algorithm since it is well known that any conjunction of antimonotone constraints is also an antimonotone constraint [10]. The $\text{Th}_{\mathcal{D}}(\mathcal{C}_{\text{sup}} \wedge \mathcal{C}_{\overline{\text{sen}}})$ that we are looking for, is then a downward closed theory which means that if an itemset $X$ is part of this theory, then all subsets of $X$ belong to this theory, too. This reminds us of the antimonotone heuristic in Apriori which will be utilized by our hiding algorithm as well, for efficiently computing the theory of itemsets satisfying the conjunction of the two constraints. The algorithm is presented in the sequel.

## 4.3   A Constraint-Based Mining Algorithm

The constraint-based itemset mining algorithm (see Fig. 2) will generate the $\text{Th}_{\mathcal{D}}(\mathcal{C}_{\text{sup}} \wedge \mathcal{C}_{\overline{\text{sen}}})$ – itemsets in the theory along with their support information – in order to create the positive border $\mathcal{B}d^+(\text{Th}_{\mathcal{D}}(\mathcal{C}_{\text{sup}} \wedge \mathcal{C}_{\overline{\text{sen}}}))$ of the itemsets that satisfy both constraints $\mathcal{C}_{\text{sup}}$ and $\mathcal{C}_{\overline{\text{sen}}}$. Initially, the mining algorithm stores in $C_1^{\mathcal{B}}$ all the candidate items from the set of items $\mathcal{I}$ that satisfy the Boolean formula $\mathcal{B}$. Then it stores in $L_1$ these items from $C_1^{\mathcal{B}}$ which were found to be frequent, after counting them through the first pass in the database. In the subsequent for-loop, the level-wise operation of the algorithm unfolds. Based on the specific level $k$, the algorithm computes in $C_k^{\mathcal{B}}$ the candidate itemsets of the $k$-th level by applying the Apriori-genB procedure to the set of frequent and non-sensitive itemsets of size $k-1$, that comprises the collection of itemsets $L_{k-1}$. Apriori-genB has been slightly modified from the original Apriori-gen in our approach so that it performs a 2-way pruning: first it removes from $C_k^{\mathcal{B}}$ candidates of size $k$ with either infrequent or sensitive subsets of size $k-1$, and then it removes sensitive candidates of size $k$. A sensitive candidate of size $k$ is a candidate generated by Apriori-genB that does not satisfy $\mathcal{C}_{\overline{\text{sen}}}$, even if all of its subsets are frequent and non-sensitive (that is, all of its subsets belong to $L_{k-1}$). Next, the support of candidates in $C_k^{\mathcal{B}}$ is counted and all those candidates, that are found to be frequent, are placed into $L_k$. When $L_k$ becomes empty, the algorithm terminates by returning the union of $L_k$ set collections generated so far. Apparently, the time complexity of the algorithm is bounded by an exponent to the size of the largest itemset of the revised negative border.

We demonstrate the steps of the algorithm now, by applying it to our example scenario. Recall that $\mathcal{I} = \{a, b, c, d\}$. In the first step we get $C_1^{\mathcal{B}} = \{a, b, c, d\}$, as all the items in $\mathcal{I}$ satisfy $\mathcal{B}$, while in the second step $L_1 = \{a, b, c, d\}$, since all items in $C_1^{\mathcal{B}}$ are also frequent. In steps 3 to 11 we have repetitive calls to Apriori-genB corresponding to increasing levels of collections of itemsets for generating the $C_k^{\mathcal{B}}$ collections of sets. $C_2^{\mathcal{B}}$ is generated first and it contains initially the collection of itemsets $\{ab, ac, ad, bc, bd, cd\}$. Itemsets from $C_2^{\mathcal{B}}$ are pruned either because their subsets do not belong to $L_1$, or because they do not satisfy $\mathcal{B}$. In our case, $ac$ and $bd$ are taken out because of the latter reason, and $C_2^{\mathcal{B}}$ becomes $\{ab, ad, bc, cd\}$. Then $L_2$ is computed by counting the support of the itemsets in $C_2^{\mathcal{B}}$, where we finally get $L_2 = \{ab:3, ad:3, bc:2, ad:3\}$. $C_3^{\mathcal{B}}$ is generated next, containing only the 3-itemset $abd$, which is immediately pruned since one of its

**Input:**
$\mathcal{D}$: transaction database
$\sigma$: the minimum support threshold
$\mathcal{B}$: Boolean formula representing $\mathcal{C}_{\overline{sen}}$
**Output:**
$L$: frequent itemsets satisfying $\mathcal{B}$

1: **Description:**
2:   $C_1^{\mathcal{B}}$ the candidate items that satisfy $\mathcal{B}$
3:   $L_1$ the frequent items in $C_1^{\mathcal{B}}$
4: **for** $(k = 2; L_{k-1} \neq \emptyset; k{+}{+})$
5:     $C_k^{\mathcal{B}} = $ Apriori-genB$(L_{k-1})$;
6:     **for each** transaction $t \in \mathcal{D}$
7:         $C_t = $**subset**$(C_k^{\mathcal{B}}, t)$;
8:         **for each** candidate $c \in C_t$
9:             $c.count{+}{+}$;
10:    **end**
11:     $L_k = \{c \in C_k^{\mathcal{B}} \mid c.count \geq \sigma\}$;
12: **end**
13: **return** $L = \bigcup_k L_k$;

**Fig. 2.** The constraint-based mining algorithm

subsets (2-itemsets), which is $bd$, does not belong to $L_2$. Based on the application of the constraint-based algorithm to the example database, we can now compute the positive border of the frequency theory $Bd^+(\mathrm{STh}_{\mathcal{D}}(\mathcal{C}_{\mathrm{sup}} \wedge \mathcal{C}_{\overline{sen}}))$ and the corresponding negative border, more specifically $Bd^+(\mathrm{STh}_{\mathcal{D}}(\mathcal{C}_{\mathrm{sup}} \wedge \mathcal{C}_{\overline{sen}})) = \{ab: 3, ad:3, bc:2, cd:3\}$ and $Bd^-(\mathrm{STh}_{\mathcal{D}}(\mathcal{C}_{\mathrm{sup}} \wedge \mathcal{C}_{\overline{sen}})) = \{ac : 4, bd : 2\}$.

## 5 Experimental Evaluation of the Constraint-Based Mining Algorithm

In this section, we evaluate the proposed Constraint-based Mining Algorithm and we compare it with the conventional Level-wise Apriori Algorithm. We evaluate both algorithms on real and synthetic datasets. Real datasets along with *T10I4D100K* and *T40I10D100K* synthetic datasets are available in the Frequent Itemset Mining Dataset Repository [20]. The rest of the synthetic datasets were generated using the IBM Basket Data Generator [26]. We utilized datasets with a variety of characteristics in terms of the number of transactions, number of items, and average transaction length. The *mushroom* dataset was prepared by Bayardo [7]. The *BMS1* and *BMS2* datasets were used for the KDD Cup 2000 [29]. Finally, the *kosarak* dataset [8] contains anonymized click-stream data of a Hungarian online news portal. The synthetic datasets were generated so as to study the results given by datasets with different average transaction length (*T10I4D100K, T40I10D100K*) and even larger datasets (*1M, 5M*). We summarize the details of the datasets in Table 2.

**Table 2.** Characteristics of the datasets

| Dataset | Number of transactions | Number of items | Aver. Trans. Length |
|---|---|---|---|
| mushroom | 8,124 | 119 | 23 |
| BMS1 | 59,602 | 497 | 2.5 |
| BMS2 | 77,512 | 3,340 | 5.6 |
| kosarak | 990,002 | 41,270 | 8.1 |
| T10I4D100K | 100,000 | 870 | 10.10 |
| T40I10D100K | 100,000 | 942 | 39.60 |
| 1M | 1,000,000 | 2398 | 4.58 |
| 5M | 5,000,000 | 1468 | 4.07 |

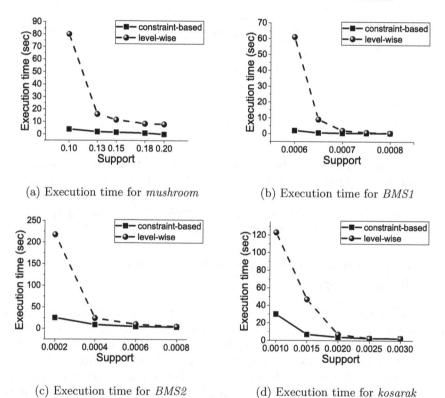

(a) Execution time for *mushroom*        (b) Execution time for *BMS1*

(c) Execution time for *BMS2*            (d) Execution time for *kosarak*

**Fig. 3.** Execution time in seconds for the level-wise algorithm (grey line) and the constraint-based algorithm (black line), for the real datasets.

We implemented both algorithms by using or extending the PyFIM extension module of Borgelt [12], so as to compute efficiently the non-sensitive frequent itemsets and the corresponding positive border. All experiments were performed

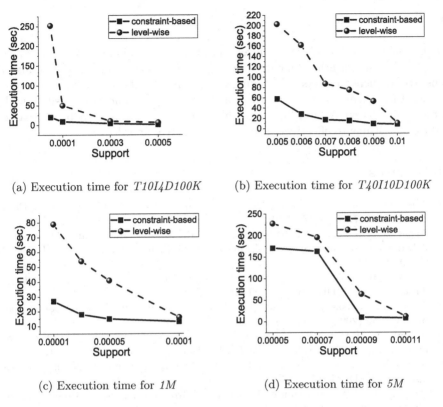

(a) Execution time for *T10I4D100K*

(b) Execution time for *T40I10D100K*

(c) Execution time for *1M*

(d) Execution time for *5M*

**Fig. 4.** Execution time in seconds for the level-wise algorithm (grey line) and the constraint-based algorithm (black line), for the synthetic datasets.

on a personal computer with an Intel Core i5 at 3.4 GHz processor, under Windows 7. Both algorithms take as input the dataset $\mathcal{D}$, the set of sensitive itemsets $\mathcal{S}_{\mathcal{D}}^{\sigma}$ and the support threshold $\sigma$. The evaluation metric we used is the execution time required by each algorithm in order to give output, which is the set of non-sensitive frequent itemsets $\widetilde{\mathcal{F}}_{\mathcal{D}}^{\sigma}$, and in extension its positive border $\mathcal{B}d^{+}(\widetilde{\mathcal{F}}_{\mathcal{D}}^{\sigma})$. Moreover, we used a steady number of 500 sensitive itemsets for all experiments.

Figure 3(a)–(d) present the execution time (in seconds) for both Level-wise and Constraint-based algorithms, for the *mushroom*, *BMS1*, *BMS2*, and *kosarak* dataset respectively. Observe that in all scenarios, the Constraint-based algorithm outperforms the Level-wise algorithm. The execution time of the Level-wise algorithm increases exponentially, as the support threshold decreases. Although for some datasets the Constraint-based algorithm seems to follow the same behavior, the algorithm is significantly faster and more scalable than the Level-wise algorithm. Finally, Fig. 4(a)–(d) demonstrate the results for the *T10I4D100K*, *T40I10D100K*, *1M*, and *5M* datasets respectively. Again, the proposed algorithm outperforms the Level-wise algorithm.

# 6   Conclusions

In this paper, we introduced a novel constraint-based hiding model to reduce the preprocessing overhead incurred by border-based techniques in the hiding of sensitive frequent itemsets. The hiding model lends itself to the efficient computation of the theory of itemsets which are both frequent and non-sensitive with a constraint-based Apriori-like algorithm. These can be used in border-based hiding algorithms to effectively conceal the sensitive knowledge.

# References

1. Abul, O., Gökçe, H.: Knowledge hiding from tree and graph databases. Data Knowl. Eng. **72**, 148–171 (2012)
2. Aggarwal, C., Yu, P.: Privacy-Preserving Data Mining: Models and Algorithms. Advances in Database Systems. Springer, Boston (2008). https://doi.org/10.1007/978-0-387-70992-5
3. Agrawal, R., Srikant, R.: Fast algorithms for mining association rules in large databases. In: VLDB, pp. 487–499 (1994)
4. Agrawal, R., Srikant, R.: Privacy-preserving data mining. In: SIGMOD Conference, pp. 439–450 (2000)
5. Atallah, M., Bertino, E., Elmagarmid, A., Ibrahim, M., Verykios, V.: Disclosure limitation of sensitive rules. In: KDEX Workshop, pp. 45–52. IEEE (1999)
6. Atzori, M., Bonchi, F., Giannotti, F., Pedreschi, D.: Anonymity preserving pattern discovery. VLDB J. **17**(4), 703–727 (2008)
7. Bayardo, R.: Efficiently mining long patterns from databases. In: Proceedings of SIGMOD 1998, pp. 85–93 (1998)
8. Bodon, F.: A fast APRIORI implementation. In: Proceedings of the IEEE ICDM Workshop on Frequent Itemset Mining Implementations, FIMI 2003, vol. 90, pp. 56–65 (2003)
9. Bonchi, F., Ferrari, E.: Privacy-Aware Knowledge Discovery: Novel Applications and New Techniques. Chapman & Hall/CRC Data Mining and Knowledge Discovery Series. CRC Press Inc., Boca Raton (2011)
10. Bonchi, F., Lucchese, C.: On condensed representations of constrained frequent patterns. Knowl. Inf. Syst. **9**(2), 180–201 (2006)
11. Bonchi, F., et al.: Privacy in spatiotemporal data mining. In: Giannotti, F., Pedreschi, D. (eds.) Mobility, Data Mining and Privacy, pp. 297–333. Springer, Heidelberg (2008). https://doi.org/10.1007/978-3-540-75177-9_12
12. Borgelt, C.: Frequent item set mining. Wiley Interdisc. Rev.: Data Min. Knowl. Discov. **2**(6), 437–456 (2012)
13. Boulicaut, J.-F., Jeudy, B.: Constraint-based data mining. In: Maimon, O., Rokach, L. (eds.) The Data Mining and Knowledge Discovery Handbook, pp. 399–416. Springer, Boston (2005). https://doi.org/10.1007/0-387-25465-X_18
14. Bu, S., Lakshmanan, L.V.S., Ng, R.T., Ramesh, G.: Preservation of patterns and input-output privacy. In: ICDE, pp. 696–705 (2007)
15. Clifton, C.: Protecting against data mining through samples. In: Atluri, V., Hale, J. (eds.) Research Advances in Database and Information Systems Security. ITIFIP, vol. 43, pp. 193–207. Springer, Boston, MA (2000). https://doi.org/10.1007/978-0-387-35508-5_13

16. Dasseni, E., Verykios, V.S., Elmagarmid, A.K., Bertino, E.: Hiding association rules by using confidence and support. In: Moskowitz, I.S. (ed.) IH 2001. LNCS, vol. 2137, pp. 369–383. Springer, Heidelberg (2001). https://doi.org/10.1007/3-540-45496-9_27
17. Delis, A., Verykios, V.S., Tsitsonis, A.A.: A data perturbation approach to sensitive classification rule hiding. In: SAC, pp. 605–609 (2010)
18. Evfimievski, A.V., Srikant, R., Agrawal, R., Gehrke, J.: Privacy preserving mining of association rules. Inf. Syst. **29**(4), 343–364 (2004)
19. Fredman, M.L., Khachiyan, L.: On the complexity of dualization of monotone disjunctive normal forms. J. Algorithms **21**, 618–628 (1996)
20. Frequent Itemset Mining Dataset Repository. http://fimi.ua.ac.be/data/
21. Gkoulalas-Divanis, A., Verykios, V.: Association Rule Hiding for Data Mining. Advances in Database Systems. Springer, Boston (2010). https://doi.org/10.1007/978-1-4419-6569-1
22. Gkoulalas-Divanis, A., Verykios, V.S.: An integer programming approach for frequent itemset hiding. In: CIKM, pp. 748–757 (2006)
23. Gkoulalas-Divanis, A., Verykios, V.S.: Exact knowledge hiding through database extension. IEEE Trans. Knowl. Data Eng. **21**(5), 699–713 (2009)
24. Gkoulalas-Divanis, A., Verykios, V.S.: Hiding sensitive knowledge without side effects. Knowl. Inf. Syst. **20**(3), 263–299 (2009)
25. Gurvich, V., Khachiyan, L.: Hiding sensitive knowledge without side effects. Discrete Appl. Math. **96–97**, 363–373 (1999)
26. IBM Basket Data Generator. http://sourceforge.net/projects/ibmquestdatagen/
27. Kantarcioglu, M., Clifton, C.: Privacy-preserving distributed mining of association rules on horizontally partitioned data. IEEE Trans. Knowl. Data Eng. **16**(9), 1026–1037 (2004)
28. Kantarcioglu, M., Jin, J., Clifton, C.: When do data mining results violate privacy? In: KDD, pp. 599–604 (2004)
29. Kohavi, R., Brodley, C., Frasca, B., Mason, L., Zheng, Z.: KDD-Cup 2000 organizers' report: peeling the onion. SIGKDD Explor. **2**(2), 86–98 (2000). http://www.ecn.purdue.edu/KDDCUP
30. Lindell,Y., Pinkas, B.: Privacy preserving data mining. In: CRYPTO, pp. 36–54 (2000)
31. Menon, S., Sarkar, S.: Minimizing information loss and preserving privacy. Manag. Sci. **53**(1), 101–116 (2007)
32. Menon, S., Sarkar, S., Mukherjee, S.: Maximizing accuracy of shared databases when concealing sensitive patterns. Inf. Syst. Res. **16**(3), 256–270 (2005)
33. Moustakides, G.V., Verykios, V.S.: A maxmin approach for hiding frequent itemsets. Data Knowl. Eng. **65**(1), 75–89 (2008)
34. Oliveira, S.R.M., Zaïane,O.R.: Algorithms for balancing privacy and knowledge discovery in association rule mining. In: IDEAS, pp. 54–65 (2003)
35. Oliveira, S.R.M., Zaïane,O.R.: Protecting sensitive knowledge by data sanitization. In: ICDM, pp. 613–616 (2003)
36. Rizvi, S., Haritsa, J.R.: Maintaining data privacy in association rule mining. In: VLDB, pp. 682–693 (2002)
37. Saygin, Y., Verykios, V.S., Clifton, C.: Using unknowns to prevent discovery of association rules. SIGMOD Rec. **30**(4), 45–54 (2001)
38. Srikant, R., Vu, Q., Agrawal, R.: Mining association rules with item constraints. In: KDD, pp. 67–73 (1997)
39. Stavropoulos, E.C., Verykios, V.S., Kagklis, V.: A transversal hypergraph approach for the frequent itemset hiding problem. Knowl. Inf. Syst. **47**(3), 625–645 (2016)

40. Sun, X., Yu, P.S.: A border-based approach for hiding sensitive frequent itemsets. In: ICDM, pp. 426–433 (2005)
41. Sun, X., Yu, P.S.: Hiding sensitive frequent itemsets by a border-based approach. JCSE **1**(1), 74–94 (2007)
42. Verykios, V.S., Elmagarmid, A.K., Bertino, E., Saygin, Y., Dasseni, E.: Association rule hiding. IEEE Trans. Knowl. Data Eng. **16**(4), 434–447 (2004)
43. Verykios, V.S., Pontikakis, E.D., Theodoridis, Y., Chang, L.: Efficient algorithms for distortion and blocking techniques in association rule hiding. Distrib. Parallel Databases **22**(1), 85–104 (2007)

# E-Government

# A Smart Cross Border e-Gov Primary Health Care Medical Service

Alexander B. Sideridis[(✉)]

Agricultural University of Athens, 11855 Athens, Greece
as@aua.gr

**Abstract.** Nearly two years ago, the European Commission of the European Union provided to the Authorities of Member States the appropriate regulation and systems for the development of services necessitating cross border transactions. So far, unfortunately, Member States have shown certain reluctance. This may be justified particularly for systems involving processes or necessitating transfers of confidential and personal data. Nevertheless, the proposed by the European Commission systems guarantee (as far as recent developments in network and cloud securities can do it) efficient validation of data, through authentication procedures. On the other hand, in Europe, cannot be ignored the accumulated and increased interest by Public Administrations and Organizations' of public and private interest in using systems of cross border nature. This tendency is quite justified by citizens increased mobilization, from one State to another. No need to notice that free movement of the Europeans is one of the basic principles of the European Union! All this effort has led literature to the presentation of a few systems of cross border nature for health, social services, environment and life sciences, in general.

In this paper, a cross border authentication service linking primary health units of public or private status is proposed. This service, at its final implementation, will fully exploit, freely available by the European Commission, platforms. By now, the first phase of this service, a local primary health care system, securing access to medical records of citizens moving throughout Europe, is used by public, primary health service units of Greece. The full satisfaction of this service will allow its proposition as a standard to interested Member States. At a later stage, module systems, similar to the proposed ones, will be nodes of the joining in organizations to a European Smart Cross Border Primary Health Care System.

**Keywords:** e-Government systems · Authentication · Electronic identification · Cloud Computing · Primary health care service

## 1 Introduction

Recent papers elaborate on the need to design and implement e-government systems offering online services to citizens irrespective of their mobility to various countries. Actually, such systems have managed to eliminate manual work in areas of continued globalization, such as e-commerce, e-banking, e-health, e-justice, e-forensics, and e-crime. These systems are mainly autonomous and simply connect to each other over

© Springer Nature Switzerland AG 2020
S. Katsikas and V. Zorkadis (Eds.): e-Democracy 2019, CCIS 1111, pp. 67–78, 2020.
https://doi.org/10.1007/978-3-030-37545-4_5

the internet without providing particular security conditions. Models used are usually of mixed structure involving automated and manual procedures [26–28].

The development of systems, as the above described, raised organizational problems, since the first attempts were made of transforming our societies to digital ones [19]. Over the years, in spite to dystopia syndromes and raised anxieties, many efforts in reshaping administration models, improving security techniques and reforming protective confidentiality laws, with regard personal data and data integrity, have managed to combat lurker's immovability [15, 17, 20, 22–24]. Public and private agencies of certain European countries and especially those of south Europe are -even if until now- trying to catch up and join in the process of reshaping their complete organization modules [37]. In general, initial reluctance, alert to change and binding to bureaucratic chaos have been gradually replaced by an optimistic attitude to achieve full automated procedures. Smart initiatives, aiming to alleviate the burden of bureaucracy and offer to citizens services needed, are issues daily proclaimed by policy makers. All benefited stakeholders came across problems of integrity, privacy and security [1, 28, 39, 40]. The initial main aim of removing administrative burdens and improve time response, when citizens were coming across a governmental agency, through a Government to Citizen (G2C) service, is replaced by increased upgrade effort as the complexity of the supporting systems and new mobile e-Government services demand [25, 42]. Full systems integration, citizens mobility across Europe, increased awareness of security fraud dangers, create an atmosphere of continuous upgrade needs. Even if this service is offered within a citizen's home country, the outcome in many cases, may be questioned. Is this G2C service secure enough with regard to data integrity? Is any danger behind this service of violating my personal data? These questions are immense when private Business to Citizens (B2C) or Business to Government (B2G) are involved or when services required necessitate the use of personal and confidential data. Obviously, these fears are magnified proportionally when, citizens of their need, are moving out of their home to a foreign country (e.g. the case of Europeans moving from one State of the European Union (EU) to another).

Various initiatives by the EU encouraging mobility of Europeans (e.g. Erasmus programmes) quite often come across bureaucracy barriers. Authenticated documents are required in support of cases bound to happen when Europeans are freely moving to look for entries in foreign educational institutions, getting jobs, looking for new opportunities, in general. To the continuous evolution regarding the mobility of these people, a relatively new social phenomenon should be added. Legal refugees mobility cannot be ignored anymore [28]. Waves of the latest require special attention. Conformity rules exist and would severely be applied. In addition to these circumstances, personal health obstacles restrict or eliminate any chance of mobility for major categories of citizens, as above. Actually, personal health is a common denominator to all the categories of citizens. Although online services and e-government systems have been implemented in response to mostly commercial and banking procedures, the case of personal health and mobilizes' corresponding needs are ignored.

Of course, e-government services processing and/or providing especially sensitive information to stakeholders when and where it is required, in accordance with citizens free movement, are of the most delicate nature. The need may be unprecedented, the response time may be a decisive factor for life-saving services. Medical files, recent additional diagnoses, certain medical examination reports, and tests may be safety certified and authenticated. Obviously, all this strictly confidential information is of great importance if and when is available to the appropriate personnel.

Encouragement for designing e-government systems of such complex structure, in dialing with technical and organizational problems, and especially of securely exchanging personal or confidential information, has been boosted by certain outcomes of major European Commission (EC) projects. Software platforms are available since the year 2016, when e-AUthentication (e-AU), e-SIGNature (e-SIGN) and e-IDentification (e-ID) were publicly presented to Member States of the European Union (EU) [30–36]. In parallel to these developments, advances in Cloud Computing and Smart Cross Border e-Government (SCBeG) systems [27] present alternatives in designing systems offering services to citizens in cross border environments. Also, existing autonomous systems, aiming to offer e-government services within territorial limits, are now updated for expanding business frontiers or/and facilitating the legitimate movement of citizens between the EU Member States [28].

In the present paper, we concentrate on a primary health care medical service offered by health care medical organizations to citizens looking for immediate treatment -at any time or place- he or she may be of need. For reasons of simplicity and state forward application, we concentrate to the medical e-government service aiming to fully cover medical needs of Europeans during their mobility around the EU's States. The conceptual design of the proposed such a service will be based on the safety and authenticity precautions directed by Cloud Computing and the existing software platforms such as those provided by the European project STORK. It may be capable of meeting the requirements of any European citizen for primary health care help and treatment's arrangement [1, 12, 14, 43], as he/she is moving around the EU, regardless his/her state of origin. Apart from the Europeans, the service should also cover primary health care needs of any eligible citizen, like legal refugees, being on mobility, within the European States. Supporting to such a service systems should overcome problems related to the unavailability of his/her medical files, needed for immediate medical attention [38]. In such cases, systems create the appropriate medical records and register them to the State of the initial requirement of the corresponding service.

Apart from the general concept and design prerequisites of the proposed e-government primary health care service, in this paper, we also elaborate mostly to the implementation of a module being the kernel of supporting systems. This module has been proposed as a deliverable of the project YGEIA1 [29] and is fully implemented and used by the Greek e-Government of Social Security Service [16]. It is actually an extended citizen's medical file, the so called *Patient's Medical Protocol* (PMP). PMPs contain fully authenticated, through STORK platforms, medical information and further documentary evidence (diagnostic tests, hospital treatment reports, etc). A PMP should be the basic entity of the appropriate data base developed and kept by each European State on a central or distributed form. The PMP should be the silent companion of any citizen, ready to be used and updated by especially authorized medical personnel of linked to the system health care organizations.

The structure of the paper is as follows. Section 2 describes the functional organization of the service provided by a typical Primary Health Care Centre system's organization, its subsystems and platforms. In Sect. 3, the architecture, functionality and implementation requirements are presented. Discussion follows in Sect. 4 where, at the same time, an attempt is made to encourage researchers to participate in similar projects and stimulate further ideas, discussions and implementations.

## 2  Primary Health Care Organization

### 2.1  Primary Health Care Services

Primary Health Care in most of the EU Member States is usually provided by Local Community Health Centres (LCHC). The medical personnel of a LCHC usually employs general practitioners as family doctors and, in most of the cases, specialists covering the basic medical doctor's specialties. LCHCs are functioning under the umbrella of integrated National Public Health Care (NPHC) systems. In absence of LCHC's services, or even if complementary to them, private enterprises, usually called Diagnostic Centres (DCs) are filling the gap (a DC is consisting of a number of medical doctors of the basic specialties forming a consortium). In urban areas and cities patients are usually directly addressing to Outpatient Departments or, in case of emergency, the Emergency Units of nearby Hospitals. All health organisations (LCHCs, DCs, hospitals etc.) are accommodated, in most cases, under the umbrella of the respective NPHC system of each Member State of the EU [41].

In all cases above, by this first aid step health service provision, patients are locally treated or guided to secondary and tertiary care in accordance with a diagnosis made by health professionals of the above units. Patients are so addressed in allied health professions chiropractic, physicians, physician associates, dentistry, midwifery, nursing, medicine, optometry, pharmacy, psychology etc. Prior and during the actual patient's guidance, a *"front-office primary health care service"*, apart from being capable to decide who the appropriate addressee is by checking his social security number and verifying identity data, it should also provide to him patient's medical record and file. Then, the specialist, or any health advisor acting as the addressee, should be able to properly advice, treat or redirect his/her patient as appropriate.

Recently, a Greek initiative aiming at automating the front-office service offered so far to patients by the administration of LCHCs manually [41] had been proposed. In parallel, the Greek e-Government of Social Security Service [16] has proceeded to its implementation. By this initiative, a simple e-government service has alleviated administrative burden of both administration and patient and accelerated the decision process of the actors (patient-administrator-specialist) and the final outcome (diagnosis, treatment or guidance for help outside the LCHC). In other words, the service suggests to patients the selection of the appropriate specialist, arranges the appointment with him/her in accordance to his/her availability and carries out the necessary transfer of patient's medical record. There is a number of legal and technical issues to be carefully considered, like the proper consideration of medical record's upgrading by eligible persons, as well as the capability of DCs to directly upload to patient's medical file their examination results.

The implementation of the above described *e-Government front-office primary health care service* to patients looking for a proper advice and treatment in LCHC or any other similar organization, is put into practice in Greece for the last two years and its use is considered as satisfactory [16].

## 2.2 Networking Primary Health Care Services

We now proceed to the design of the appropriate network infrastructure of primary health care centres so that they will provide corresponding services to citizens being in mobility. According to such G2C service, when a European citizen or any other legitimate person of Member State (MS) A, is moving to MS B, should be offered health care services in a more efficient and direct way while his medical file will be available to authorised personnel [29]. Steps followed are shown in Fig. 1 where:

- Any authorized user of the **MS A** can access a protected resource (medical file) from the **MS B** through the NPHC system.
- The system forwards the request to the Cross-Border Authentication System.
- If the authentication is valid then the medical file of the specific individual is accessed in the **MS B** NPHC system.
- Consequently, the medical file is sent to the **MS A's** authorized user.

During the first stages of implementing the *e-Government front-office primary health care service* described above, a question was raised with regard to system's commitment to provide such a service in case of a patient's mobility to a different EU country or, even if elsewhere, than that of his/her own state of origin. Smart Cross Border e-Gov Systems providing such services seem to present the appropriate basis in

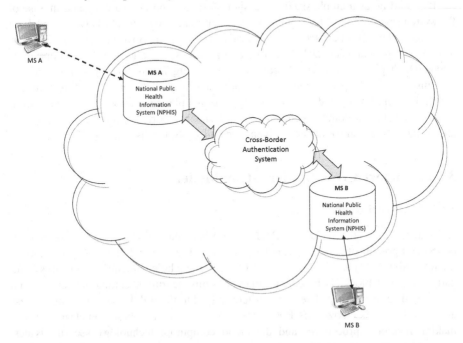

**Fig. 1.** Medical file authentication process in primary health care services.

also dealing with *"cross-border front-office primary health care services"* of a kind such that described above [27]. Security issues and strict national law with regard medical record's sensitive personal data, authentication of data, final patient's identification and more general interoperability problems are very effort consuming problems under serious consideration. Obviously, e-government services necessitating merge of heterogeneous computer environments, as those of the European States, needed to cooperate in offering primary health care services to European citizens moving around the EU, will face difficult interoperability problems. Cloud computing incorporation will elevate and adequately help [29, 43].

### 2.3   Mobility Services Through Smart Cross-Border e-Gov Systems

Security and privacy are key enablers of Smart Cross Border e-Gov systems while, one of their main objectives is to provide secure citizen mobility by utilizing state-of-the-art tools. Cloud Computing Privacy and Security techniques and models should be used by the relevant health care organizations [24, 37, 40, 43]. Certified authentication of diagnoses and medical documents or info of any form, included to Patient's Medical Protocol and issued by secondary and tertiary health care units, are online available when and iff are required by eligible actors. These transactions are safely accompanying citizens, while they are moving across Member States, using the existing platforms on e-AU and e-SIGN. STORK 2.0 platforms. Thus, the proposed systems could significantly support the authorities, utilizing national e-IDs, under improved security measures and enhanced capabilities [28].

It should be also emphasized the design of the appropriate strategy and the use of the system, without any discrimination, by legitimate movements of Syrian and Iraqi refugees across Europe (decision of Heads of States or Governments, Summits of March the 7th and 18th, 2016, in Brussels) [2–8, 28]. Due to nature and conditions under which people of warring countries are looking for asylum in Member States, systems like the proposed one, are of immediate need. Obviously, certification and authentication of medical data of this category of people are of importance since a lot of cases of villains exploiting them have already been reported (details of prerequisites and refugees legal movement are given in detail by Sideridis et al in [29].

## 3   The Smart Cross Border e-Gov Model

### 3.1   The Architecture

A Smart Cross Border e-Gov (SCBeG) system is actually a Decision Support System (DSS) comprising of three structural blocks: The I/O, the Validation-Authentication-Identification (VAI) and Processing blocks [26]. The whole authentication process, and part of the I/O block, is based on smart, machine learning, comparing, curing and checking data procedures. These smart items added to the full decision-making process are enough to characterize a SCBeG system as a smart system based on clear decision-making methods, procedures and the cloud computing technology security issues. The VAI block provides additional capabilities in authenticating personal and sensitive data. Obviously, a fundamental part of the VAI block consists of the platforms developed by STORK 2.0 project. These platforms include two identity models: The Pan-European Proxy Services (PEPS) & MiddleWare (MW) models (Fig. 2). It is noted that these models are based on established international standards, such as OASIS web SSO, ISO/IEC 27001, and OASIS DSS [27].

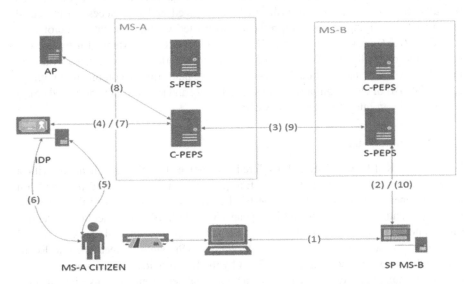

**Fig. 2.** Cross Border Authentication through STORK 2.0 [33, 34].

The authentication process is actually performed in two steps:

(a) Data submitted are collected by the system using various validity tests and/with data available from original sources. In most cases, this is the most difficult step, since original sources may not be available or, if there are any, may be of questionable validity;

(b) Authentication is performed, among public/local agencies or any other local supervising organisation of the service provided, both at citizen's State or enterprise's origin and the State in connection abroad. During this step, and in particular its Infrastructure as a Service (IaaS) model, should also be added to the system computer resources (software, hardware, servers) over the Internet. Public, local administrations and any third party are providers to the system. They should not only host the appropriate user's applications and personal files for testing but they should also handle maintenance, backup and upgrading services. Policy based services and automation of administrative tasks should also be main tasks of this IaaS.

The Processing block of the SCBeG system includes the appropriate Databases and a DSS mechanism while, two-way links exist with the VAI block. Subsequently, e-ID platforms and required programmes facilitate Interoperability Solutions for European

Public Administration (ISA), Connect European Facility (CEF) and guarantee availability of e-ID as a trust Service (IDaaS) [2–5]. Actually the European Commission, in an attempt to encourage Member States to extent their services with cross border functionalities, launched through the CEF programme the Digital Single Web Portal, where all needed information on Building Blocks (BB) can be found. The service required is an e-ID of citizens, businesses (natural or legal persons) and public servants by authenticating themselves in order to be authorized and gain access to protected resources by verifying in a secure, reliable and trusted way their identity and/or their role. STORK1.0 provided the first e-ID BB while STORK2.0 extended it by demonstrating the capability of the provision of additional attributes by trusted Attribute Providers (AP). All the structural blocks of the above platforms, in combination with the appropriate BB of cloud computing, are strengthening and transform the proposed cross-border tool in an integrated SCBeG system.

## 3.2   The Functionality

While STORK 1.0 & STORK 2.0 offered the first e-ID BB solution along with a software reference implementation, the European Commission covered the needs on legal interoperability by introducing the EU Regulation No 910/2014 of the European Parliament and the Council of the European Union [13, 14]) on "Electronic identification and trust services for electronic transactions in the internal market (eIDAS Regulation)" that repeals the Directive 1999/93/EC (Signature Directive). The Regulation, which has been adopted in July 2014 by the EU, provides the legislative and the regulatory framework for the creation of an appropriate environment, in which citizens, businesses and public administrations can interact securely, promoting and strengthening cross-border authentication. Key points of the Regulation are the mandatory cross-border recognition of the authentication schemes of all the Member States in public administration services, the provision of trusted services without cost and the association of the already existing authentication schemes with pre-established assurance Levels of Authentication.

The regulation is also taking into account the STORK 1.0 & STORK 2.0 e-ID Interoperability Framework, established during the implementation of these projects. The framework is consisting of several national nodes acting as Pan-European Proxy Services (PEPS) or Middle Wares (MW Solution) depending on the architectural solution that has been followed by the Member States [31, 35]. The main objectives of these nodes are to conceal the complexity of the national systems and to be a link of confidence for the creation of a *Circle of Trust* in Europe. Moreover, these nodes have to guarantee scalability, since any change within a Member State should be transparent to the other Member States.

The identification and authentication processes are based on message exchanging using the appropriate implementation profiles and technical specifications provided by STORK projects. The messages include personal and technical attributes. Details on the profiles, protocols and technical specifications used are beyond the scope of this paper and are omitted. By digitally signing the requesting and receiving assertions the requestor or sender are being authenticated, ensuring the integrity of the exchanged assertions.

Figure 2 demonstrates a STORK 2.0 scenario where the user from MS A needs to be authenticated to a Service Provider (SP) established in MS B. PEPS architecture is followed by both the MSs. The MS where the SP is established and the MS of origin of the user. PEPS are acting, according specific scenarios, either as Citizen's PEPS (C-PEPS) or as Service PEPS (S-PEPS). In a number of cases, PEPS is acting as C-PEPS and S-PEPS also. In this scenario the PEPS of MS A is acting as C-PEPS while PEPS in MS B (service provider) as S-PEPS. The C-PEPS of MS A and the S-PEPS of MS B have a trusted relation by sharing their digital certificates. The same applies between S-PEPS and the SP.

The Service Provider supports cross border authentication through STORK 2.0 and provides the user with the ability to choose that option [27]. Users are authenticated through their national PEPS. Obviously, user's consent is required by PEPS before transferring his personal data to the SP. Thus, the whole authenticated process consent is in full compliance with the "Data Protection Directive" [14]. It may be cases requiring more than identity attributes. In such cases, users will be asked to choose the source of the attributes, authenticate again to the source, and give their final permission so that the process will be completed by the service provider.

The authentication process can be completed following the 9 steps below [27]:

a. A safely protected resource of the SP is asked for access by the user A (1);
b. The outcome of the authentication process is sent by the SP to the corresponding S-PEPS (2);
c. The S-PEPS forwards the outcome of the authentication process to the relevant C-PEPS (3) of the Member State of origin of the user;
d. The authentication of the user takes place through C-PEPS to a national Identity Provider (IDP) (4,7);
e. Authentication of the user himself to the chosen IDP is taking place (5,6);
f. C-PEPS may retrieve (with the consent of the user) additional identification information or attributes from an AP (8);
g. Authenticated user's information and user's identification is transferred from the C-PEPS of Member State A to S-PEPS of Member State B (9);
h. S-PEPS forwards the information of step (7) to the service provider (10), see Fig. 2;
i. Access to the requested resource is permitted to the user.

## 4  Discussion

Integration and connection of national e-ID infrastructures, necessary for the type of systems like those proposed recently is still faced with reservation and remains an open issue although seven years have passed already since their first trial of implementation [38]. Actually, it was Austria's first attempt to take the challenge to deploy national e-ID modules in online processes by creating the legal basis for acceptance of foreign e-ID. This attempt has proved to be very successful and has managed, during its deployment, to satisfy several national legal requirements which had to be taken into account. By now, according to the Austrian Law, foreign citizens are registered in the so-called supplementary register by the means of qualified certificates and are treated equally like local residents. A similar approach using direct registries merge, rather than creating supplementary ones, has been adopted in this work.

Recently proposed e-government systems, combined with the results of the STORK 2.0 project, have contributed significantly to the implementation of innovative and reliable cross-border e-services, which enhance the improvement of the daily life of European citizens, increase the transparency of electronic transactions and ultimately contribute to the further development of the EU internal market. These e-services, coupled with the latest emerging technologies, e.g. e-identification, are "equipped" with supplementary security protection to face a potential online attack for the loss of personal data.

It is obvious that full implementation of the above systems is still a difficult task. Still, they will bring many benefits in key areas, such as health and social services in general. Although they have often been so far criticized for their poor contribution to efficiency and transparency in service provision [22]; recent advances promise successful implementation results. The proposed applications like the present one of a *cross-border primary health care system* can fill the gap in cross-border environment when European citizens move to various EU Member States and are of need of immediate medical care services. The need to improve the way of health care delivery and the recovery of the medical history of the patient is critical, as any possible delays in the delivery of the required treatment can be disastrous. Although the European Union has laid the foundations at a technical level through the STORK project and its individual pilots, and similar systems appear a few years back, the important advantage of our proposed system is that the medical history of a patient will always be up to date and readily recoverable at any level of care (primary, Secondary and tertiary). The primary health care service can be quite demanding in its implementation, as there are too many legal aspects that still need to be taken into account and laboriously clarified. As medical data are predominantly sensitive and have often been a target of online attacks, reassurance of high level safety of systems providing services of such a nature is always under very serious consideration.

# References

1. Alguliyev, R., Yusifov, F.: Electronic health as a component of G2C services. IJACSA **8**(3), 201–206 (2017)
2. European Commission (a). http://ec.europa.eu/information_society/apps/projects/. Accessed 23 Apr 2016
3. European Commission (b). http://ec.europa.eu/digital-agenda/en/connecting-europe-facility/. Accessed 17 Apr 2016
4. European Commission (c). https://ec.europa.eu/dgs/connect/en/content/electronic-identification-and-trust-services-eidas-regulatory-environment-and-beyond/. Accessed 17 Apr 2016
5. European Commission (d). http://ec.europa.eu/isa/. Accessed 17 Apr 2016
6. European Commission (2016). http://ec.europa.eu/digital-agenda/en/digital-agenda-europe-2020-strategy/. Accessed 17 Apr 2016

7. European Commission.: The European eGovernment Action Plan 2011-2015-Harnessing ICT to promote smart, sustainable & innovative Government in ICT for Government and Public Services. In: EC Publications, Brussels (2010). http://eur-lex.europa.eu/legal-content/EN/TXT/PDF/?uri=CELEX:52010DC0743&from=en/. Accessed 22 Apr 2016
8. European Commission.: Towards interoperability for European public services. In: T.C. Communication from the Commission to the European Parliament, the European Economic and Social Committee and the Committee of the Regions, Brussels (2010). http://ec.europa.eu/isa/documents/isa_iop_communication_en.pdf. Accessed 22 Apr 2016
9. European Council (a). [online] General Secretariat of the Council, EU International Summit, EU-Turkey Statement of the EU Heads of State or Government, Brussels (2016). http://www.consilium.europa.eu/en/press/. Accessed 24 Apr 2016
10. European Interoperability Framework For Pan-European eGovernment Services. Brussels (2004). http://ec.europa.eu/idabc/servlets/Docd552.pdf?id=19529/. Accessed 19 Apr 2017
11. European Parliament and the Council of the European Union.: Regulation (EU) No 910/2014 on electronic identification and trust services for electronic transactions in the internal market and repealing Directive 1999/93/EC 27. In: Official Journal of the European Union, L 257/73, Brussels (2014)
12. European Patients - Smart open Services, epSOS. http://www.epsos.eu/. Accessed 20 Apr 2016
13. European Union.: A Common European Asylum System, Luxembourg: Publication Office. ISBN 978-92-79-34626-2
14. European Union.: Directive 2011/24/eu of the European Parliament and of the Council on the application of patients' rights in cross-border healthcare. http://eur-lex.europa.eu/LexUriServ/LexUriServ.do?uri=OJ:L:2011:088:0045:0065:EN:PDF. Accessed 17 June 2017
15. Höchtl, J., Polycek, P., Schölhammer, R.: Big data in the policy cycle: policy decision making in the digital era. J. Organ. Comput. Electron. Commer. 25(4), 147–169 (2015)
16. IDIKA. http://www.idika.gr. (in Greek). Accessed 29 June 2019
17. Janowski, T., Estenez, E., Baguma, R.:. Platform governance for sustainable development: reshaping citizen - administration relationships in the digital age. Gov. Inf. Q. 35(4), 1–16 (2018). https://doi.org/10.1016/j.giq.2018.09.002
18. National Organization for the Provision of Healthcare Services, [online], Law 4213/2013 - Adaptation of national legislation to the provisions of Directive 2011/24 / EU of the European Parliament and of the Council of 9 March 2011 on the application of patients' rights in cross-border healthcare (L 88/45/4.4.2011) and other provisions. https://www.taxheaven.gr/laws/law/index/law/565. (only available in Greek). Accessed 28 June 2017
19. Parycek, P., Schossböck, J.: The uni brent movement. A successful case of mobilising lurkers in a public sphere. Int. J. Electron. Gov. 4(1/2), 43–68 (2011)
20. Parycek, P., Höchtl, J., Ginner, M.: Open government data implementation evaluation. J. Theoret. Appl. Electron. Commer. Res. 9(2), 80–100 (2014)
21. Parycek, P., Rinnerbauer, B., Schossböck, J.: Democracy in the digital age: digital agora or dystopia. Int. J. Electron. Gov. 9(3/4), 185–209 (2017)
22. Pimenidis, E., Georgiadis, C.K.: Can e-government applications contribute to performance improvement in public administration? Int. J. Oper. Res. Inf. Syst. 5(1), 48–57 (2014)
23. Pimenidis, E., Iliadis, L.S., Georgiadis, C.K.: Can e-Government Systems Bridge the Digital Divide? In: Proceedings of the 5th European Conference on Information Management and Evaluation (ECIME 2011), Dipartimento di Informatica e Comunicazione, Università dell'Insubria, Como, Italy, pp. 403–411 (2011)

24. Posch, K.C., Posch, R., Tauber, A., Zefferer, T., Zwattendorfer, B.: Secure and privacy-preserving eGovernment—best practice Austria. In: Calude, C.S., Rozenberg, G., Salomaa, A. (eds.) Rainbow of Computer Science. LNCS, vol. 6570, pp. 259–269. Springer, Heidelberg (2011). https://doi.org/10.1007/978-3-642-19391-0_19

25. Reiter, A., Prünster, B., Zefferer, T.: Hybrid mobile edge computing: unleashing the full potential of edge computing in mobile device use cases. In: Proceedings of the 17th IEEE/ACM International Symposium on Cluster, Cloud and Grid Computing, pp. 935–944 (2017)

26. Sideridis, A.B., Protopappas, L.: Recent ICT advances applied to smart e-government systems in Life Sciences. In: Proceedings of Information and Communication Technologies in Agriculture, Food and Environment. 7th HAICTA, Kavala, Greece (2015)

27. Sideridis, A.B., Protopappas, L., Tsiafoulis, S., Pimenidis, E.: Smart cross-border e-Gov systems and applications. In: Katsikas, S.K., Sideridis, A.B. (eds.) e-Democracy 2015. CCIS, vol. 570, pp. 151–165. Springer, Cham (2015). https://doi.org/10.1007/978-3-319-27164-4_11

28. Sideridis, A.B., Protopappas, L., Tsiafoulis, S., Pimenidis, E.: Smart cross-border e-Gov Systems: an application to refugee mobility. Int. J. Electron. Gov. (2017)

29. Sideridis, A.B., Pimenidis, E., Costopoulou, K., Yialouris, C.P., Savvas, I., Maliappis, M., Ntaliani, M., Karetsos, S., Tsiafoulis, S., Protopappas, L., Chatziandreou, A.: e-Gov. In: Proceedings of Recent Advances in Life Sciences & EE's Project Proposals (Medical, Animal, Plant, Food Sciences and Environmental Protection), Doctoral Consortium, HAICTA 2017, Chania, Crete (2017)

30. STORK 1.0 (a). https://www.eid-stork.eu/. Accessed 20 Apr 2016

31. STORK 1.0 (b) eID Consortium, D2.3 Quality authenticator schem. http://www.eid-stork.eu/. Accessed 22 Apr 2016

32. STORK 1.0 (c) eID Consortium, D 3.2.1 SAML. http://www.eid-stork.eu/. Accessed 22 Apr 2016

33. STORK 2.0 (a). https://www.eid-stork2.eu/. Accessed 12 Apr 2016

34. STORK 2.0. (b) https://www.eidstork2.eu/images/stories/documents/ETSI%202015%20presentation%20-STORK%202.0.pdf/. Accessed 14 Apr 2016

35. STORK 2.0 (c). https://www.eid-stork2.eu/. Accessed 20 Apr 2016

36. STORK 2.0 (d) eID Consortium, D4.3 First Version of Technical Design. https://www.eidstork2.eu/. Accessed 22 Apr 2016

37. Stranacher, K., Krnjic, V., Zefferer, T.: Trust and reliability of public sector data. In: Proceedings of World Academy of Science, Engineering and Technology (WASET), pp. 384–396 (2013)

38. Tauber, A., Zefferer, T., Zwattendorfer, B.: Approaching the challenge of eID interoperability: an Austrian perspective. Eur. J. ePractice 14, 22–39 (2012)

39. Viale, P.G., Cunha, M.A., Lampoltshammer, T., Polycek, P., Testa, M.G.: Increasing collaboration and participation in smart city governance: a cross case analysis of smart city initiatives. Inf. Technol. Dev. 23(3), 526–553 (2017)

40. Viale Pereira, G., Polycek, P., Falco, E., Kleinhans, R.: Smart governance in the context of smart cities: a literature review. Inf. Policy 23(2), 143–162 (2018)

41. Yialouris, C.P., Chatziandreou, A.: Implementing YGEIA1. TR/258, InfoLab, AUA, (in Greek), Athens, Greece (2017)

42. Zefferer, T.: Mobile Government: e-Government for mobile societies. Stocktaking of current trends and initiatives. Vienna Secur. Inf. Technol. Center 14, 1–58 (2011)

43. Zwattendorfer, B., Zefferer, T., Stranacher, K.: An overview of cloud and identity management models. WEBIST 1, 82–92 (2014)

# Blended Learning and Open Courseware for Promoting Interoperability in Public Services

Anastasia Papastylianou[1], Antonios Stasis[1(✉)], Konstantinos Rantos[2], and Victoria Kalogirou[3]

[1] National Centre of Public Administration and Local Government in Greece, Athens, Greece
apapas@ekdd.gr, an.stasis@gmail.com
[2] Department of Computer Science, International Hellenic University, Kavala, Greece
krantos@cs.ihu.gr
[3] Department of Information and Communication Systems Engineering, University of Aegean, Samos, Greece
vickalogirou@gmail.com

**Abstract.** Public Administrations invest a lot to improve their public services by making them more efficient and effective. In parallel, a significant effort is invested in training for Digital skills. However, the desired result is not yet achieved since a transformational approach for the primary users of the services, the Public Administration officials, is still missing. A combined approach for the training and the transformation of the services that need to reach certain criteria for interoperability and thus better public cross border cross sector services is presented in this paper. The Greek National Centre of Public Administration and Local Government (EKDDA) identified the need and created a learning model for Public Administration officials. The solution was proposed and implemented to address both issues, with the use of blended learning trainings, open courseware material and tools to assess and evaluate electronic public services via the Interoperability Maturity Assessment Model for a Public Service (IMM-IMAPS). A blended learning model for promoting interoperable government services will not only facilitate digital skills enhancement but will also help create a "digital services interoperability culture". The level of the evaluation and the assessment of the 98 real case examples of Public services examined during the training sessions, helped organizations identify actions needed to increase the interoperability maturity of their services. An important parameter that was further elaborated is the high percentage of satisfaction of the trainees regarding the presented content and the methods. These methods and practices were also reused by other countries.

**Keywords:** Blended learning · Open CourseWares (OCWs) · Slidewiki · Interoperability Maturity Assessment model (IMAPS) · Public services · e-Learning · Project Based Learning (PBL) · Moodle · eGovernment

© Springer Nature Switzerland AG 2020
S. Katsikas and V. Zorkadis (Eds.): e-Democracy 2019, CCIS 1111, pp. 79–93, 2020.
https://doi.org/10.1007/978-3-030-37545-4_6

# 1    Introduction

Interoperability is a crucial and critical success factor to forge ahead in the online provision of public services [1,2]. In the Digital Single Market (DSM) Strategy for Europe the role of interoperability in cross-border and cross-sector connections between communities, public services and public administrations has been widely recognized [3]. The European Interoperability Framework (EIF) was called as one of the legal instruments for eGovernment [3,4].

The Public sector is an enabler for the digitization of the economy and society in European Union (EU) [5,6], hence its wide support by several initiatives and policies developed by the European Commission (EC). The interoperability requirements in Public Administrations is also evident, considering the numerous government programs, action plans, and policy documents published in recent years at national and European levels [7].

ISA$^2$ programme, a funding instrument for the digitization of public administrations in the EU [8], in 2014 developed and updated as a reusable solution to assess the maturity of electronic public services, the Interoperability Maturity Model-IMAPS (former IMM) to assist interoperability according to the EIF conceptual model. In addition, proper training and digital skills, are an essential combination to eGovernment management, hence the strong need for Digital skills in public administration [11], while more advanced skills are essential to deliver electronic interoperable services [12]. As the training needs on interoperability in public administration are great and immediate, open and massive courses are under consideration. The awareness of such courses among users and the popularity of systems providing such courses are increasing [13]. Open CourseWare (OCW) is frequently cursory, outdated or non-reusable. Many of the courses contain only a syllabus and are only available in one language or format, making them difficult to reuse [14].

The National Centre of Public Administration and Local Government (EKDDA), identified the gap in understanding interoperability issues and the strong need to train public servants on it, and further, the need to raise awareness among organizations about the importance of interoperability in public services. The actions to implement the need started in 2015 with the initiation of training programs with e-learning modules and services at European level [15], on three different levels: "Basic Interoperability Concepts and Issues", "Interoperability Framework" and "Interoperability Assessment of Public Services (IMAPS)". EKDDA, with this action helped Greece to be one of the first countries that implemented the IMM and IMAPS in the assessment of real public services. The expectation of the implementation of the IMAPS was not only to improve interoperability of the assessed public services and affect positively the quality of the concerned public administration, but also to enhance the skills of public officials. Moreover, EKDDA promoted the policy of collaboration within other organizations and developed the Open Educational resources (OER), related to Interoperability and more specifically to the IMAPS model via blended learning programs and Open Coursewares (OCWs) using Moodle and Slidewiki platforms.

This paper focuses on the impact that these actions had to the Greek Public Administration with regards to the promotion of interoperability and the evolution of IMAPS. The authors were the main actors in the implementation of EKKDA actions such as specific training activities, consultations, as well as training evaluation and training impact assessment, in order to identify the impact that the training program had to the trainees and the respective Public Administration Bodies.

The paper describes the authors involvement and view and is structured as follows. Section 2 provides the interoperability assessment base and the new collaborative learning tools. Section 3 presents the training methodology and programs, with the related supporting and dissemination activities. Section 4 provides the main results, considering the evolution of the IMAPS model and the improvement of interoperability maturity in public services and training evaluation. The paper concludes with Sect. 5 where proposals for future work are also presented.

## 2    Background

The first version of the European Interoperability Framework (EIF) was published by European Commission (EC) in 2004 [16]. Following its first revision in 2008 [17], the National Interoperability Framework Observatory - NIFO was established in 2009 [18] for monitoring the implementation of National Interoperability Frameworks, and for the assessment of the compatibility with the EIF. In 2010 EC communicated the first European Interoperability Strategy defining strategic priorities and objectives for Interoperability[1] in European public services. EIS laid the foundation for a systematic approach to govern interoperability at EU level. In 2014 the first European Interoperability Reference Architecture [19] was announced to facilitate the EIF implementation. EIF was revised in 2017 [20] considering the experience gained by its implementation. All these years the main European Programme that was focusing on interoperability was the Interoperable Solutions for European Public Administrations programme (ISA) and its successors (e.g. ISA2 [21]).

To assist stakeholders in assessing the interoperability maturity of their digital public services and provide them guidance in improving it, the European Commission has also developed under the ISA program the Interoperability Maturity Model (IMM) which was succeeded by the Interoperability Maturity Assessment for Public Services (IMAPS) model. Both models adopt five levels to indicate the maturity of a public service as shown in Table 1 [22], with the desirable maturity level being at least 4: Sustainable.

The assessment of public services is focused on implementation aspects of the following three functional areas [22], also depicted in Fig. 1:

- **Service Delivery:** it includes issues related to the public channels available for the delivery of the service to the targeted end users group, i.e. citizens, businesses, or other administrations.

---

[1] http://ec.europa.eu/isa/documents/isa_annex_i_eis_en.pdf.

**Table 1.** Interoperability maturity levels

| Maturity level | Maturity stage | Interpretation |
|---|---|---|
| 1 | Ad Hoc | Poor interoperability - the service has almost no interoperability in place |
| 2 | Opportunistic | Fair interoperability - the service implements some elements of interoperability best practices |
| 3 | Essential | Essential interoperability - the service implements the essential best practices for interoperability |
| 4 | *Sustainable* | *Good interoperability - all relevant interoperability best practices are implemented by the public service* |
| 5 | Seamless | Interoperability leading practice - the service is a leading example for others |

- **Service Consumption:** it addresses issues related to the consumption (reuse) of existing services for the needs of processing of information towards the delivery of the service outcome. The more extensive is the reuse of information consumed from existing services, the more interoperable is considered the service.
- **Service Management:** it includes aspects related to managing the service during its life-cycle and service execution, such as procurement, service level management, and controlling and monitoring the process flow.

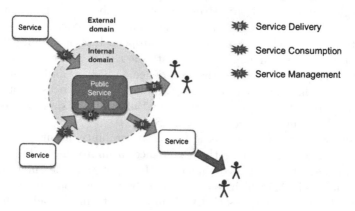

**Fig. 1.** Interoperability areas of the IMAPS model [22]

IMAPS consists of a set of questions which address the above three functional areas accompanied by an initial section which defines the scope of the public service under assessment, all available as an online self-assessment survey. The questions seek to assess the maturity with regards to all layers of interoperability, as these are defined in the new EIF, i.e. legal, organisational, semantic, and technical interoperability [17].

# 3    Promoting Interoperability

## 3.1    Methodologies to Promote Interoperability

Three (3) training programs' curriculums were designed and developed open educational resources (OER) including text with open licence, questions, case studies, media, and other freely accessible digital assets, organized for training, workshops, and dissemination info days. Various open and collaborative learning methods and tools were used for this purpose. During the development and delivery of the training periods, the EKDDA has cooperated very closely with ISA to create systematic actions to promote interoperability.

The implementation of interoperability training project included actions covering (a) Identification of training needs, (b) Instructional design of programs, (c) Development of learning material, (d) Development of evaluation material (e) Delivery of the training and other activities for the entire public sector and local government (f) IMAPS implementation in real public services, and (g) Implementation of Training Impact Assessment.

The training needs analysis demonstrated that interoperability, although recognized as an important aspect by digitally aware employees, it is not in organizations' top priorities. Therefore, dissemination activities, open consultations, interactive communications were developed and supported to raise awareness, promote interoperability and increase participation.

Different learning methods such as classroom training, e-learning, blended learning, open coursewares, support the activities to evolve the results. Especially for the IMAPS implementation, EKDDA has chosen the blended learning and open courseware techniques. Moreover EKKDA maintains an internal database with the staff of all organizations in Greece that are active in e-government and interoperability initiatives. EKDDA is supporting this domain for almost two decades, using face to face programs. EKDDA initially invited for IMAPS the staff of the organizations that are responsible for interoperable e-government services, relevant to the Digital Policy of EU and are included in the EIF action plan [20].

**Blended Learning Program.** EKDDA initially organized a training program for IMAPS that was divided in three parts. The first part was a typical two days classroom training course aiming to familiarize the trainees with the main interoperability concepts, the structure of the IMAPS model and the use of the e-learning tools that would be used during the second part of the training program. During the first part of the program the trainees were separated in groups that had similar interests or belonged to the same organization. The instructors assigned to each group a specific public service for evaluation using IMAPS. The public services were selected in collaboration with the participants taking into account (a) the interoperability policy areas of EU, (b) the competencies, responsibilities and priorities of the organizations that the participants worked for, (c) the popularity of an e-services, (d) the potential reuse of data and functions from other e-services.

During the second part of the training program each group worked on the assigned subject while an e-learning platform (moodle) was used for asynchronous e-learning with all the necessary material of the program, guidelines, specific forums for discussion and online support by the instructors. Moreover, synchronous e-learning sessions were organized using Big blue button in order to discuss complicated issues that could arise. Each group had to accomplish the evaluation of the public service, and provide supporting to the evaluation information, together with their conclusions which were focusing on (a) the interoperability maturity improvement of the public service and (b) potential amendments to IMAPS so that it can better cover the needs of a specific domain or a specific organization. These conclusions, were communicated to ISA as a valuable feedback to the EIF's implementation and suggestions for future enhancements.

The third part of the program was a workshop with presentations and discussions regarding the evaluated public services, the potential synergies and next actions. Specific questionnaires were used in order to get the appropriate feedback by the trainees regarding IMAPS and the training program. The questionnaires included qualitative research, training needs collection and peer evaluation. Each training group had approximately 20–25 trainees. The methods that were utilized in this blended learning program were Project Based Learning and Open and Collaborative Learning. Figure 2 summarizes the structure of the training program.

**1st Phase : Basic Concept and Presentation of the model** (Two days face to face )
- ✓ Main interoperability issues and concepts
- ✓ Introduction to the Interoperability Maturity Model for electronic public services
- ✓ Detailed presentation of methodology, criteria and rating scale of the model
- ✓ Presentation of objectives, deliverables of essays and form working groups

**2nd Phase : Practical Implementation** (10 days, e-Learning )
- ✓ Implementation and support

**3rd Phase : Presentations and Proposals for Improvement** (Two days face to face)
- ✓ Essay presentations
- ✓ Suggestions for configuring / extent the model to the National or Sectoral

**Fig. 2.** The structure of the IMAP training program

Following the training programs, special innovative workshops and conferences were organized mainly addressed at the public sector. The best cases from each course were presented and inspired the audience for further collaboration and synergies. This was crucial since the interoperability implies close collaboration among different organizations. The purpose of these workshops was to inform, explore and promote methods, techniques, practices, tools and conditions required for the promotion of interoperability in the public administration and enhance relevant services, as well as to jointly experiment on the IMAPS implementation. With these activities a special human network was established with focus on interoperability.

**Open Courseware for IMAPS and Interoperability.** The blended learning methods and the conferences although important, had a slow pace in the engagement and training of all the public sector bodies in interoperability issues and in IMAPS. Therefore, it was decided to offer these courses in an open courseware platform and invite other organizations for further improvement and collaboration.

The Open CourseWare (OCW) concept arose from the success of open source software by expanding the concept of openness to the educational context [26]. A vast amount of OCW is being published online to make educational content more attainable. Therefore it was decided the creation, translation and evolution of highly-structured remixable OCW for interoperability that would be shared via the open-source wiki platforms SlideWiki[2]. Currently EKDDA offers the following training courses as an open courseware in the Slidewiki platform and as Open Courses on Moodle[3]: Open Government [23], Basic Interoperability Concepts [24], and Interoperability Maturity Assessment Model for a public service [25].

The training path that EKDDA offered to the participants consisted of the following steps:

1. Basic Interoperability Issues and Concepts.
2. Interoperability Framework and Toolkit.
3. Interoperability Maturity Assessment of Public Services - IMAPS.

The open courseware material had additional requirements such as specific supporting videos [27] and special assessment questionnaires [28], all offered in English. The Interoperability related courses on SlideWiki allow users to:

- collaboratively create comprehensive OCW (curricula, slide presentations, self-assessment tests, illustrations etc.) online in a crowdsourcing manner,
- semi-automatically translate this content into more than 50 different languages and to improve the translations in a collaborative manner and
- support engagement and social networking of educators and learners around that content.

The main drawback of the open courseware programs is that they do not offer a certification for the successful completion of the courses and do not offer additional support apart from the material that is being presented. Nevertheless, the value of the open courseware was not questionable since a lot of stakeholders that have a tight schedule can follow the course with their own pace and provide their additional resources to improve it and update it.

**Training Evaluation and Training Impact Assessment.** EKDDA applies a transformed training two level evaluation method based on Kirkpatrick's

---

[2] Slidewiki is a project funded by the Horizon 2020 programme (GA: 688095).
[3] https://elearning.ekdd.gr/course/index.php?categoryid=21.

Four-Level Training Evaluation, including the Reaction, Learning, Behaviour & Results[4].

**Level 1: Evaluation of Reaction and Learning** - The degree to which participants find the training useful and relevant to their jobs and the degree to which participants gain the knowledge, skills and attitude based on their participation in the training.

**Level 2: Impact Assessment** - The degree to which participants apply what they learned during training after two months, when they are back on the job, and the degree to which specific outcomes and behaviours occur as a result of the training.

At the end of each program, in the first level, an online evaluation gives the direct results of the training. The evaluation includes 44 questions and is organized in 5 different sections except the demographical data. The sections include characteristics regarding the Organizational, Educational Resources, Instructors, Instructional Design and Reaction, including between them usefulness, satisfaction and the general evaluation. After two months of training another online form, with five sections and 144 questions, measures the outcomes and results of training. The data includes the degree of awareness, the degree of training implementation, specific actions etc.

### 3.2   Implementation of IMAPS

Interoperability applies to different sectors in Public Administration therefore the services that were selected for evaluation during the training courses should (a) be suitable for evaluation with IMAPS i.e. not a machine-to-machine service, (b) belong to one important sector of public administration such as Base Registries, Taxation, Health Care Services, Social Insurance, Public Procurement, Public Finance Management etc.

Each service was evaluated by a specific working group. The members of each group were mainly employees of the service owner, i.e. the authority responsible for the operation and provision of the services. It is important to mention that the groups were created in such a way, so that all stakeholder authorities views were considered in the evaluation, ensuring the holistic evaluation approach.

98 services were evaluated considering the IMAPS evaluation aspects i.e. Service Delivery, Consumption and Management. The trainees used the respective IMAPS template of the full questionnaire[5].

Following the initial assessment of each service by the group of trainees, the results were amended after presenting and discussing them with the instructors and the other trainees. Afterwards, using the IMAPS lite version online survey[6], specific recommendations were extracted for the improvement of each service. These recommendations were included in the results of each service evaluation.

---

[4] https://www.kirkpatrickpartners.com/Our-Philosophy/The-Kirkpatrick-Model.

[5] https://joinup.ec.europa.eu/sites/default/files/document/2016-03/imm_full_questio nnaire_0.pdf.

[6] https://ec.europa.eu/eusurvey/runner/IMMSurvey.

# 4 Main Results of the Implementation

## 4.1 Training Results

Three (3) Pilot courses, 15 Training Programs including 3 pilot ones, and 1 Workshop were delivered in total. The results were measured using educational indicators as training analytics and presented in many info days and conferences.

**Training Needs Results.** From the training needs analysis it became evident that interoperability is not clearly recognized in organizations, yet it's among digitally-skilled employees priorities. According to the responses to questionnaires provided to participants around 58% of them were self-motivated and had personal interest for interoperability. This result validates that the organizations in Greece do not necessarily have interoperability in their priorities. Nevertheless, the personnel of public administration is willing to contribute to the improvement of interoperability maturity in their organizations.

**Instructional Design Results.** It is worth mentioning that during the evaluation and impact assessment, as well as through open consultations, the comments from trainers, participants and contributors didn't give any proposals for program restructure, so the learning path for interoperability can be considered to be well organized.

**Training Material Results.** The training material created by EKDDA is **certified, open and available to be reused**. Notably, it is available in English and it is ready to be reused in any other country that is interested in applying IMAPS. Cyprus has already used it. As a result, the total activities for the Open Educational Resources of EKDDA were the following.

- **Disseminated** to a large number of Public employees (+3000 downloads).
- **Reused** by many trainees and trainers to create their own material (+300).
- **Augmented** by contributors and new educational material have been occurred with case studies.
- **Commented** by users and contributors and continuously improved.

**Training Delivery Results.** EKDDA trained 350 public servants through 15 courses from 2016 until 2018. The main results of the training process were the following.

- The programs **raised awareness** among Public Administrations and public servants regarding interoperability, service modelling and re-design and provided the ability to implement the IMAPS.
- Trainees can recognize how a service interacts with other services and how it could **be re-designed**.

– The consultation phase ensures better understanding and collaboration among public servants and promotes the efficient resolution of various issues regarding the **interaction** among public services
– The consultation phase maps the various implementations done across public administrations and public services, revealing cases of duplicate implementations on the one hand, i.e. bad interoperability examples, but also cases of **reusable components**, practices and services that can be reused in various other contexts, saving unnecessary costs in time and effort.

The great challenge faced in the training process was the ability to collaborate and make **synergies** and to act as a **human network** of Public Administration representatives and interested parties for interoperability. In that way, comments and input can continually improve the IMM-IMAPS.

Furthermore, this work inspired the Foundation of Research and Technology (FORTH) to create an additional flavour for the use of IMAPS in e-health care services in Greece [17]. They reused the open courcewares for interoperability and IMAPS on Slidewiki and created a new transformed open courseware for interoperability in Health, which has been awarded in SlideWiki's Open Course-Ware competition[7].

**Training Evaluation and Impact Assessment Results.** The participants evaluation of the training program is summarized in Fig. 3, showing that overall the participants were satisfied with the approach.

## Training Evaluation

| Learning Evaluation (scale 1-10) | Impact Assessment of Learning (scale 1-10) |
|---|---|
| **Usefulness = 8.7** | **Interoperability awareness = 8.8** |
| **Satisfaction = 8.8** | **Necessity for organization = 8.9** |

Fig. 3. Training program evaluation

### 4.2 Interoperability Maturity Results

EKDDA trainees evaluated 98 public administration services. 83 of the services have been further analysed and the analysis of the rest is still in progress. The analysis followed the process described in Sect. 3.

The interoperability maturity of the services are shown in Table 2. The services have been classified according to the domain that they belong and the rows of the table show the average results per domain. The selected domains

---

[7] https://slidewiki.eu/2018/12/12/read-the-interview-of-dimitrios-g-katehakis-angel ina-kouroubali-and-ioannis-karatzanis-winners-of-slidewikis-open-courseware-comp etition/.

were influenced by the National Public Policy, the priorities of Digital Single Market and Europe 2020. Whenever an e-service was applicable to more that one domain the classification was based on the potential target user group. For instance 11 services, related to Base Registries were evaluated and the average maturity level for Service Delivery, Consumption and Management were **3.3**, **3.6**, and **3.2** respectively.

**Table 2.** Interoperability maturity

| Domain | Number of services | IMAPS maturity level | | |
|---|---|---|---|---|
| | | Delivery | Consumption | Management |
| Base registry | 11 | 3,3 | 3,6 | 3,2 |
| Citizen services | 2 | 4,2 | 3,3 | 3,2 |
| Education | 10 | 3,6 | 3,3 | 3,6 |
| Health care services | 6 | 3,0 | 3,9 | 4,0 |
| Horizontal A2A | 5 | 3,2 | 3,7 | 3,6 |
| Public finance management | 6 | 3,7 | 3,2 | 2,8 |
| Public procurement | 3 | 3,0 | 3,8 | 2,9 |
| Social security | 20 | 3,5 | 3,1 | 3,2 |
| Taxation | 12 | 3,4 | 3,5 | 3,1 |
| Transportation | 5 | 3,1 | 3,7 | 2,9 |
| Business | 3 | 2,0 | 4,2 | 3,5 |
| **Total/Average** | **83** | **3,3** | **3,6** | **3,3** |

Moreover, in Table 3 we can see how similar services can be compared regarding interoperability maturity level. This comparison will help public authorities identify good practices and examples and be able to reuse them in order to improve the quality of the services provided.

**Table 3.** Maturity comparison for similar services

| Organization | IMAPS consumption | IMAPS management | IMAPS average |
|---|---|---|---|
| Hospital 1 | 3,77 | 3,77 | 3,77 |
| Hospital 2 | 4,30 | 4,45 | 4,375 |

In total, the average maturity level of the services that were evaluated in Greece during this period according to IMAPS was 3.3, as shown in Fig. 4.

Figure 5 demonstrates an example of a diagram that can be derived from the database in order to justify the potential policy decision that can be made for interoperability. One can see that the health care and base registry services are more interoperable than other services of Public administration.

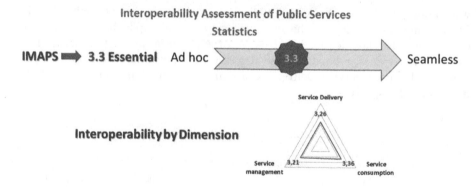

Fig. 4. Average interoperability maturity level of the evaluated services

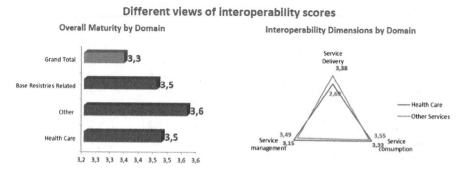

Fig. 5. Average interoperability maturity per domain considering the aspects of IMAPS

It is important to mention that although IMAPS refers to interoperability among different organizations, there are several cases, where different systems that are being supported by different vendors, according to specific different contracts, are using interoperability as a means of communication although they belong to the same organization. In these cases the other systems are considered as external environment, although in the same administration body.

## 5  Conclusions and Future Work

Interoperability is a key success factor for offering high quality public services with the minimal cost by reusing data, functions, processes of other services. IMAPS is a tool that can help public administrations to assess the maturity of the services they provide regarding interoperability. IMAPS is a generic assessment tool that can be applied in different domains and type of services. In some cases, specialization to the initial model has been identified as a need during the training courses for specific domains. The standards that are being used in each domain can further elaborate and specify the current generic version of the

IMAPS model. This need will create different versions for different domains e.g. health, procurement. This has also been proposed by European Commission.

The systematic - regular evaluation of the public services can improve interoperability maturity. Moreover, it can allow the comparison among similar service of different organization and different countries. At this stage IMAPS is too generic to allow this to happen. Specialization is also required for different organizations considering their practices related to internal application-system development, outsourcing and the different types of systems that they operate. Last but not least, although IMAPS is focusing on the evaluation of an existing service is very useful for the new service design, since it provides hinds for the better exploitation of existing services of other organization and promotes collaboration for the creation of an interoperable service that will be able to be reused by other organizations.

Considering the training methods, it was revealed that blended project based learning and Open coursewares are crucial for establishing collaboration among different organizations that can increase interoperability in the near future. OCW, Blended learning and PBL have increased collaboration within organizations (from 24% to 80%) and better engagement results have been achieved. Additionally, a new participation level has appeared because participants act as Champions (30% activate owners and contributors to the training material). Teamwork can have better results both in the objective evaluation of the service and the creation of a common understanding for the improvements that need to be made. Open courseware material can enhance collaboration and involve apart from public administration experts more stakeholders and citizens. This can lead to the creation of a Social network focusing on interoperability issues and creating promoting the culture of interoperability. During the training courses it was obvious that the different departments of the same public organization may need to collaborate using interoperability principles, mainly due to the way that the legacy systems have been developed and the organizational barriers. For instance, different contracts and different head of departments in the same organization may require interoperable approach for offering aggregated public services.

The next steps required are (a) the handling, supporting and management of the interoperability network and synergy with the social partners and all the Public Agencies, as well as the Local Government organizations, (b) further adaptation of the IMAPS model for specific domains that will allow benchmarking, comparison of similar services, and reuse of good practices, (c) IMAPS can also be used for promoting the interoperability concepts e.g. the public service in a practical and tangible way, (d) the specialization in targeted programmes for the development of the human resources within the context of a digital environment and Certification of interoperability skills in order to response to real organizational and training needs with determined targets and expected results for the improvement of the services delivered to the citizens, (e) Innovative activities through the use of internationally acknowledged methods, good practice and know-how transfer. So activities of promoting and applying IMAPS in Public Administration needs to provide not only methods or material per se, but also the appropriate digital knowledge and skills in public organization to evolve the interoperability. The focus was put upon training, collaboration, openness, sharing -reuse and finally, on the creation of a Social Interoperability Culture.

**Acknowledgement.** The information and views set out in this paper are those of the author(s) and do not reflect the official opinion of the EKDDA or European Commission. Moreover the authors would like to thank the trainees that participated in the training programs that significantly contributed to the implementation of this work.

# References

1. Kubicek, H., Cimander, R.: Eur. J. ePractice (2009). http://www.dlorg.eu/uploads/External%20Publications/6.1.pdf
2. CEPS: Evaluation Study supporting the interim evaluation of the ISA$^2$ programme ISA$^2$, European Union (2019). ISBN 978-92-76-02074-5, https://www.ceps.eu/wp-content/uploads/2019/06/NO0119341ENN.en_.pdf
3. EC COM(2015) 192. A Digital Single Market Strategy for Europe, Brussels, 06 May 2015. https://eur-lex.europa.eu/legal-content/EN/TXT/?uri=celex%3A52015DC0192
4. Rosic, Z., Lognoul, M., De Streel, A., Hocepied, C.: Contribution to Growth: European Digital Single Market: Delivering improved rights for European citizens and businesses. European Parliament (2019). http://www.crid.be/pdf/public/8449.pdf
5. Decision (EU) 2015/2240 of the European Parliament and of the Council of 25: establishing a programme on interoperability solutions and common frameworks for European public administrations, businesses and citizens (ISA2 programme) as a means for modernising the public sector, Brussels, 4 December 2015
6. European Parliament: Entertainment x.0 to boost broadband deployment, WIK, TNO, RAND Europe (2013). http://www.europarl.europa.eu/document/activities/cont/201310/20131017ATT72946/20131017ATT72946EN.pdf
7. Cordella, A., Bonina, C.M.: A public value perspective for ICT enabled public sector reforms: a theoretical reflection. Gov. Inf. Q. **29**(4), 512–520 (2012). ISSN 0740–624X, https://doi.org/10.1016/j.giq.2012.03.004
8. Directive (EU) 2019/1024 of the European Parliament and of the Council of 20 June 2019 on open data and the re-use of public sector information, PE/28/2019/REV/1. http://data.europa.eu/eli/dir/2019/1024/oj
9. Soares, D., Amaral, L.: Information systems interoperability in public administration: identifying the major acting forces through a Delphi study. J. Theoret. Appl. Electron. Commer. Res. **6**(1), 61–94 (2011). https://doi.org/10.4067/S0718-18762011000100006
10. Ministerial Declaration on eGovernment - Tallinn declaration (2017). https://ec.europa.eu/digital-single-market/en/news/ministerial-declaration-egovernment-tallinn-declaration
11. EC COM/2010/0682. An Agenda for new skills and jobs: A European contribution towards full employment
12. OECD: Digital Government Toolkit (2015). www.oecd.org/officialdocuments/publicdisplaydocumentpdf/?cote=GOV/PGC/EGOV(2015)2&docLanguage=En
13. Atkins, D., Seely Brown, J., Hammond, L.: A Review of the Open Educational Resources (OER) Movement: Achievements, Challenges, and New Opportunities, Report to The William and Flora Hewlett Foundation (2007). https://hewlett.org/wp-content/uploads/2016/08/ReviewoftheOERMovement.pdf

14. Vahdati, S., Lange, C., Auer, S.: OpenCourseWare Observatory - Does the Quality of OpenCourseWare Live up to its Promise? In: Fifth International Conference on Learning Analytics and Knowledge, pp. 73–82 (2015). https://arxiv.org/abs/1410. 5694

15. Training material for "Interoperability Maturity Assessment for Public Services", National Center of Public Administration and Local Government (2019). http://resources.ekdd.gr/gnosis/index.php/3-26/88-interoperability-maturity-asse ssment-for-public-services

16. European Interoperability Framework (2004). https://ec.europa.eu/idabc/servle ts/Doc4ee4.pdf?id=18060. Accessed 22 Aug 2019

17. European Interoperability Framework (EIF) for European public services (2010). http://ec.europa.eu/isa/documents/isa_annex_ii_eif_en.pdf. Accessed 22 Aug 2019

18. National Interoperability Framework Observatory (NIFO) (2009). https://ec.eur opa.eu/idabc/en/document/7796.html. Accessed 22 Aug 2019

19. European Interoperability Reference Architecture (EIRA) (2019). https://joinup. ec.europa.eu/solution/eira. Accessed 22 Aug 2019

20. European Interoperability Framework - Implementation Strategy (2017). https:// eur-lex.europa.eu/legal-content/EN/TXT/?uri=COM%3A2017%3A134%3AFIN. Accessed 22 Aug 2019

21. ISA2 - Interoperability solutions for public administrations, businesses and citizens (2019). https://ec.europa.eu/isa2/home_en. Accessed 22 Aug 2019

22. Interoperability Maturity Assessment for a Public Service. IMAPS v1.1.1 User Guide (2018). https://ec.europa.eu/isa2/solutions/imaps_en. Accessed 22 Aug 2019

23. Slidewiki, Open Government (2018). https://slidewiki.org/deck/113098-1/anoik th-diakybernhsh-open-governance/deck/113101-1/113101-1:2/view?language=el. Accessed 22 Aug 2019

24. Slidewiki, Interoperable Public e-Services - Main interoperability issues and concepts (2017). https://slidewiki.org/deck/4507-8/interoperable-public-e-services-main-interoperability-issues-and-concepts?language=en. Accessed 22 Aug 2019

25. Slidewiki, IMM-Interoperability Maturity Assessment for Public Services (2018). https://slidewiki.org/deck/108796-2/imm-interoperability-maturity-assessment-for-public-services?language=en. Accessed 22 Aug 2019

26. Vladoiu, M.: State-of-the-art in open courseware initiatives worldwide. Inform. Educ. **10**, 271–294 (2011)

27. Slidewiki videos (2018). slidewiki.org/deck/108796-2/imm-interoperability-maturit y-assessment-for-public-services/slide/758164-14/110560-2:1;116012–1:2;758164– 14:1/view?language=en. Accessed 22 Aug 2019

28. Slidewiki evaluation questionnaire (2019). slidewiki.org/deck/108796-2/imm-intero perability-maturity-assessment-for-public-services/slide/758631-8/116094-1:10;75 8631–8:1/view?language=en. Accessed 22 Aug 2019

# How to Do It Right: A Framework for Biometrics Supported Border Control

Mohamed Abomhara[1(✉)], Sule Yildirim Yayilgan[1(✉)],
Anne Hilde Nymoen[1(✉)], Marina Shalaginova[1(✉)], Zoltán Székely[2(✉)],
and Ogerta Elezaj[1(✉)]

[1] Department of Information Security and Communication Technology,
Norwegian University of Science and Technology, Gjøvik, Norway
{mohamed.abomhara,sule.yildirim,anne.nymoen,
marina.shalaginova,ogerta.elezaj}@ntnu.no
[2] Faculty of Law Enforcement, National University of Public Service,
Budapest, Hungary
dr.szekely.zoltan@gmail.com

**Abstract.** Complying with the European Union (EU) perspective on human rights goes or should go together with handling ethical, social and legal challenges arising due to the use of biometrics technology as border control technology. While there is no doubt that the biometrics technology at European borders is a valuable element of border control systems, these technologies lead to issues of fundamental rights and personal privacy, among others. This paper discusses various ethical, social and legal challenges arising due to the use of biometrics technology in border control. First, a set of specific challenges and values affected were identified and then, generic considerations related to mitigation of these issues within a framework is provided. The framework is expected to meet the emergent need for supplying interoperability among multiple information systems used for border control.

**Keywords:** Biometrics · Border control · Ethical challenges · Legal challenges · Social challenges

## 1 Introduction

Biometrics technology [18,20] refer to automated methods of identification and verification of the identity of individuals based on their physiological or behavioral attributes. Examples of biometrics include fingerprints, facial features, iris scans, etc. They are used to support the border police on making decisions by providing automated identification, verification and cross-checking of individuals based on their biological and behavioral traits [5]. Identification is a process to associate a person with an identity (who are you?). Verification is a process to determine whether someone is who he/she claims to be (are you who you claim to be?). Cross-checking is a process of verifying information by using

© Springer Nature Switzerland AG 2020
S. Katsikas and V. Zorkadis (Eds.): e-Democracy 2019, CCIS 1111, pp. 94–109, 2020.
https://doi.org/10.1007/978-3-030-37545-4_7

alternative European Union (EU) information systems. Biometrics technology is increasingly being used by countries worldwide and is a highly adopted technology at the EU borders [12, 32]. It aim is to help achieving an automated, rapid and highly secure border clearance process, such that an increasing passenger throughput does not compromise border control reliability.

On the one hand, biometrics technology has been proven to be cost-effective to enhance border security, detect fraud and help to improve border crossing efficiency as well as facilitate an effective migration control and enforcement. On the other hand, biometrics technology can lead to some challenges and conflicts with fundamental human rights and can be a cause of ethical, social and legal challenges [11, 32]. The key challenge is related to individual rights, such as respect for personal privacy [37, 38], human dignity [16], bodily integrity [26], equity and personal liberty [31, 36]. Personal data protection is also an issue, especially when biometrics information is stored in centralized databases [8, 29].

Another major concern with biometrics technology is the seemingly immutable link between biometric traits and persistent personal information storage about individuals [9]. The tight link between personal records and biometrics can have both positive and negative consequences for individuals and the society overall. Recent research [10] on biometrics data shows that it can reveal personal information, such as gender, age, ethnicity and even critical health problems like diabetes, vision problems, Alzheimer's disease, etc. Such confidential information might be used for example to discriminate among individuals when it comes to border crossing enforcement.

People have the right to choose to what extent and how to engage with the systems and devices (e.g., biometric sensors). For example, some people may refuse to have their photographs taken by a face recognition system due to the concerns about the purpose of the use of the images [9]. Moreover, others may refuse to or feel uncomfortable to undergo iris scans or provide fingerprints due to permanent or temporary disability. A study of biometric enrollment and verification in the United Kingdom showed that 0.62% of the sample group of people with disabilities were unable to enroll any of the three biometrics tested: fingerprints, facial scans, and iris scans [25]. Moreover, according to the European health and social integration survey (EHSIS), in 2012 there were 70 million people with disabilities in EU [15]. If 0.62% of all disabled in EU were unable to provide this data, approximately 434000 Europeans would be unable to provide any of the three most common types of biometric data. Such concerns may impact these people and also people belonging to different groups with varying cultural beliefs, values and specific behaviors on how they interpret the requirements of being exposed to biometrics technologies. In general, a range of complex and interconnected issues must be addressed while deciding on the use of biometrics as a technology for border control [30]. Also, ethics guidelines and a regulatory framework for the use of biometrics technology in border control must be formulated in order to avoid any harmful impact on the society while allowing for the continuous development of this technology to benefit the society [11].

In this paper, Sect. 2 discusses the potential benefits of using biometrics in EU borders and the ethical theories around it. Section 3 investigates the key ethical, social and legal challenges of using biometrics technology and demonstrates vulnerabilities and risks related to these challenge categories, followed by a discussion of moral considerations with regards to human rights, right to privacy, right to data protection etc. Section 4 presents a discussion on ethical reasoning and decision making. Section 5 concludes the study.

## 2      Background

This section provides a background of benefits of biometrics in EU borders and a discussion on moral, ethics and ethical theories.

### 2.1    Potential Benefits of Using Biometrics in EU Borders

Freedom of movement is restricted by closed or controlled borders in order to protect other fundamental rights such as security or health, national or regional political, societal, cultural or economic interests of the political entities within that bordered area. The Schengen Border Code (SBC) (Regulation (EU) 2016/399) and its amendment (Regulation (EU) 2017/458) set out the rules governing the movement of people across EU's internal and external borders. The main aim of border checks is to ensure that the persons and goods crossing the border are entering or leaving the area with the permission (authorization) of the political entity of SBC. This permission for travel is currently manifested in a travel document having a physical form as well as a record on the authorization in the national travel document database.

Identification and verification procedures at the border are to ensure that entry-to or exit-from a country will be granted to the right persons. In recent years, Member States have seen an increased use of biometric identification and authentication systems at EU's borders including airports and land borders [2,24]. More significantly, the large-scale EU information systems such as Visa Information System (VIS), Second-generation Schengen Information System (SIS II), European Asylum Dactyloscopy Database (EURODAC) and Entry Exit System (EES) etc. [22] employ biometrics for migration and border control and management. Such systems involve several highly complex processes, leading to a number of ethics and privacy challenges [11,31]. The integration of biometric at border control provides benefits for travelers, political entities (states), authorities responsible for border control as well as individual border guards. Such benefits include accuracy, integrity, robustness and efficiency.

- **Accuracy:** Accuracy of travelers' identification and verification means the ability to recognize genies person and reject imposters person correctly [17]. During manual border checks, border guards seek to gain knowledge about the subject (traveler) and associate it with his/her identity. For example, the border guard looks at the traveler and verifies with the picture on the travel document (on bio-data page) to determine if the person standing in front of him/her is the same that is pictured in the travel document. However, the accuracy of identification and verification depends on lighting, age of the picture, perception capabilities, tiredness, make-up etc. In addition, spreading culture of having aesthetic surgery poses a further challenge to manual identification. Moreover, a human border guard is usually very efficient during the start of the shift, then diminishing attention appears as the officer gets tired. In this case, biometrics can enhance and support these practices. A selective and differentiated application of multimodal biometrics identification results in a higher average accuracy during the whole shift as well as facilitates cross-checking of personal data with greater accuracy [17].

- **Integrity:** Integrity of the identification is the ability to confirm that the collected data and its components (e.g., passport picture and passport information) have not been altered from that created by the issuing State or organization [17]. Use of biometrics enhances the reduction of identity fraud impersonation ( e.g., fake IDs and passports) as the identification and verification processes do not rely on the human agent. To the best of our knowledge, a reduction in fraud means an increase in accuracy. Therefore, using biometrics eliminates a quite considerable integrity threat that the border guards face and benefits the authority responsible for border control.

- **Robustness:** Biometrics systems are easy to operate, maintain, update, replace, redeploy or decommission compared to border control units/booths consisting of human agents only. Long years to achieve full competence and repetitive training is not required and experience is not lost with a single unit. From the traveler's view, utilizing multimodal biometrics allows the traveler to (theoretically) decide which biometric modality (e.g., fingerprints, face, iris) will be used for identification based on his/her preferences.

- **Efficiency:** The processing capacity of Automated Border Control (ABC) gates is sustained over time as ABCs don't get tired. Additionally, ABCs conduct an objective repeatable set of checks to complete identity and document verification can be more accurate and quicker to complete than similar checks conducted by humans [17]. This results in a higher number of low-risk travelers' throughput without losing accuracy or integrity and allows human resources to be focused on potentially higher-risk travelers.

As these benefits are all potential, the actual benefits highly depend on how biometric systems are integrated into the border management and how control systems help facilitate the correct identification and verification of persons and contribute to fighting identity fraud.

## 2.2 Moral, Ethics and Code of Ethics

Morals are the general views, thoughts and convictions of people in making judgments about what is right or wrong. According to Kizza [23], morality is defined as "a set of rules (code) of conduct that governs human behavior in matters of right and wrong, good and bad." Ethics, on the other hand, concerns the way we can come to moral judgments of what is right and wrong for individuals and society. The ethical judgment of what is good or bad and right or wrong is often based on a set of shared rules, principles, and duties applicable to all in a group or society and this is called code of ethics. A code of ethics is a written set of ethical principles and guidelines that govern decisions and behaviors in an organization (e.g., border management authorities) according to its primary values and ethical standards and theories [3,6].

There are many ethical theories, each of which emphasizes different points, such as predicting an outcome and carrying out one's duties to others to reach an ethically correct decision. Consequentialism theory (result-based ethics) emphasizes the consequences of human actions, whether good or bad, right or wrong. Deontological ethics does not concern the consequences of an action but rather it considers the will and the motivation for undertaking an action [21,23,28]. It is sometimes described as duty-based or rule-based ethics. Even though the distinction between deontological and consequentialism is often clear, the two theories are fundamentally different. They are both normative, and as a result, code of ethics are formulated as guidelines rather than prescriptions and prohibitions. The aim of the code of ethics is to provide a moral basis for emerging professional choices and provide adequate protection for all those who act in a statutory manner, and to recognize the unworthy practices associated with the police profession. The following are examples of the ethical principles for border guards which provide moral guidance during service shifts and out of service shifts.

1. **Respect of dignity and rights:** Respecting the rights of every person and avoid the use of torture, inhuman or degrading treatment.
2. **Fairness:** Treating of persons must be equal and having no preference, bias or prejudices based on race, background, ethnicity, gender, religion, personal and social status or property status etc.
3. **Duty of confidentiality:** Respecting for privacy and guaranteeing the security of the data and the information obtained.
4. **Responsibility:** Taking responsibility for actions and decisions in legal and moral terms. If misconduct takes place, take steps to ensure it is not repeated.

## 3   The "How to Do It Right" Framework

This section presents a framework (Fig. 1) which helps to point out the types of challenges, the specific vulnerabilities and risks which the stated concerns/challenges lead to and the generic considerations for handling these challenges raising due to the use of biometric technologies. The focus on ethical, social and legal challenges constitute the topmost layer of the framework. The next layer of the framework is the values affected due to the presence or uprising of the challenges. The third layer from the top is the impact assessment layer. That is, what are the consequences of a value being affected? What vulnerabilities and risks arise correspondingly and what are the mitigation plans? Then, the bottom most layer lists the corresponding considerations that the border control

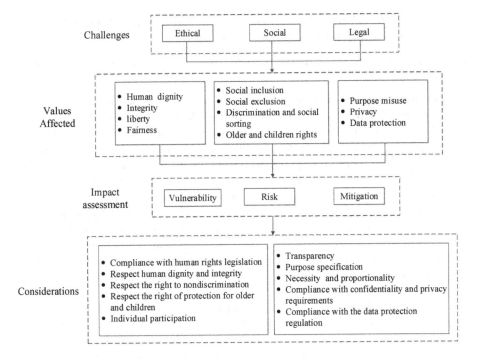

**Fig. 1.** The proposed framework for specifying biometric technologies related challenges and the considerations

police are expected to comply with. The framework provides a what to do and how to do it right guideline for border control police when various challenges are met by providing a link from the challenge, to the value(s) affected and an impact assessment on the values affected as well as pointing out the considerations that must be in place. Below, we provide examples of which values maybe affected under varying challenges and how.

### 3.1   Challenges Level

Biometrics technology is acknowledged to potentially raise critical ethical, social and legal challenges. Ethical challenges generate situations that requires a person or organization to choose between alternatives that must be evaluated as right (ethical) or wrong (unethical). Social challenges create problems that engaging in normal social behaviors and may influence a large number of individuals within a society. Legal challenges refer to formal questioning of the legality of an act and whether or not the act is being taken in accordance with the law.

Challenges layer provides information to help border officer or border authorities think through basic ethical, social and legal concepts and considerations. It will not provide specific answers for the specific challenges but will help bring to conscious awareness some understandings that help in thinking through these issues.

## 3.2 Values Level and Examples of How Values Are Affected by Ethics, Social and Legal Challenges

Below, we give examples of how several values may be affected due to the arisen of such challenges.

(I) **Human dignity:** The capability to verify travelers' identities is extremely important and regards human dignity [16,23,31]. People may feel uncomfortable (or humiliated to some extent) when authorities like the border police are recording body features algorithmically. Many factors, for example physical work or physical incapacity (e.g., physical disabilities, sight impairment and mental health problems), can make it hard for some people to provide biometrics or they may simply be unwilling to do so. For instance, damaged fingers due to manual work can impact the way people are treated when providing fingerprint data [13]. In these cases, challenges with collecting biometrics data and remaining respectful of human dignity may emerge. People who cannot provide fingerprints or other biometrics data sometimes face a greater risk of negative consequences than people who can [25].

Biometrics data collection from vulnerable persons including those with disabilities requires particular attention. Human dignity is evidently a complex notion of the individual and biometrics data is strictly linked to the human body, whose integrity (physical and psychological) constitutes a key element of human dignity.

(II) **Social inclusion/exclusion and risk of discrimination:** The introduction of biometrics to improve identity verification at land borders raises serious objections to the potential to facilitate discriminatory social profiling [36]. For example, the biometrics enrollment of injured and disabled travelers could lead to higher false rejection rates than average. Moreover, senior citizens and children who have particular problems with using biometrics enrollment devices (e.g., fingerprint scanner, iris recognition reader) may face enrollment difficulties. Although discrimination of vulnerable individuals might be involuntary and unintentional, it may deeply affect them and impact the principle of equity. Furthermore, religious aspects (e.g., beard, headscarf) or interpersonal contact (e.g., photographs, touching, exposing parts of the body) may render a biometrics system an unacceptable intrusion. For example, those of faith who wear head or face coverings have difficulties with enrolling facial biometrics. Verification of such biometrics in public (e.g., at the border crossing points) may lead to embarrassment or offense, causing avoidance of situations where this is necessary. Therefore, mandatory encouraged use of such system may undermine religious authority and create de facto discrimination against certain groups whose members are not allowed to travel freely or obtain certain services without violating their religious beliefs and privacy. In positive terms, respecting a person's intrinsic worth requires recognizing that the person is always entitled to participate in social and community life regardless of age, beliefs, disability, health, etc.

(III) **Children rights:** Biometric technology also present several ethical questions regarding children's rights. These include the right to information, the right to privacy, security and the right to no discrimination, etc. With respect to children and biometric technology, the main concern is that children will not fully know or understand the implications of the accessibility to, and subsequent use of the data collected. While children (and indeed their parents) may be aware of basic privacy settings and risks, even sophisticated users face great difficulties. Moreover, child identification introduces the requirement for greater levels of care. The problem is that there are several reasons why not all biometrics can be used for child identification and biometric recognition of toddlers. For example, a study by Basak et al. [4] found that "capturing fingerprints for children less than three years is hard due to very small fingerprint area, smooth skin, and thin fingers." Therefore, very young kids with small fingerprints might not be identified efficiently.

Furthermore, children are particularly entitled to effective privacy protection. This is because children cannot develop privacy expectations for reasonable legal protection. Moreover, biometric match accuracy diminishes as children grow. Fingerprinting young children affects the quality and reliability of future matches to the initial fingerprints [19]. The risk of a wrong match increases when the fingerprints or facial images are compared more than five years after the initial collection.

(IV) **Purpose misuse:** Function or purpose creep occurs when the biometrics data is collected for one specific purpose and subsequently used for another unintended or unauthorized purpose without the user's consent. A famous example of a large-scale biometric function creep is the European Dactyloscopy (EURODAC) fingerprint database. The original purpose of this EURODAC was to compare fingerprints for the effective application of the Dublin convention. It enables EU countries to identify asylum applicants as well as illegal immigrants within the EU. However, soon after the database was established, other police and law enforcement agencies were also granted access. Similar concerns may also arise in the case of other large-scale, centralized EU national and international databases, such as SIS II, VIS and EES. Biometrics are likely to strengthen the potential for function creep due to the very sensitive nature of the data collected and the possibility to use centrally stored biometric data for purposes other than the original purpose.

(V) **Right to privacy and data protection:** Every individual has the right to privacy protection and personal data protection when his/her data is collected and shared. The use of biometrics technology as a border control tools introduces problems with maintaining individuals' privacy and protection of their personal data. Such a technology will probably increase the risk of available information misuse as a result of unethical and/or illegal practices if personal data are not protected adequately.

The main concerns include unnecessary and unauthorized collection of biometrics data for traveler identification and verification [8,38]. GDPR [35], among other legislation, state that to best preserve an individual's privacy and right for data protection, the amount of personal data collected should always be kept to a minimum. Moreover, personal data like biometrics data should only be used when individuals or authorities will benefit from the collection. Cameras, for instance, are now widely used to monitor our everyday life. People often benefit from such monitoring, especially at borders to control people flows and detect suspicious activities (e.g., illegal border crossing). However, extensive data collection and analysis can also lead to privacy violations.

Information linkage and compromise of anonymity is another concern [38]. Various kinds of information about individuals stored in a range of databases (e.g., SIS II and VIS) have the potential to become yet another means through which information can be linked to purposes ranging from commercial marketing to law enforcement. Recent research [10] explores the possibility of extracting supplementary information from primary biometric traits, face, fingerprints, hand geometry and the iris. Such information includes personal attributes like gender, age, ethnicity, hair color, height, weight and so on.

Despite all the benefits of using biometrics technology in border control, privacy concerns have become widespread because each time a person's biometric data is checked, a trace is left that could reveal personal and confidential information. Biometric data should essentially be well-protected against unnecessary and unauthorized collection, access and disclosure etc.

### 3.3   Impact Assessment Level

Table 1 summarizes values that may be affected and maps them to vulnerabilities, risks and possible mitigation measures in comparison to the current systems authorized in EU border control and other solutions already on the market.

### 3.4   Considerations Level

This section presents ethical, social and legal considerations.

1. **Ethical considerations for human rights:** According to Article 7, Regulation (EU) 2016/399 (amended in Regulation (EU) 2017/458), competent authorities should ensure that the human dignity and integrity of persons whose data are requested are respected and should not discriminate against persons on grounds of sex,religion, disability, age etc. Thus, biometric platform at border should be designed to support human right-compliant systems, related to technological, ethical and sociological aspects. For biometric technologies to be successful with its use and actual implementation, they should not only consider the security and privacy of personal data, but it also need

**Table 1.** Values and the corresponding vulnerabilities, risks and mitigation measures.

| Values | Vulnerability | Risk | Potential mitigation measure |
|---|---|---|---|
| Respect to human dignity | Current systems do not afford individual a choice of what biometrics data they prefer to enroll or use | Violation of right to human dignity, cultural or religious customs etc. | Border control biometrics must provide information about what and why biometrics used as well as allow choice policies and procedures, unless choice is inapplicable |
| Right to the person integrity | Current systems do not adapt or lack informed consent policies | Violation of the right to integrity | Border control biometrics must ensures a collection of free and informed consent form individuals according to rules laid down by regulations such as GDPR |
| Right to person liberty | Current systems may lack of policy, procedures and ethical guidelines for data collection and processing or may allow unauthorized processing of individuals data; e.g., use of force to collect biometrics data | Violation of the right to liberty of an individuals | Border control biometrics must apply policy to restrict the procedures of data collection and processing, balancing between lawful interest and personal liberty |
| Right of protection for children | Current systems does not address/deal with children vulnerability and special needs | Violation of the children rights which may lead to high levels of discrimination due to children lack of knowledge about the systems | Border control biometrics must envisages adoption of devices and procedures to ensure children' needs. Also, the biometric data of children should be treated with enormous care and the procedures need to comply with data protection legislation such as GDPR [35]. Parents must always be notified when their children's biometric data is to be collected or used, and written consent must be obtained in advance |
| Right to no discrimination | Current systems may be discriminated based on sex, race, ethnic or social origin, genetic features, religion or belief, political opinion, disability, age or sexual orientation etc. | Discrimination, social inclusion/exclusion and social sorting of individuals | Border control biometrics must ensure nondiscrimination policy that comply with human rights legislation |
| Respect for private and family life | Current systems do not adapt an adequate family related consent and procedures | Violation of right to respect for private and family life | Border control biometrics must adopt appropriate measures for family consent and procedures |
| Right to no information tracking | Current systems lack of notices and information about tracking of individuals | Violation of personal right and legitimate purpose requirements leading to surveillance of individuals and/or other members of the family | If within the purpose and the law, surveillance should be authorized and consistent with EU and national laws |
| Right to personal data protection | Current systems may allow personal data to fall into the wrong hands or/and shared across organizations | Violation of right to security principles such as confidentiality, integrity, and availability | Border control biometrics must ensure Security by Design to guarantee the ongoing confidentiality, integrity, availability and resilience of processing systems and services |
| Right to privacy and confidentiality | Current systems may breach confidentiality, allowing unauthorized disclosure of personal information | Violation of personal privacy | Border control biometrics must ensures implementation of privacy-enhancing technologies to protect data in accordance with the law |

to guarantee that the users can interact with the systems and make the user experience acceptable. To do so, system designers and policy makers must consider all challenges, vulnerabilities and risks (Table 1) related to the system design. Moreover, border control biometrics platforms must pay particular attention to minors, whether traveling accompanied or unaccompanied and must respect the specific needs of children and their interests must be protected in ways supplementary to the general treatment of adult subjects.

2. **Considerations for travelers with physical or mental impairment:** As mentioned above, EU Regulation (EU) 2016/399 specifies equal rights for border crossing. Therefore, border control biometrics platforms should consider travelers with special needs/categories including individuals who physically or mentally impaired etc. An extra attention should be given to, among many others:

   (a) People with temporary injuries who might have difficulties to provide biometric sample due to temporary wound (e.g., injured face and/or broken arm/fingers) [25]. In this case, Border control biometrics platforms should not discriminate against such people and shall use biometric devices (e.g., fingerprints scanner) which perform acquisition in a greater number of situations.

   (b) People with total permanent disability whom have difficulties to freely move their limbs due to sensory damage and/or muscle damage. For example, in case of fingerprints verification, travelers with a hand disability may lack the ability to place the required finger and keep it steady for a sufficient time on the fingerprints scanner. Moreover, in case of face recognition/iris scanning, people with neck disabilities may have difficulties in correctly placing their face near the iris scanning device/face recognition camera. Thus, border control biometrics devices should be able to work in off-axis acquisitions and be adjustable to support such people with biometrics recognition and make it more comfort.

   (c) People with technological illiteracy, for example, elderly people and children who lack knowledge of using technology/tools (e.g., automated border control gates) would have a difficulty to use and interact with devices. In this case, border control biometrics devices should design an interface that taking into consideration elder's and kids' needs.

3. **Considerations for privacy and data protection:** As mentioned earlier, biometric data can be used to recognize individuals automatically with greater accuracy. On the other hand, a misuse of such biometric data can have dangerous consequences which pose several security and privacy challenges such data destruction and/or unauthorized disclosure of, or access to personal data, to name a few. Thus, border control biometrics platforms should be designed to support privacy-compliant biometric systems. Perceived risks are related to how people view the biometric technology, whether they trust it, and whether they like to use it. With respect to this, EU regulation (e.g., GDPR [35]) prohibit the use of special categories personal data such as biometric data without the user's awareness and permission. Also, prohibit the use of the biometric data different from the purpose of the system (purpose

misuse issue discussed in Sect. 3.2). For example, biometric data stored in e-passports can only be used for issuing electronic documents and verification of document holder (Regulation (EC) 444/2009).

Border control biometrics platforms should consider several privacy aspects for protecting the privacy of personal data. These aspects include:

(a) The purpose of biometric data: The legitimate purpose of biometric data collection and processing used only for verifying the identity of the individual during the border crossing procedure. Article. 13 (1) of the GDPR stipulates that "information to be provided to data subject where personal data are collected from the data subject." This information shall include, purpose of the system, the enrollment and verification processes, and the methods used for data protection, among other.

(b) People control of their personal data: According to Article. 32 (2) of the GDPR [35], the data subject has the right to ask for removal or erasure of biometric data in electronic documents. Also, the data subject should have the possibility to decide when he/she no longer be authenticated and verified using the biometrics system and choice to proceed with manual checks (when applicable).

(c) Data protection measures: Article. 32 (2) of the GDPR stipulates that *"the controller and processor must implement appropriate technical and organizational measures to protect personal data against destruction, loss, alteration, unauthorized disclosure of, or access to personal data transmitted, stored or otherwise processed and against all other unlawful forms of processing."* Therefore, border control biometrics system shall deploy a privacy enhancing technologies and secure access control techniques to avoid any misuse of personal data.

(d) Reuse of data for law-enforcement purposes: According to Regulation (EU) 2016/399 and its amendment Regulation (EU) 2017/458, citizens should be checked in criminal databases such as SIS II and SLTD on a systematic and non-systematic basis. As the majority of these travelers are presumably innocent individuals. Therefore, saving and cross checking their data on a systematic basis with law-enforcement databases would be disproportionate. Any reuse of personal data done for the purpose of law enforcement should be done in accordance with Directive (EU) 2016/680 [1], which aims to ensure more consistent and higher level of protection of the personal data of natural persons in the areas of criminal matters and public security.

# 4 Discussion on Ethical Reasoning and Decision Making

In view of the ethical theories (discussed in Sect. 2.2) and the open dilemma of what is right and what is wrong, it is clear that the situation is similar, particularly surrounding the use of biometric technology. On the one hand, one group of people (travelers, border officers etc.) may see biometrics technology used in border control as a liberator, believing in the power of technology to bring convenience (e.g., avoid queues) and efficiency (e.g., cut costs) and increase mobility (e.g., convenient border-crossing for citizens). This group may also welcome more powerful surveillance to improve border security (e.g., monitor migration, combat identity theft and fraud etc.). We may agree with this group. First and foremost, the use of biometrics in the border control aims to improve security and detect fraud (discussed in Sect. 2.1) which will leads to maximizing the benefits for the society (e.g., travelers) and minimizing the human workload (e.g., border police officers). With respect to the consequentialism theory (discussed in Sect. 2.2), every society member (travelers, border police officers etc.) must benefit the same and it is not specific to any individual. Furthermore, the reason one individual must promote the overall good is the same reason why anyone else has to promote the good. Hence, it can be said that the ethics of the border control biometrics is related to consequentialism. The consequentialism theory places a group's interest and happiness above those of an individual for the good of many.

On the other hand, other groups of people may object and perceive biometrics technology as a threat to their personal life and privacy. Such groups might believe that surveillance technology is untrustworthy and destructive to liberty, dignity and privacy. For example, collecting biometric data such as iris scanning from veiled Muslim women [27] in stressful situations (e.g., inappropriate police behavior due to exhaustion or stress) may undermine the dignity of the women being scanned. An FRA report "Under watchful eyes: Biometrics, EU IT systems and fundamental rights" [14] showed that disproportionate force has been used when fingerprinting asylum seekers and migrants in irregular situations. Considering deontological ethics (duty-based or rule-based ethics discussed in Sect. 2.2) and given the vulnerability of the people concerned as well as the obligation to use the least invasive means, it is difficult to justify the use of physical or psychological force solely to obtain biometrics for the purpose of identification and verification. When it comes to border control and border rules, ethical theories might change according to circumstance. Border officers have a duty to do the right thing (verify the identity of a traveler before entering/exiting the border etc.) even if it produces an undesirable outcome. In the case of veiled Muslim women or any other cases, it would be difficult to judge the action of an officer based on the outcome.

From the review, it could be concluded that ethics are not absolute, and clearly, views on biometrics technology vary according to the differing needs of people and institutions. However, different perceptions of biometrics technology reflect the diverse value judgments as influenced by many factors: age, gender, cultural beliefs, education, moral imagination etc. Remarks over the use of biometrics technology for large populations, especially if the consequences lead to social exclusion, either as a result of the individual being unable to reliably enroll or verify their data, or simply not having confidence in the system and avoiding having to interact with it. Certainly, when it comes to border control and the use of biometrics technology to increase border security, monitor migration and combat identity theft and fraud etc., the argument is essentially utilitarian (consequentialism theory) where the collective right of a group (group interest) is balanced against the rights of the individual. It makes the individual simply a means to the ends of the majority. However, this could be a wrong argument. Wickins in [36] and Townend in [34] argue that public interest must be judged by considering the balance between individuals, i.e. the rights of single individuals must be balanced against other single individuals if individuals are not to be used instrumentally.

## 5  Conclusions

An important conclusion to this paper is that we are not attempting to provide an answer to what is ethical and what is not, or what is right and what is not. We see biometrics technology usage in border control with two sides. One side is the main intention and aim of biometrics technology to improve border control management and enhance people flow etc. The other side represents the risk of violating personal rights. As said, conflicts with decisions based on what to choose (e.g., privacy versus security, autonomy versus solidarity) make it difficult to have a broad and consistent position in favor of, or against expanding or restricting biometric technologies.

Individual acceptance of biometrics technology should be actively promoted through ensuring transparency of decision-making, clear policy regarding the purpose of biometric technology and how it is used, as well as increased measures dedicated to preserve personal rights and personal data protection. Since greater use of personal data impacts upon human rights, there needs to be an honest and assertive study of what the risks are to personal rights and privacy as well as how these risks are mitigated. Border control biometrics should comply with human rights legislation to encourage respect for fundamental rights in the implementation of biometrics technologies. Also, they should respect human dignity and protect personal integrity, preserve individual freedom and self-determination (i.e., choice and consent with respect to which biometrics data he/she prefers to use), respect privacy and family life, and safeguard against harm and unreasonable force for data processing. Moreover, border control biometrics should comply with security requirements and data protection legislation to ensure data confidentiality, integrity and availability when collecting and processing personal related data.

In the future, we shall investigate the use of ontologies for knowledge representation and enhancement of knowledge discovering using machine learning techniques. Ontologies provide a formal, explicit specification of a shared conceptualization of a domain that can be communicated between people and heterogeneous and widely spread application systems [33]. We aim to propose a semantic based framework for biometrics integration in border control systems relying on ontologies and machine learning techniques [7] to tackle ethical, social and legal challenges.

**Acknowledgements.** This work is carried out in the EU-funded project SMILE (Project ID: 740931), [H2020-DS-2016-2017] SEC-14-BES-2016 towards reducing the cost of technologies in land border security applications.

# References

1. Directive (EU) 2016/680 on the protection of natural persons with regard to the processing of personal data by competent authorities for the purposes of the prevention, investigation, detection or prosecution of criminal offences or the execution of criminal penalties, and on the free movement of such data, and repealing council framework decision 2008/977/jh. Official Journal of the European Union (2016). https://eur-lex.europa.eu/legal-content/EN/TXT/PDF/?uri=CELEX:32016L0680&from=EN
2. Anand, A., et al.: Enhancing the performance of multimodal automated border control systems. In: 2016 International Conference of the Biometrics Special Interest Group (BIOSIG), pp. 1–5. IEEE (2016)
3. Banks, C.: Criminal Justice Ethics: Theory and Practice. Sage Publications, Thousand Oaks (2018)
4. Basak, P., De, S., Agarwal, M., Malhotra, A., Vatsa, M., Singh, R.: Multimodal biometric recognition for toddlers and pre-school children. In: 2017 IEEE International Joint Conference on Biometrics (IJCB), pp. 627–633. IEEE (2017)
5. Bhatia, R.: Biometrics and face recognition techniques. Int. J. Adv. Res. Comput. Sci. Softw. Eng. **3**(5) (2013)
6. Boddington, P.: Towards a Code of Ethics for Artificial Intelligence. Springer, Cham (2017). https://doi.org/10.1007/978-3-319-60648-4
7. Buitelaar, P., Cimiano, P., Magnini, B.: Ontology Learning from Text: Methods, Evaluation and Applications, vol. 123. IOS Press, Amsterdam (2005)
8. Campisi, P.: Security and Privacy in Biometrics, vol. 24. Springer, London (2013). https://doi.org/10.1007/978-1-4471-5230-9
9. National Research Council, Whither Biometrics Committee, et al.: Biometric Recognition: Challenges and Opportunities. National Academies Press, Washington, DC (2010)
10. Dantcheva, A., Elia, P., Ross, A.: What else does your biometric data reveal? A survey on soft biometrics. IEEE Trans. Inf. Forensics Secur. **11**(3), 441–467 (2015)
11. De Hert, P.: Biometrics and the challenge to human rights in Europe. Need for regulation and regulatory distinctions. In: Campisi, P. (ed.) Security and Privacy in Biometrics, pp. 369–413. Springer, London (2013). https://doi.org/10.1007/978-1-4471-5230-9_15
12. Díaz, V.: Legal challenges of biometric immigration control systems. Mex. Law Rev. **7**(1), 3–30 (2014)
13. Drahansky, M., Dolezel, M., Urbanek, J., Brezinova, E., Kim, T.H.: Influence of skin diseases on fingerprint recognition. J. Biomed. Biotechnol. **2012**, 62614 (2012)
14. European Union Agency for Fundamental Rights: Under watchful eyes - biometrics, EU IT-systems and fundamental rights (2018). https://fra.europa.eu/en/publication/2018/biometrics-rights-protection
15. Eurostat: Disability statistics - need for assistance (2017). https://ec.europa.eu/eurostat/statistics-explained/pdfscache/34419.pdf
16. Floridi, L.: On human dignity as a foundation for the right to privacy. Philos. Technol. **29**(4), 307–312 (2016)
17. International Civil Aviation Organization (ICAO): ICAO TRIP guide on border control management (2017). https://www.icao.int/Meetings/TRIP-Jamaica-2017/Documents/ICAO%20TRIP%20Guide%20on%20BCM-For%20validation-16-11-2017.pdf

18. Jain, A., Hong, L., Pankanti, S.: Biometric identification. Commun. ACM **43**(2), 90–98 (2000)
19. Jain, A.K., Arora, S.S., Cao, K., Best-Rowden, L., Bhatnagar, A.: Fingerprint recognition of young children. IEEE Trans. Inf. Forensics Secur. **12**(7), 1501–1514 (2017)
20. Jain, A.K., Ross, A., Prabhakar, S., et al.: An introduction to biometric recognition. IEEE Trans. Circuits Syst. Video Technol. **14**(1), 4–20 (2004)
21. Kagan, S.: Normative Ethics. Routledge, Abingdon (2018)
22. Kenk, V.S., Križaj, J., Štruc, V., Dobrišek, S.: Smart surveillance technologies in border control. Eur. J. Law Technol. **4**(2) (2013)
23. Kizza, J.M., et al.: Ethical and Social Issues in the Information Age, vol. 999. Springer, London (2007). https://doi.org/10.1007/978-1-4471-4990-3
24. Labati, R.D., Genovese, A., Muñoz, E., Piuri, V., Scotti, F., Sforza, G.: Biometric recognition in automated border control: a survey. ACM Comput. Surv. (CSUR) **49**(2), 24 (2016)
25. Lee, T.: Biometrics and disability rights: legal compliance in biometric identification programs. J. Technol. Law Policy 209 (2016)
26. Van der Ploeg, I.: Genetics, biometrics and the informatization of the body. Annali-Istituto Superiore di Sanita **43**(1), 44 (2007)
27. Rahman, Z., Verhaert, P., Nyst, C.: Biometrics in the humanitarian sector (2018)
28. Ronzoni, M.: Teleology, deontology, and the priority of the right: on some unappreciated distinctions. Ethical Theory Moral Pract. **13**(4), 453–472 (2010)
29. Sprokkereef, A.: Data protection and the use of biometric data in the EU. In: Fischer-Hübner, S., Duquenoy, P., Zuccato, A., Martucci, L. (eds.) Privacy and Identity 2007. ITIFIP, vol. 262, pp. 277–284. Springer, Boston (2008). https://doi.org/10.1007/978-0-387-79026-8_19
30. Sprokkereef, A., De Hert, P.: Ethical practice in the use of biometric identifiers within the EU. Law Sci. Policy **3**(2), 177 (2007)
31. Sutrop, M.: Ethical issues in governing biometric technologies. In: Kumar, A., Zhang, D. (eds.) ICEB 2010. LNCS, vol. 6005, pp. 102–114. Springer, Heidelberg (2010). https://doi.org/10.1007/978-3-642-12595-9_14
32. Tanwar, S., Tyagi, S., Kumar, N., Obaidat, M.S.: Ethical, legal, and social implications of biometric technologies. In: Obaidat, M.S., Traore, I., Woungang, I. (eds.) Biometric-Based Physical and Cybersecurity Systems, pp. 535–569. Springer, Cham (2019). https://doi.org/10.1007/978-3-319-98734-7_21
33. Taye, M.M.: Understanding semantic web and ontologies: theory and applications. J. Comput. **2**(6) (2010)
34. Townend, D.: Overriding data subjects' rights in the public interest. In: The Data Protection Directive and Medical Research Across Europe, pp. 89–102. Routledge (2017)
35. Voigt, P., Von dem Bussche, A.: The EU General Data Protection Regulation (GDPR). A Practical Guide, 1st edn. Springer, Cham (2017). https://doi.org/10.1007/978-3-319-57959-7
36. Wickins, J.: The ethics of biometrics: the risk of social exclusion from the widespread use of electronic identification. Sci. Eng. Ethics **13**(1), 45–54 (2007)
37. Yu, S.: Big privacy: challenges and opportunities of privacy study in the age of big data. IEEE Access **4**, 2751–2763 (2016)
38. Zeadally, S., Badra, M.: Privacy in a Digital, Networked World: Technologies, Implications and Solutions. Springer, Cham (2015). https://doi.org/10.1007/978-3-319-08470-1

# A Method for Assessing the Openness of Semi-Open Data Initiatives: Applied to the Justice Domain

Mortaza S. Bargh[1,2(✉)], Sunil Choenni[1,2], Ronald Meijer[1], and Sharvin Choenni[3]

[1] Research and Documentation Centre, Ministry of Justice and Security, The Hague, The Netherlands
{m.shoae.bargh, r.choenni, r.f.meijer}@minvenj.nl
[2] Rotterdam University of Applies Sciences, Creating 010, Rotterdam, The Netherlands
{m.shoae.bargh, r.choenni}@hr.nl
[3] Call2, Zoetermeer, The Netherlands
s.r.m.choenni@gmail.com

**Abstract.** Some public organisations, despite being committed to attain the ideals of Open Data, struggle to meet the Open Data requirements fully. Often this is the case when their data are of low quality, have (potentially) sensitive information, or have non-interoperable format and semantics. These restrictions, for example, apply quite often to the datasets of justice domain. In practice, nevertheless, many of such public organisations do share their data in a way that partially satisfies the Open Data Requirements in order to be, e.g., transparent. To acknowledge such data opening initiatives, we advocate and describe a method to assess the degree of data openness, as a first step for recognizing such so-called Semi-Open Data initiatives. The proposed method relies on a multi-dimensional method to quantify these initiatives in terms of their adherence, i.e., distance, to the Open Data requirements. We carry out eight case studies and present the results in a way that it shows how to construct and fine-tune the parameters of the proposed method incrementally in a sense making way (i.e., based on consensus among stakeholders involved in a given domain). We report on the feasibility and applicability of the proposed model in practice and the encountered challenges.

**Keywords:** Assessment · Indicator · Measurement · Method · Open Data · Openness · Semi-Open Data

## 1 Introduction

Gaining public trust, achieving transparency, stimulating innovations, and delivering economic growth have been considered as some of the driving-forces behind Open Data initiatives for public organisations in recent years. Open data initiatives can even foster democratic processes when they are designed appropriately (i.e., via transforming raw data into meaningful information by public administrators and citizens collectively) [1].

S. Katsikas and V. Zorkadis (Eds.): e-Democracy 2019, CCIS 1111, pp. 110–125, 2020.
https://doi.org/10.1007/978-3-030-37545-4_8

Open Data initiatives have also gained momentum in the justice domain. Within the justice domain, the notion of Open Justice has been recognised even long before transparency (via Open Data) became an important aspect of governance [2]. Open Justice refers to making courts and their proceedings open and public so that what is done in the name of justice can be scrutinised and criticised. Nowadays, however, Open Data within the justice domain extends the scope of Open Justice to beyond simply court proceedings and judgments and it includes also the data gathered within the administration processes and the judicial procedures of the whole justice branch of government.

Opening Data, particularly in the justice domain, is subject to privacy, misinterpretation and misleading challenges with adverse impacts on individuals, the public and the society at large. Therefore, many public organisations, particularly those in the justice domain [3, 4], have been hesitant or unable to open their data in a way that satisfies Open Data requirements, e.g., the data being opened as raw as possible (or as they are), for everybody, in a timely way, with primacy, permanence and appropriate metadata. Actually, nevertheless, a large number of public organisations, particularly those in the justice domain, do share a modified form of their data with the public after putting a lot of efforts to address the privacy, misinterpretation and misleading challenges of the data [5–7]. For example, the shared data are processed, aggregated, and offered to specific data consumers (e.g., scientists) in order to protect privacy of data subjects or to enhance the quality of data. Actually, fostering democratic processes (i.e., monitorial, deliberative and participatory processes) asks for transforming raw Open Data into meaningful information collectively by public administrators and citizens [1]. Despite all these efforts, these data sharing initiatives are not classified as Open Data and these organisations cannot position themselves as Open Data compliant. Therefore, such organisations cannot demonstrate their dedication towards the ideals and objectives of Open Data in being, for example, transparent and supportive of innovations and economic growth. This (negative) image can be costly for public organisations, as they may not gain (or even lose) the public trust. Being unable to share their data according to the full requirements of Open Data and not being recognised when sharing their processed data are two sides of the same problem that public organisations, particularly those in the justice domain, face today.

In order to acknowledge the efforts of those organisations that share their data in a not-fully-Open-Data-compliant way (while they basically push the frontiers of information sharing towards the ideals of Open Data), Bargh et al. [8] coin the term of Semi-Open Data for those initiatives. More specifically, "Semi-Open Data paradigm includes those data sharing solutions that aim at Open Data Objectives (like transparency, compliance, innovation, decision support, cost reduction, participation, and collaboration) but do not fulfil all conditions of Open Data" [8, p. 10]. We note that the term Semi-Open Data refers to a wide spectrum of the types of data sharing initiatives that fall between the two extremes of closed/confidential data and Open Data. A main step to make Semi-Open Data initiatives visible is to somehow indicate their positions on this spectrum between these two extreme points. To this end, we propose assessing the degree of adherence of these Semi-Open Data initiatives to the requirements and objective of Open Data. We use the term 'degree of openness' to refer to how much Semi-Open Data initiatives adhere to the requirements of Open Data.

In this contribution we aim at devising a systematic method for assessing the degree of openness of a dataset shared by an organisation. The proposed method determines the degree of openness of Semi-Open Data initiatives based on the Open Data requirements, which, in turn, are based on the Open Definition [9]. The existing assessment methods either (a) indicate whether a data sharing initiative fulfils all requirements of Open Data or not, thus making a binary decision on data openness (like [10]), or (b) consider the degree of openness of a data sharing initiative in combination with the degree of data usage, thus providing an integrated measure of data openness and data utility (like [11] and [12]). Unlike these existing methods, our proposed method aims at providing a more granular indication of openness with respect to exiting binary assessment methods and at making the efforts of the public organisations behind those data opening initiatives visible within the Open Data landscape. As a consequence of the latter advantage, our method is not affected by how the data are utilised by the public or third parties, thus just aiming at transparency at the supply side.[1] This visibility not only encourages such organisations to continue opening (more of) their data, but also provides a (more) realistic view on the landscape of Open Data [8].

The contributions of this paper are threefold. Firstly, we build on the results of [8] and [13] about Semi-Open Data by specifying how to assess the degree of data openness in Semi-Open Data initiatives. Our proposed method adopts a multi-dimensional measurement approach to quantify Semi-Open Data initiatives in terms of their adherence to the Open Data requirements. Secondly, we report on the results of applying the assessment model in practice to eight datasets made open already in the Netherlands (four datasets) and four other countries (one dataset per country). Thirdly, we raise the importance of a data openness measure that is not binary (i.e., the data being open in its generic sense or not) and not closely intertwined with data usage aspects.

Our study touches the justice domain in two ways: (1) most datasets in the justice domain are prune to high-impact privacy and misinterpretation implications on individuals potentially, which makes Semi-Open Data relevant for these datasets, and (2) for our case studies we choose some datasets from the justice domain to illustrate the feasibility of applying the proposed method in practice. The justice domain here denotes the whole justice branch of government, not just courts and judgements. Other than the two aspects mentioned, the proposed method is generic and applicable to all datasets from any domain. The research methodology used for this study is based on three processes. Firstly, the proposed assessment method of data openness draws on the authors' experience to share data in the justice domain for many years. Secondly, we use a number of case studies to validate the feasibility of, and to illustrate how to define and fine-tune the proposed method. Thirdly, the study is grounded in the body of literature.

---

[1] Note that one can define a similar measure to make the demand side transparent. Considering such a demand figure next to the supply figure defined in this contribution (especially in a longitudinal manner), one can gain insight in the impact of transparency in data opening in the two-dimensional plane of data openness versus data impact. This perspective is, however, out of our scope in this contribution.

This paper is organised as follows. In Sect. 2, we present the method proposed for assessing the degree of data openness. In Sects. 3, we report on applying the assessment method to eight open datasets from the justice domain. In Sect. 4 we discuss the potentials and limitations of the proposed method. Finally, in Sect. 5 we present our conclusion and future research directions.

## 2 Proposed Method for Assessing Data Openness

In this section we present the proposed method for assessing the degree of data openness also for those initiatives that partially satisfy Open Data requirements.

### 2.1 Open Data Characteristics

A number of requirements have been defined for achieving the objectives of Open Data by various governments and organisations. These requirements determine the characteristics of Open Data. Bargh et al. [13] investigate these requirements from four sources, namely: Canadian government [9, 14], US government [15], Dutch government [16], and from South Africa's Open Data Research Network [17].

The sources investigated in [13] agree on some of the Open Data requirements. All these sources, for example, require open datasets to be license free and reusable. The sources, however, do not have the same viewpoint on the aggregation level of the data opened, for example, with respect to the "as it is" requirement of Open Data. In our method, all of these requirements are included in order to accommodate the viewpoints of all the sources considered. This inclusiveness can be extended readily, should one decide to comply with also the new requirements of other sources.

### 2.2 Indicators of Openness

In order to compare entities, one can use a benchmarking tool with a set of defined indicators [18]. For measuring the degree of openness, Veljković et al. [19] used eight characteristics of Open Data from Open Government Working Group [20] as indicators. These indicators are to be complete, primary, timely, accessible, machine processable, non-discriminatory, non-proprietary and license free [20]. Similarly, our method relies on defining a number of indicators of data openness, but our proposal bases them on the identified requirements of Open Data, as summarised in [13]. Our indicators are quite similar to the generally accepted requirements of Open Data because of making them (a) meaningful – as they are backed up and promoted by some prominent sponsors and proponents of Open Data ideals – and (b) actionable – as we investigate and show the feasibility of their implementation in practice in this paper by applying them to a range of open/shared datasets from the justice domain (see the following sections). Further, we are careful not to define too many indicators as the curse of high dimensionality may result in meaningless distance measures [21].

We structure our indicators at two hierarchical levels, inspired by our experience in Open Data research as well as our daily practice of opening justice domain datasets. The proposed high-level and low-level indicators are:

- Category *who* (denoted by $I_1$) which captures the target group for data opening and the entity in charge of data opening. The low-level indicators of category who are:
  - *For whom* indicator (denoted by $I_{1,1}$) that determines who may receive the data. Ideally the data should be available for everybody without any discrimination, without any need for identification, or without any need for usage justification. This access is restricted to the extent that is permitted by law and regulations (i.e., subject to privacy, confidentiality, security, or other valid restrictions).
  - *By whom* (or primacy) indicator (denoted by $I_{1,2}$) that determines the source primacy of the data. Ideally the data should be published by its primary sources in order to, among others, enable a proper control of data collection and storage.
- Category *how* (denoted by $I_2$) that captures how the data are made available and how the data may be used. The low-level indicators of category how are:
  - *Access easiness* indicator (denoted by $I_{2,1}$) that determines how easy the process of data access is. Ideally the data should be accessible without any technological (e.g., requiring browser-oriented technologies) and procedural restrictions.
  - *Via a web portal* indicator (denoted by $I_{2,2}$) that determines how to download the data. Ideally the data should be accessible via an Application Programming Interface (API) for automatic data processing and be accessible via a web portal (e.g., in the Netherlands via www.Opendata.nl).
  - *Timeliness* indicator (denoted by $I_{2,3}$) that determines how fresh the data are published. Ideally the data should be opened timely (i.e., as quickly as possible).
  - *Intellectual Property Rights* (IPR) indicator (denoted by $I_{2,4}$) that defines the conditions under which the data should be used. Ideally the data should be license-free and reusable for data recipients in order to enable (commercial) innovations and (commercial) reuse of the data.
  - *Monetary costs* indicator (denoted by $I_{2,5}$) that determines how much one should pay in order to access the data. Ideally the data should be accessed free of charge.
  - *Permanence* indicator (denoted by $I_{2,6}$) that determines how sustainably the data are made available. Ideally the data should remain online with appropriate version tracking, archiving, and history logging over time.
- Category *what* (denoted by $I_3$) that captures the content and format of the data to be opened as well as what the accompanying data should be. The low-level indicators of category what are:
  - *Machine-readability* indicator (denoted by $I_{3,1}$) that defines how easy the data can be used by automated processes. Ideally machine-readable datasets are based on common file formats, like CSV (Comma-Separated Values) and XML (Extensible Markup Language), which are suitable for machine processing.
  - *Standardised data format* indicator (denoted by $I_{3,2}$) that determines how well defined the schemata of the data is. Ideally the data format should be standardised well for efficient data storage and processing.

- *Originality* indicator (denoted by $I_{3,3}$) that determines how much processing is done on the data. Ideally data should be made open as it is, as much as possible.
- *Completeness* indicator (denoted by $I_{3,4}$) that determines how complete the data bulk should be opened. Ideally no part of the data should be removed.
- *Metadata richness* indicator (denoted by $I_{3,5}$) that determines how self-contained the opened data are. With rich metadata the data recipients obtain sufficient information to understand the strengths, weaknesses, analytical limitations, and security and privacy requirements of the data. Through this understanding data recipients can interpret and process the data appropriately. For example, data processors can treat the data correctly if they are provided with additional descriptions of the purpose of data collection, the population of interest, the characteristics of data samples, and the method of data collection.
- *Content discoverability* (denoted by $I_{3,6}$) indicator that captures how easy it is to locate the data objects. Ideally the data objects should be provided with (persistent) URIs (Unified Resource Identifiers) to enable locating data objects.
- Category *what-not* (denoted by $I_4$) that captures whether the data may be opened from the viewpoint of law, regulations and ethics. We observe that (privacy) sensitive information falls out of the scope of Open Data in all Open Data requirements lists that we have investigated. For example, the exceptions of Open Data in the Netherlands include those datasets that contain privacy sensitive data, national security data, and business sensitive data.
  - *Information sensitivity* (denoted by $I_{4,1}$) indicator for a dataset should be none to open the data. As such it is the key indicator (not) to go for opening the data.

## 2.3  Indicator Levels and Values

Our approach for assessing the degree of data openness is based on defining some meaningful and actionable levels for each indicator defined in Subsect. 2.2. According to this approach, every indicator can eventually be characterised by a number of ordinal levels based on some agreed upon guidelines, principles and standards. For example, indicator 'for whom' defines the scope of data recipients, i.e., for which groups the data are opened. The 'for whom' indicator can subsequently be specified in the range between 'share with no one' corresponding to confidential data and 'share with the public' corresponding to the common setting of Open Data. The example intermittent levels of the 'for whom' indicator could be: 'share the data within a specific group', 'share the data within a department of an organisation', 'share the data within an organisation/ministry', and 'share the data among a federation of organisations'. As another example, for the 'standard data format' indicator, which relates to data interoperability and link-ability, one can think of the following levels: 'without any specific data format', 'with a data format of acceptable convertibility' (applicable within data space environments, see [22] for the definition of data space), 'with a data format of high/precise convertibility' (applicable within data warehouse environments [23]), and 'with a standardised data format' (applicable within a database management system).

Defining multiple ordinal levels for the indicators of our method should be done based on the consensus of domain experts and stakeholders, given the set of (already opened) Semi-Open datasets in a domain. Defining these levels per indicator is out the scope of this contribution, as creating the consensus among all stakeholders in domain is generally a time-consuming process. This process could resemble those processes for product standardisations, which are guided by also subjective and business interests.

For every ordinal level of an indicator, as defined above, one must subsequently assign a numeric value between 0 and 1. These assigned values should be meaningful in indicating meaningful distances to the ideal level for that indicator. Note that the ideal level for an indicator, which is assigned a value 1, is defined by Open Data requirements for that indicator (e.g., the ideal level of indicator 'for whom' is 'share with the public'). Ratio values 0 and 1 mean maximum and minimum distances to the ideal value, respectively. Like assigning indicator levels, assigning the values per indicator should be based on the consensus of domain experts and stakeholders, given the set of (already opened) Semi-Open datasets in a domain. A comprehensive and advanced method for assigning these values is out the scope of this contribution.

For the purpose of illustrating the approach (i.e., as a proof of concept), we will define these levels for and based on those datasets that we have considered as our case studies. Our intention here is not to be comprehensive but to show the feasibility of the proposed method and our approach for defining its parameters. With a widespread adoption of the proposed assessment method for Semi-Open Data in a certain domain, the stakeholders within a concerned domain could agree upon a comprehensive, actionable and meaningful data model for quantifying every indicator, considering all partially opened datasets as well as the preferences of the corresponding stakeholders.

## 2.4   Proposed Measurement Method

Instead of making a binary decision whether a data sharing initiative fulfils all conditions of Open Data or not, in [13] we advised to adopt a multi-dimensional multi-level measurement method for measuring the degree of openness for those initiatives that push the data sharing frontiers towards the Open Data ideals. In this section, we elaborate on the measurement method in more details as follows.

Let $I_{m,n}$ denote the Open Data indicator representing the $m^{th}$ high-level and the $n^{th}$ low-level indicator as defined in Subsect. 2.2. We assume that indicator $I_{m,n}$ takes a number of ordinal levels from $\{i_{m,n}\}$, which are defined based on some agreed upon criteria (See Subsect. 2.3). Further, we assume that every defined ordinal level $i_{m,n}$ is mapped to a value between 0 and 1, represented by value $|i_{m,n}|$ or $|I_{m,n}|$ alternatively.

We define the Degree of Openness (DO) for a dataset D, for which indicator $I_{4,1}$ has an indicator level value of 1 (i.e., the information is not sensitive), based on:

$$DO = \left( \sum_{m<4} \sum_{n} |i_{m,n}| \right) / (\|I\| - 1), \tag{1}$$

where $\|I\|$ is the total number of indicators and $|i_{m,n}|$ is the assigned level-value to indicator $I_{m,n}$ of dataset D. One can also define the Degree of Openness per each high-level indicator as

$$DO_m = \left(\sum_n |i_{m,n}|\right) / \|I_m\|, \tag{2}$$

where $m < 4$ and $\|I_m\|$ is the total number of indicators within category m.

Note that the last indicator (i.e., $I_{4,1}$ representing information sensitivity) has a veto role for opening data (go vs. no-go). If a dataset contains sensitive data, then it cannot be opened due to legal or policy reasons. One can also assume similar roles for any of the other indicators. For example, according to [15] processed, also derived or aggregate data may be considered as Open Data only if the data dissemination includes the corresponding primary data. Further, some indicators may affect each other, depending on how they are defined. For example, if data suppression is the processing carried out on the data, then data completeness is affected adversely. Such data processing means that indicators $I_{3,3}$ and $I_{3,4}$ affect each other. Studying elaborated models that capture these restrictions and impacts is left for future studies.

One can assign weights to the indicators in Relation (1), based on the relative importance of corresponding Open Data requirement as:

$$DO^w = \left(\sum_{m<4} \sum_n w_{m,n} \cdot |i_{m,n}|\right) / (\|I\| - 1), \tag{3}$$

where $\sum_{m<4} \sum_n w_{m,n} = 1$. For our case studies we assume all indicators are equivalent. Thus, we used Relation (1) instead of Relation (3).

## 3   Case Studies

For evaluating the proposed method, we apply it to eight datasets from the justice domain to assess their openness, as described below. We choose these justice domain datasets to illustrate the feasibility of the proposed method and to illustrate how its parameters can be finetuned. The intention is by no means to compare the performances of the organisations/countries responsible in releasing these datasets.

### 3.1   Datasets

The analysed datasets are denoted by $DS_1$, ..., $DS_8$, which are arbitrarily chosen from different sources from the justice domain (i.e., they are not representative for the corresponding organisations or countries and they are of different types, formats and sizes). We assume that, as these datasets are already open, they do not have privacy issues. In other words, the corresponding indicator value $|I_{4,1}| = 1$. The first four datasets are from the Netherlands and the other four datasets are from India, the USA, Australia and Canada. In the following we briefly provide more information about these datasets and the organisations that have shared (or partially opened) them.

Dataset $DS_1$ [24] presents the crime statistics at the national level in The Netherlands. This dataset is based on the microdata from a large number of organisations involved in the Dutch criminal justice system. The dataset is published by Research and Documentation Centre of the Dutch Ministry of Justice and Security (WODC) and Statistics Netherlands (CBS). It has been published annually since 1985 on topics related to crime and law enforcement in the Netherlands [25] and to the local police and city councils [26]. The data are presented in 36 tables with different number of attributes and records. The total number of the attributes is about 550.

Dataset $DS_2$ [27] contains an elaborated selection of verdicts from different courts in the Netherlands (e.g., the verdicts of the High Court and Courts of Appeal, as well as the full bench of the court and mediatised verdicts). The Council for the Judiciary of the Netherlands publishes the database. The verdicts are accessible via a web portal and are stored in an XML format. Each record contains nine attributes. Seven attributes present structured data and two attributes provide semi-structured data. The structured attributes are: Authority, verdict date, published date, case number, formal relation, law branch, and extraordinary distinguishing values. The semi-structured attributes are a summary of the verdict and the verdict itself.

Dataset $DS_3$ [28] provides data about vandalism and public order problems leading to public space degradation in Amsterdam police jurisdiction and four police districts. The dataset compares these regional problems with those in the whole Netherlands. The dataset pertains to 2016 and is published by the Department for Research, Information and Statistics of the municipality of Amsterdam (OIS). The source of the data is the Safety Monitor (VM) of the CBS. This dataset contains five attributes: clutter on the street, public property destroyed, graffiti against walls and buildings, dog excrement on the streets and other depletions.

Dataset $DS_4$ [29] contains information about recent (attempted) burglary in the Netherlands. This dataset is published by the Dutch Police. The data can be accessed only via the web-portal of the Dutch Police by entering a postal code of a house. The results are aggregated at least on 4 digits postal code level (out of maximum 6 digits). The results are plotted on a map and may be grouped on higher aggregation level by choosing between five predefined ranges, varying from 500 m to maximum 25 km.

Dataset $DS_5$ [30] is published by the Ministry of Home Affairs, Department of States, and National Crime Records Bureau of India. It contains data on crimes against scheduled castes[2], consisting of three attributes: States/Union Territories (UTs), crime head and one attribute called 2014. Every record in this dataset represents how often a certain type of crime has occurred in a specific state in 2014. The crime data are accessible via a web-platform and may be downloaded in CSV format.

Dataset $DS_6$ [31] presents crime statistics in the United States at a national level by its volume and rate per 100,000 inhabitants for the period of 1997–2016. This dataset, which is published by the FBI's Criminal Justice Information Services (CJIS), is build up from the data of a large number of organisations involved in the US criminal justice system. The data are presented on an online platform and can be downloaded in an

---

[2] Scheduled castes (and scheduled tribes) are various officially designated groups of historically disadvantaged people in India.

XLS file format with different number of attributes and records. The dataset is structured and has more than 20 attributes.

Dataset $DS_7$ [32] presents crime statistics at the national level in Australia. The dataset, published by the Australian Bureau of Statistics (ABS), contains data about the victims of selected offences, recorded by national police agencies within each state and territory in 2016. Conforming to Australia's National Crime Recording Standard (NCRS), the dataset is presented in five tables, each with a different number of attributes and records.

Dataset $DS_8$ [33] presents crime statistics in British Columbia in Canada. The dataset, published by Statistics Canada, contains 14 attributes and is only accessible by downloading a file which can be done in several formats (XLS, CSV or SCSV format).

### 3.2    Illustration of the Approach and the Results

Our proposed method aims at providing a simple, meaningful, and pragmatic way of assessing the degree of data openness. Therefore, we defined the indicators similarly to the generally accepted requirements of Open Data as they are promoted by prominent sponsors and proponents of Open Data ideals. In order to enhance the feasibility and meaningfulness of the proposed method, we further propose to define the indicator levels and to assign their values in a sense making way, based on, among others, the characteristics of a wide range of partially opened/shared datasets. In the following, we illustrate our approach for defining the indicator levels and their values by applying the approach to datasets $DS_1, \ldots, DS_8$, see also Table 1 for a summary of the results.

As the datasets are accessible online, i.e., they are 'for the public', we set Indicator 'for whom' to the value of one (denoted by $|I_{1,1}| = 1.0$) for all of the datasets without attempting to specify any other ordinal levels (and the corresponding ratio values) for indicator $I_{1,1}$. Note that, from now on, we shall similarly assign the maximum value 1.0 for those indicators that assume their ideal level possible. For datasets $DS_1, \ldots, DS_8$, therefore, we have $|I_{2,1}| = |I_{2,4}| = |I_{2,5}| = |I_{2,6}| = |I_{3,6}| = |I_{4,1}| = 1.0$.

Open Data initiatives normally use a number of attributes as metadata to describe datasets. For determining the value of metadata indicator, we required that the metadata should provide the following information about the data: What the data are about as well as when, where, by whom, how and why the data are collected. We note that in this way we adopt a more specific definition for metadata, compared to the definitions used in database community. We identify the following eight metadata-items in the datasets we studied: title, description, language, theme, keywords, license, publisher, and references. To score the corresponding indicator $I_{3,5}$ we gave values 0.00 or 1.00 if all of these items are missing or present, respectively, and deduce 0.125 per missing metadata item. For example, dataset $DS_5$ and $DS_8$ have two metadata items missing, therefore their $|I_{3,5}| = 0.75$.

Only datasets $DS_2$, $DS_4$ and $DS_6$ can be accessible from a web-portal directly (thus their indicator $|I_{2,2}| = 1.00$). The other datasets should be downloaded before one can access their content (thus the corresponding indicator $|I_{2,2}| = 0.00$).

For the standard format indicator $I_{3,2}$, we assign value 1.0 to those data formats that are interoperable with any other format (such as XML or CSV). Standard formats that are not interoperable with other standards (such as the XLS format) obtain value 0.50. For all the other cases, the indicator value 0.00 is assigned. Datasets $DS_2$, $DS_4$, $DS_5$ and $DS_8$ are in XML of CSV format (so their $\left|I_{3,2}\right| = 1.0$) and the rest of the datasets are in XLS format (so their $\left|I_{3,2}\right| = 0.5$).

For the timeliness indicator $I_{2,3}$, it appeared difficult to verify whether the investigated datasets are published in a reasonable timeframe, noting that most of these datasets are published in a rather long timeframe. Therefore, we assign $\left|I_{2,3}\right| = 0.50$ for all these datasets except for dataset $DS_4$ that we give a perfect score because it has a much better time frame than the other datasets.

For the originality indicator $I_{3,3}$, we assigned a value of 1.00 for those datasets that contain only plain numbers or strings. For those datasets with edited data in a way that we can somehow trace back to the original data values, we gave a value of 0.75. For those datasets with edited data items that we cannot trace back to the original data values, we gave a rating of 0.5 or lower. For example, if there is not enough information available to compute from a given percentage the absolute original number, the indicator value 0.5 is assigned.

As we searched for open datasets, the found and investigated dataset are appeared to be incomplete in some way. For example, we could see all crime statistics, but we can't find all police reports about those statistics. Therefore, we concluded that all of the investigated datasets are in fact incomplete and assigned a value of 0.75 for their completeness indicator $I_{3,4}$.

Regarding the machine-readable indicator $I_{3,1}$, the question is how clean, for example, XLS files should be in order to be considered as machine-readable. We determined our rating as follows. If the XLS file can be opened with another format than XLS, for example if one can open an XLS file as a CSV file, then we consider it as clean (thus machine readable $\left|I_{3,1}\right| = 1.00$). If the file is not a CSV file, i.e., cannot directly be opened with any tool, but there is some pre-processing needed to open the file and make it machine-readable, then $\left|I_{3,1}\right| = 0.50$ or 0.25 depending how much pre-processing is needed, for example, ranging from removing a mark-up layer to adapting binary codes. For datasets $DS_1$, $DS_3$, $DS_6$ and $DS_7$ there was a significant amount of pre-processing necessary in order to make them machine-readable (like adapting binary codes). Therefore, for these datasets we assigned $\left|I_{3,1}\right| = 0.25$. For the other datasets in XML and CSV files, the readability is the highest, i.e., $\left|I_{3,1}\right| = 1.00$.

To score by whom (i.e., primacy) indicator, we assign $\left|I_{1,2}\right| = 0.50$ if a dataset is the product of the data collected from several organisations and assign $\left|I_{1,2}\right| = 1.0$ if a dataset is published by an organisation that also produces the dataset.

**Table 1.** A summary of the scoring results for the 8 datasets studied.

| High and low level indicators | | From the Netherlands | | | | From other countries | | | |
|---|---|---|---|---|---|---|---|---|---|
| | | $DS_1$ | $DS_2$ | $DS_3$ | $DS_4$ | $DS_5$ | $DS_6$ | $DS_7$ | $DS_8$ |
| Who | For whom | 1.00 | 1.00 | 1.00 | 1.00 | 1.00 | 1.00 | 1.00 | 1.00 |
| | By whom | 0.50 | 1.00 | 1.00 | 1.00 | 1.00 | 0.50 | 0.50 | 1.00 |
| How | Ease of access | 1.00 | 1.00 | 1.00 | 1.00 | 1.00 | 1.00 | 1.00 | 1.00 |
| | Via a web portal | 0.00 | 1.00 | 0.00 | 1.00 | 0.00 | 1.00 | 0.00 | 0.00 |
| | Timeliness | 0.50 | 0.50 | 0.50 | 1.00 | 0.50 | 0.50 | 0.50 | 0.50 |
| | IPR | 1.00 | 1.00 | 1.00 | 1.00 | 1.00 | 1.00 | 1.00 | 1.00 |
| | Monetary costs | 1.00 | 1.00 | 1.00 | 1.00 | 1.00 | 1.00 | 1.00 | 1.00 |
| | Permanence | 1.00 | 1.00 | 1.00 | 1.00 | 1.00 | 1.00 | 1.00 | 1.00 |
| what | Mach. readable | 0.25 | 1.00 | 0.25 | 1.00 | 1.00 | 0.25 | 0.25 | 1.00 |
| | Standard format | 0.5 | 1.00 | 0.50 | 1.00 | 1.00 | 0.50 | 0.50 | 1.00 |
| | Originality | 0.75 | 1.00 | 0.50 | 1.00 | 1.00 | 0.75 | 0.75 | 0.75 |
| | Completeness | 0.75 | 0.75 | 0.75 | 0.75 | 0.75 | 0.75 | 0.75 | 0.75 |
| | Metadata | 1.00 | 1.00 | 1.00 | 1.00 | 0.75 | 1.00 | 1.00 | 0.75 |
| | Discoverability | 1.00 | 1.00 | 1.00 | 1.00 | 1.00 | 1.00 | 1.00 | 1.00 |
| What n. | Info sensitivity | 1.00 | 1.00 | 1.00 | 1.00 | 1.00 | 1.00 | 1.00 | 1.00 |
| Degree of Openness (DO) | | 0.73 | 0.95 | 0.75 | 0.98 | 0.86 | 0.80 | 0.73 | 0.84 |

# 4 Discussion

In this section we discuss the potentials and limitations of this study and elaborate on some future research directions.

The proposed assessment method to determine the degree of data openness can make it possible to learn about and consider also not fully Open Data initiatives. Further, such a measurement can make it possible to compare organisations in how their Open Data initiatives are, relative to one another and relative to the average (in a specific sector/domain). A longitudinal comparison of Semi-Open Data initiatives within a given context or organisation can also become more fine-grained using the assessment method proposed. Having such views on the progress of Open Data in time (i.e., a longitudinal view) and space (i.e., among peer organisations) can help organisations to form their Open Data policies and strategies optimally. By setting the two openness and usage dimensions next to each other, one can also gain insight in how much data openness leads to maximum data use; and thereby make a cost-benefit trade-off possible.

This study showed that assessing the degree of data openness is feasible. Further, the assessment method is flexible and extensible in the sense that it can be enhanced as needed (for example, by improving upon the indicators, the structure of the indicators, and the levels and their values per indicator). Through adapting the weighing factors of the indicators, see relation (3), appropriately the assessment method can also be tuned to various contextual situations and viewpoints. Fine-tuning of the assessment method and its weighing factors is subject of our future research. Nevertheless, the way that we carried out our case studies shows a way for constructing and fine-tuning the parameters of the method incrementally in a sense making way (i.e., based on consensus among parties/stakeholders involved in a given domain and based on iterative application of the method to a sufficient number of datasets in that domain). When these parameters are well defined and agreed upon by the experts/stakeholders in a domain, we foresee the possibility of applying some of them automatically to datasets.

In this contribution we took the first step towards defining the degrees of openness for Semi-Data initiatives for and based on eight datasets from justice domain. This is not a one-shot and strictly top-down operation. It requires going through iterations, by reflecting on the results obtained and learning from the feedback given by practitioners, domain experts, and peers. Building upon this initial work, we should improve our data model (i.e., the appropriate levels and their values per indicator) by investigating the characteristics of more datasets.

Although the datasets/cases considered in this paper were (close to) Open Data in the justice domain, they could not be marked as Open Data in its traditional sense if one considers the scores that the datasets received in Table 1. According to [34], for example, a dataset was considered as Open Data if the dataset met all requirements of the definition of Open Data fully. Therefore, considering the scores in Table 1, the efforts that are spent to share the datasets that are investigated as case studies in this paper, could not be recognised within the scope of Open Data initiatives. While, according to the Semi-Open Data assessment method, one can easily see that these datasets are actually quite close to the ideal definition of Open Data.

In this work we defined high-level indicators based on their logical similarities (who, how, what and what-not). It is for future research to validate the hierarchical structure proposed or to advance the structure among the indicators so that a more insightful measure of semi-openness can be delivered. Due to the fact we considered a few partially opened datasets, some of the indicators were ideally satisfied for all datasets. Therefore, in this study we did not (attempt to) identify the possible fine-grained levels for those attributes with a score value of 1.00 for all the datasets considered (i.e., $I_{1,1}$, $I_{2,1}$, $I_{2,4}$, $I_{2,5}$, $I_{2,6}$, $I_{3,6}$ and $I_{4,1}$). For future research one should try to assign the appropriate levels and their values for these indicators as well. Eventually, after having a sufficient number of case studies, the Open Data community should reach consensus on (and standardize) the indicators, the indicator structure, and the indicator levels and values. This standardised data model can provide a uniform view on the openness of data opening initiatives in a given domain.

Assessing those datasets that are opened by other organisations (for example datasets $DS_5$, ..., $DS_8$) is not sufficiently feasible if there is no information about how the (raw) data are collected, processed and opened. This implies that the information needed to specify the degree of openness should be provided as, for example, metadata in future (Semi) Open Data releases if they want their datasets to be considered as Semi-Open Data initiative fairly. The proposed assessment method, however, can be used optimally for those organisations who know the ins and outs of how a dataset are collected, processed, and (is going to be) opened/shared (for example, in case of the organisations that directly share their datasets with others).

# 5 Conclusion

In this contribution, we provided a method to assess the degree of openness for Semi-Open Data initiatives. This assessment model empowers us to recognize and reward the extent of organisations' efforts to meet the Open Data requirements in a fine-grained way. This study showed that the proposed way of assessing the degree of data openness is feasible. Relying on the measurement results, it appeared that Semi-Open Data concept exposes beyond the tip of the iceberg, i.e., provides a means to account for those data opening initiatives that are close to Open Data. Without having the Semi-Open Data concept and without calculating the degree of openness of these initiatives it was impossible to recognize and acknowledge the (extent of the) existence of such data opening efforts.

We applied the method to a number of datasets from the justice domain and showed that the model is able to expose and quantify partially open justice datasets. This ability, in our opinion, is crucial for the justice domain as the opening of justice domain datasets in its ideal sense is not possible due to, among others, information/privacy sensitivity, misinterpretation and misleading challenges. The case studies also showed that the proposed measurement method appears to be flexible and extensible. Particularly, we proposed (and illustrated by means of our case studies) how to construct and fine-tune the parameters of the method incrementally in a sense making way, i.e., based on consensus among parties/stakeholders involved and based on iterative application of the method to a sufficient number of datasets in a given domain (in our case the justice domain).

Further, we argued that the proposed assessment method can be used to compare the data opening performances of organisations with each other and with themselves longitudinally. As such, the measurement method can guide organisations for opening their data and can enable them to move faster towards the ideals of Open Data. It is for our future research to carry out more case studies in order to fine-tune the assessment method and its weighing factors.

# References

1. Ruijer, E., Grimmelikhuijsen, S., Meijer, A.: Open data for democracy: developing a theoretical framework for open data use. Gov. Inf. Quart. **34**(1), 45–52 (2017)
2. McLachlin, B.P.C.: Openness and the rule of law (2014). https://www.barcouncil.org.uk/media/270848/jan_8__2014_-_12_pt.__rule_of_law_-_annual_international_rule_of_law_lecture.pdf. Accessed 15 Aug 2019
3. Open data trend report 2016. Technical report by The Netherlands Court of Audit, The Hague (in Dutch: Algemene Rekenkamer, Trendrapport open data 2016, Den Haag) (2016)
4. Open data trend report 2015. Technical report by The Netherlands Court of Audit, The Hague (in Dutch: Algemene Rekenkamer, Trendrapport open data 2016, Den Haag) (2015)
5. Bargh, M.S., Choenni, S., Meijer, R.: On design and deployment of two privacy-preserving procedures for judicial-data dissemination. Gov. Inf. Quart. J. **33**(3), 481–493 (2016)
6. Meijer, R., Conradie, P., Choenni, S.: Reconciling contradictions of open data regarding transparency, privacy, security and trust. J. Theor. Appl. Electron. Commer. Res. **9**(3), 32–44 (2014)

7. van den Braak, S.W., Choenni, S., Meijer, R., Zuiderwijk, A.: Trusted third parties for secure and privacy-preserving data integration and sharing in the public sector. In: Proceedings of the 13th Annual International Conference on Digital Government Research, pp. 135–144. ACM (2012)

8. Bargh, M.S., Choenni, S., Meijer, R.F.: Integrating semi-open data in a criminal judicial setting. In: Jiménez-Gómez C.E., Gascó-Hernández, M. (Eds.), Achieving Open Justice through Citizen Participation and Transparency, pp. 137–156 (2017)

9. Open Definition. http://opendefinition.org. Accessed 15 Aug 2019

10. GODI methodology. https://index.okfn.org/methodology/. Accessed 15 Aug 2019

11. Khan, S., Foti, J.: Independent reporting mechanism: aligning supply and demand for better governance, open data in the open government partnership. Report (2018). http://www.opengovpartnership.org/sites/default/files/IRMReport-OpenData.pdf. Accessed 15 Aug 2019

12. Dodds, L., Newman, A.: A guide to the open data maturity model: assessing your open data publishing and use. Technical report from Open Data Institute (ODI) (2015). http://theodi.org/guides/maturity-model. Accessed 15 Aug 2019

13. Bargh, M.S., Choenni, S., Meijer, R.: Meeting open data halfway: on semi-open data paradigm. In: Proceedings of the 9th International Conference on Theory and Practice of Electronic Governance (ICEGOV) (2016)

14. Wonderlich, J.: Ten principles for opening up government information. Sunlight Foundation Website (2010). http://sunlightfoundation.com/policy/documents/ten-open-data-principles/. Accessed 15 Aug 2019

15. Burwell, S.M., van Roekel, S., Park, T., Mancini, D.J.: Open data policy – managing information as an asset. White House Memo on Open Data Policy, 9 May 2013. https://obamawhitehouse.archives.gov/sites/default/files/omb/memoranda/2013/m-13-13.pdf. Accessed 15 Aug 2019

16. BZK: An internal draft report from the Dutch Ministry of Internal Affairs (2015)

17. Open Data Research Network (ODRN). http://www.opendataresearch.org/content/2013/566/early-insight-2-definitions-open-data. Accessed 15 Aug 2019

18. Rorissa, A., Demissie, D., Pardo, T.: Benchmarking e-government: a comparison of frameworks for computing e-government index and ranking. GIQ **28**(3), 354–362 (2011)

19. Veljković, N., Bogdanović-Dinić, S., Stoimenov, L.: Benchmarking open government: an open data perspective. Gov. Inf. Quart. **31**(2), 278–290 (2014). https://doi.org/10.1016/j.giq.2013.10.011. Accessed 15 Aug 2019

20. Open Government Working Group: Open government data principles (2007). https://public.resource.org/8_principles.html. Accessed 15 Aug 2019

21. Bishop, C.M.: Pattern Recognition and Machine Learning. Information Science and Statistics. Springer, New York (2006). Ed. by M. Jordan, J. Kleinberg, B. Scholkopf

22. van Dijk, J., Choenni, S., Leertouwer, E., Spruit, M., Brinkkemper, S.: A data space system for the criminal justice chain. In: Meersman, R., et al. (eds.) OTM 2013. LNCS, vol. 8185, pp. 755–763. Springer, Heidelberg (2013). https://doi.org/10.1007/978-3-642-41030-7_55

23. Franklin, M., Halevy, A., Maier, D.: From databases to data spaces: a new abstraction for information management. ACM SIGMOD Rec. **34**(4), 27–33 (2005)

24. https://www.wodc.nl/binaries/C%26R2015_tabellen-h03_tcm28-131083.xls. Accessed 15 Aug 2019

25. Kalidien, S.: Crime and Law Enforcement 2015 – Criminaliteit en rechtshandhaving 2015. A report/book by CBS, WODC & Raad voor de rechtspraak (2016)

26. Smit, P.R., Dijk, J.V.: History of the Dutch crime victimization survey(s). In: Bruinsma, G., Weisburd, D. (eds.) Encyclopedia of Criminology and Criminal Justice. Springer, New York (2014). https://doi.org/10.1007/978-1-4614-5690-2

27. http://data.rechtspraak.nl/uitspraken/. Accessed 15 Aug 2019

28. http://www.ois.amsterdam.nl/download/321-fysieke-verloedering-naar-veiligheidsregios-2016.xlsx. Accessed 15 Aug 2019
29. https://www.politie.nl/mijn-buurt/misdaad-inkaart?geoquery=2274&distance=5.0. Accessed 15 Aug 2019
30. https://data.gov.in/sites/default/files/datafile/crcCASc_2014_1.csv. Accessed 15 Aug 2019
31. www.ucr.fbi.gov/crime-in-the-u.s/2016/crime-in-the-u.s.-2016/topic-pages/tables/table-1. Accessed 15 Aug 2019
32. http://www.abs.gov.au/AUSSTATS/abs@.nsf/DetailsPage/4510.02016?OpenDocument. Accessed 15 Aug 2019
33. http://www5.statcan.gc.ca/access_acces/alternative_alternatif?l=eng&keng=5.94&kfra=5.94&teng=Download%20file%20from%20CANSIM&tfra=Fichier%20extrait%20de%20CANSIM&loc=http://www5.statcan.gc.ca/cansim/results/cansim-2520081-eng-8979932552853622326.csv. Accessed 15 Aug 2019
34. Trendrapport open data 2015. Technical report (in Dutch), Court of Audit of The Netherlands, 31 March 2015. https://www.rekenkamer.nl/publicaties/rapporten/2015/03/31/trendrapport-open-data-2015. Accessed 15 Aug 2019

# E-Voting and Forensics

# TrustedEVoting (TeV) a Secure, Anonymous and Verifiable Blockchain-Based e-Voting Framework

Michel B. Verwer, Ioanna Dionysiou(✉)🆔, and Harald Gjermundrød🆔

Department of Computer Science, School of Sciences and Engineering,
University of Nicosia, Nicosia, Cyprus
verwer.m@live.unic.ac.cy, {dionysiou.i,gjermundrod.h}@unic.ac.cy

**Abstract.** Research and commercial approaches on electronic voting (e-Voting) exist and the recently emerged blockchain technology has given this research area yet another boost. However, one may claim that the actual deployment of e-Voting is at its infancy, mainly due to election integrity issues such as vote non-tampering, voter anonymity, and vote verifiability (even though the last two may seem contradictory). The integration of cryptography and blockchain technology in a single framework could provide a solid foundation for secure, anonymous and still verifiable electronic voting. This paper presents the *TrustedEVoting* (TeV) framework, a blockchain-based approach, that wraps not only the required key elements for secure and verifiable e-Voting but also additional features such as support for re-voting, post-election vote check and voting channel preference. The last one is important as the transition from traditional physical voting to e-Voting is not immediate and *TeV* framework makes provision for a multiple-channel approach for voting.

**Keywords:** e-Voting · Blockchain technology · Post-election vote check

## 1 Introduction

The deployment of electronic voting (e-Voting) is still at its infancy even though, one may claim, modern internet banking systems provide much the same sort of service: secure and trusted access on internet connected devices. The main reason for not embracing e-Voting is the reluctance of the political establishment to make the transition to electronic voting systems as elections are crucial to the democratic system of a country and even a minor system mishap (technical or otherwise) could cast doubt on the integrity of the election results.

The lack of e-Voting national deployments (at least by EU member states) is evident from a recent study on the reform of the EU electoral law [12]. Only a handful of countries are deploying e-Voting nationwide or in selected parts of the country (Estonia, France, Belgium) and a few more are running (or had run

S. Katsikas and V. Zorkadis (Eds.): e-Democracy 2019, CCIS 1111, pp. 129–143, 2020.
https://doi.org/10.1007/978-3-030-37545-4_9

and discontinued) pilot programs (Germany, Ireland, UK, to just name a few). Despite the fact that there are more recent developments in some countries with regards to e-Voting (for example in Switzerland [14]), still the conclusion drawn from the survey findings holds: the vast majority of elections in EU countries is paper-based.

Interestingly enough, even though e-Voting in Estonia has been operational since 2005, the number of voters that use the electronic voting alternative has been growing in a rather slow pace. Only 1 out of 3 voters favored the e-Voting option in the elections of 2014 and 2015 [13]. This voting preference pattern is further supported by the findings of a survey conducted on various topics on democracy and elections [16], with 68% of the respondents being concerned about the potential for fraud or cyberattacks when voting electronically and 54% finding the secrecy of the ballot a matter of concern.

Taking into consideration the valid concerns on the integrity of an election process, a novel framework is proposed that addresses the core principles of e-Voting [4] while at the same time integrating new features such as re-voting, post-election vote check and multiple ways for casting a vote. The last one is important as with a diverse population and electorate not everyone will easily adopt or be willing to use new technology, therefore an e-Voting framework must supply different ways to vote to facilitate all groups. The *TrustedEVoting* (TeV) framework blends cryptographic mechanisms with the blockchain technology [11] to provide a secure, anonymous, yet verifiable e-Voting system. A *TeV* user is empowered with the ability to check his/her vote *after* the election while maintaining his/her anonymity in the system. Other benefits realized in the proposed framework include fast election results, query/audit of election results, configurable election cycle time, re-voting and independent auditing possibilities.

The rest of the paper is organized as follows: Sect. 2 describes related research efforts on e-Voting with special attention to blockchain-based implementations. Section 3 presents the *TeV* framework, that conforms with the general principles and requirements on an e-Voting system as listed in [4], followed by a use-case evaluation in Sect. 4. Section 5 concludes.

## 2   Related Work

Applying blockchain technology to facilitate e-Voting has already been investigated and there are numerous solutions ranging from systems that use the blockchain just as a ballot storage to more advanced systems that implement e-Voting based on cryptocurrencies and smart contracts. The various existing schemes utilize various types of blockchains (public and private). Public blockchains are decentralized and permissionless, accessible by everyone, whereas access in private blockchains must be explicitly granted. The restricted-access characteristic of private blockchains require centralized management, unlike the public ones. A consortium blockchain, a variation of private blockchain, is a permissioned blockchain managed by multiple parties. As the government is not per-definition a reliable entity regarding e-Voting [18], many of the proposed schemes use a public blockchain, taking advantage of the absence of a central authority and the virtually impossible alternation of data without being noticed. The taxonomy in [20] is used to categorize existing e-Voting systems based on blockchain technology.

## 2.1  e-Voting Based on Cryptocurrency

The e-Voting system under this category uses an existing cryptocurrency platform (e.g Bitcoin) as its implementation block. The main advantages include no central authority is involved, less susceptible to DDOS attacks and with enough honest nodes in the network tampering with stored records is detectable.

However, there are several issues inherent to an e-Voting system based on cryptocurrencies that could hinder its applicability. First, even popular cryptocurrencies like Bitcoin and Ethereum are not considered mature yet, making them unlike candidates to be used in an official electoral process [7]. Second, there is the matter of monetary fees. In Bitcoin every transaction has a transaction fee, leading to the question of who is going to proceed with the payment of those transaction fees in an e-Voting system. Last, but not least, one of best known security risks to the Bitcoin network is the 51% attack ( situation where one miner or a miner pool controls the majority of the POW power).

In [3] an e-Voting scheme based on the Bitcoin network is proposed where the 51% is not considered and neither are transaction fees, forking and routing attacks. These assumptions make this scheme not practically usable. In [15] ZCASH is proposed where the blockchain mechanism is used to store votes and perform voter identification. ZCASH uses a Zero Knowledge Proof (ZKP) mechanism for signing of transactions, meaning that the identity of the signer is not revealed therefore ballot secrecy is assured. In [1], the authors describe a system design for digital voting using Blockchain technology. It is different in the sense that the system supports two blockchain instances. The first instance registers the voters, and every voter can only vote once. The second blockchain instance holds the actual votes. This separates the stored votes from voter identity creating voter anonymity.

## 2.2  e-Voting Based on Smart Contracts

Smart contract are self-executing electronic contracts with programmable logic used to execute the terms of a contract between two parties. This mechanism could be used for voting as the actual votes could be programmed into a smart contract. A smart contract is considered smart as it is self executing without a central authority overseeing execution. If smart contracts are run on a public blockchain like Ethereum it has the same safeguards as a cryptocurrency scenario in relation to distributed environments. Another way is to use smart contracts as the tallying mechanism; every time a vote is cast the smart contract adds a vote to its internal counter. A big advantage of this usage is that at the end of the voting period the results are available immediately. This smart contract feature is implemented in [6], where the smart contracts tally the results for their specific district on the fly.

Ethereum blockchain is the second largest blockchain network and has smart contract features. It uses a full featured programming language, Solidity, to build smart contracts. Good examples of smart contract based e-Voting schemes with Ethereum are presented in [19] and [17]. In the latter the authors created a smart contract e-Voting solution and tested the solution in an Ethereum test environment and concluded that a small scale implementation is feasible. The proposed solution however doesn't provide voter anonymity which is a key characteristic in a general election scenario.

Other smart contract based schemes are [20] and [18] for Ethereum. The first scheme can be based on any blockchain platform supporting smart contracts. It uses the Pallier Encryption system for vote tallying. This scheme has been implemented in a test scenario on a Hyperledger Fabric platform and has been tested with a voter base of 1 million voters with, according to the authors, reasonable performance.

## 2.3   e-Voting Based on a Blockchain Ballot Box

In a blockchain ballot box scenario, blockchain is only used to securely store the votes. This could be a public blockchain solution but a private blockchain is the favorable option. In [2] a Conceptual Secure Blockchain Based Electronic Voting System is described where a chain is made per election candidate. This has the advantage that vote tallying is immediate after the election, as it is with some smart contract implementations. The first block (Genesis Block) will contain the candidate's name and each vote for this candidate is added to the chain. Anonymity is provided by hashing the information of the voter before being added to the block. As a way to decentralize a permissioned blockchain, the authors in [5] propose that the voters run blockchain nodes in the network. There is a central component, which is acting as a Central Authority (CA) server which needs to be controlled by a trusted party. The control of the voting process lies with the users but it requires voters to contribute computational resources to the voting network, something that could be seen as a weakness of the scheme.

## 3   TeV Framework

The *TeV* framework is a comprehensive approach to e-Voting that conforms to the core principles of e-Voting (Equality, Directness, Democracy, Generality, Freedom of Vote, Secrecy, Delegate Vote Rights) [4]. The following assumptions were made during the design phase of *TeV*:

- Support of multiple elections in an election cycle (e.g a parliamentary election together with a referendum on some subject)
- Existence of an already functioning DGE (Digital Government Environment), maintained by the government

- Use of DGE modules such as user authentication
- Use and update of DGE auxiliary structures such as voter registry to add voter preferences (e.g. paper ballot or electronic ballot)
- Configurable length of voting cycle, during which re-voting is allowed.

The discussion in this section starts with a *preparatory* phase, where mandatory tokens prior the commence of a particular election (election keys, voter keys, voter election ID) are generated. Selected *TeV* modules are described next. A complete and detailed presentation of the *TeV* framework could be found in [10].

## 3.1   Preparation Phase: Election Keys, Voter Keys and Voter Election ID Generation

The basic principle for the e-Voting encryption scheme is shown in Fig. 1. An anonymous vote is encrypted using an election public key $PU_e$, followed by another encryption using the voter's private key $PR_v$.

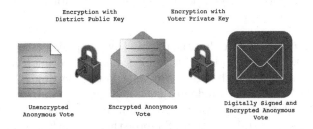

**Fig. 1.** Encrypted vote scheme

Acknowledging the catastrophic impact of a compromised election key, *TeV* framework supports multiple election keys[1], where a number of election keys is used based on a predefined categorization as set by the national Voter Registrar. This categorization could be based on the number of districts, municipalities, states, etc. For instance, a small country with *3* districts could choose to have *3* election keys, one per district (see Fig. 2). The election public keys are available to all voting stations whereas the election private keys are safeguarded. Formal procedures should exist for the election keys generation, auditing and storing. Without loss of generality, in this paper, *district* is used as the category.

Every eligible voter gets issued one set of keys per election. The private key is used for *digitally signing* his/her vote during voting time whereas the public key is used for the signature verification. In the case where there is a national Digital Government ID (DGI), the private key is coupled to the DGI for that specific election. Based on the preference of the voter, the private key is either connected to the DGI or a paper vote call is issued with the private key included.

---

[1] A key here refers to a pair of asymmetric keys.

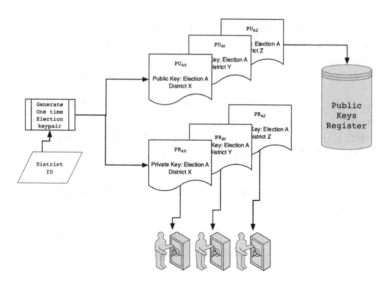

**Fig. 2.** Election keys generation for election A with 3 districts

A practical solution would be that the private key is supplied as a quick response code (QR code). This QR code can then be scanned at voting time.

In order to anonymize the vote, a unique Voter Election ID (*VEL-ID*) is generated. The *VEL-ID* is a randomly generated sequence of bytes, displayed in Base64 encoding for user readability. It could also serve as a voting token, used for limiting access to certain elections. Suppose that for the European Parliament elections the minimum voter age is 18 and for the domestic elections it is set to 16. A domestic referendum could be held simultaneously with EU parliament elections; an 18-year old would be issued two *VEL-ID*s whereas the 16-year old only one. The *VEL-ID* is utilized in the voter anonymity process, the re-vote process as well as the post-election vote checking by the voter himself/herself.

### 3.2   Vote Casting Module

**Anonymous Voter ID.** One of the challenges in casting the vote electronically is guaranteeing voter anonymity. In the *TeV* framework, this is achieved with the derivation of an anonymous voter ID *AV-ID* as shown in Eq. 1. A parameterized function $f$ returns a value, whose hash yields the *AV-ID*. Function $f$, in addition to the *VEL-ID*, uses two other parameters: *RN* and *PC*. The first quantity is a random number generated locally by the voting device and the second one is a user-supplied passcode.

$$AV - ID = H(f(VEL - ID, RN, PC))$$ (1)

The use of *RN* comes from the observation that user-supplied passcodes are usually weak, making a system vulnerable to password-guessing attacks; that was indeed reported for the Estonian e-Voting system [8]. Compromising *AV-ID* requires the possession of three elements, with no statistical or any other mathematical relationship among them, distributed on three entities (system itself, voting device, voter). The *AV-ID* is used as a proof of casting a vote and thus enables post-election vote checking.

**Re-voting.** Re-voting is the possibility of casting a vote multiple times during an election, with the last attempt being the final vote. *TeV* is a blockchain-based framework, where altering of existing records is impossible. Implementing re-voting in a blockchain setting entails addressing two issues: how to guarantee end-to-end (E2E) verifiability and how to ensure that only one vote is counted in case of casting multiple votes. The E2E verifiability is discussed later in Sect. 3.3. In order to provide one-vote count in a multiple voting setting, a *Voting Status* record is introduced that holds the status for *VEL-IDs* (Fig. 3). As this record is stored in the blockchain, the write-once characteristic implies that a new record will be created every time a voter re-votes.

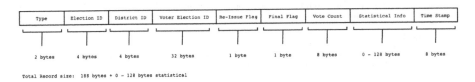

| Type | Election ID | District ID | Voter Election ID | Re-Issue Flag | Final Flag | Vote Count | Statistical Info | Time Stamp |
| --- | --- | --- | --- | --- | --- | --- | --- | --- |
| 2 bytes | 4 bytes | 4 bytes | 32 bytes | 1 byte | 1 byte | 8 bytes | 0 - 128 bytes | 8 bytes |

Total Record size: 188 bytes + 0 - 128 bytes statistical

**Fig. 3.** Voting status record

Table 1 outlines the *Voting Status* record fields and Algorithm 1 describes the process executed whenever a voter attempts to cast a vote. In order to avoid DDOS using re-voting requests, re-voting is allowed after $x$ hours have passed since the last voting.

**Table 1.** Voting Status record field description

| Field | Description |
| --- | --- |
| Type | Voting Status Record |
| Election ID | Election ID parameter (support of multiple elections) |
| District ID | District ID parameter |
| VEL-ID | Voter Election ID |
| Re-issue Flag | Used to re-issue VEL-ID |
| Final Flag | Used to signal final vote |
| Vote Count | Counter of how many times a voter with this VEL-ID has voted so far |
| Statistical Info | Sanitized voter data (e.g. age group, type of voting) for statistical purposes |
| Time Stamp | Voting Status Record creation time |

**Algorithm 1.** UpdateVoting Status Record

```
1: function UPDATE VOTING STATUS RECORD(VID VEL − ID, EID ELECTION − ID, DID
       DISTRICT − ID)
2:     if (VotingStatusRecord( VEL − ID) = null) then              ▷ Cast a vote for first time
3:         record ← CREATERECORD()
4:         Election ID ← ELECTION-ID
5:         District ID ← DISTRICT-ID
6:         Vote Count ← 1
7:         Statistical Info ← SETSTATISTICALDATA()
8:         Time Stamp ← GETCURRENTTIME()
9:         Re-issue Flag ← 0
10:        Type ← Voting Status Record
11:        if (VotingMethod = p-Voting) then                    ▷ paper-based vote is always final
12:            Final Flag ← 1
13:        else
14:            Final Flag ← 0
15:        end if
16:    else
17:        for each record with VEL − ID do
18:            if (record.Final Flag = 1) then                        ▷ Not allowed to revote
19:                Revoting ← false
20:            end if
21:        end for
22:        if (Revoting = true) then                                 ▷ Allowed to revote
23:            newrecord ← CREATERECORD()
24:            latestrecord ← GETRECORDWITHLATESTTIMESTAMP()
25:            newrecord.Vote Count ← latestrecord.Vote Count + 1
26:            set remaining record fields
27:        end if
28:    end if
29: end function
```

**Voting Client Application/App.** The client application is a vital part of any e-Voting solution. Many voting principles are incorporated in the business logic of the app. Choosing an app (for mobile platforms) or a website with mobile platform support is a development choice outside the scope of *TeV*. Thus, the term *voting app* refers to the functionality rather than the platform or application type.

Functionality-wise, at a bare minimum, a voting app for the *TeV* framework must support:

- Multiple ballots in one election cycle
- Cool down period (time period that must elapse before revoting)
- Intentionally invalid votes, blank or "abstained from voting" votes
- First time passcode automatically generated and send to mobile phone via the DGE
- Kiosk mode used at the polling stations
- Demo/practice mode (online and in Kiosk mode)
- Not allowing re-voting when a voter changes his/her passcode

In addition, several security requirements are imposed on the voting app. A comprehensive list could be found at [10].

### 3.3   Vote Storing Module

An important element of *TeV* is the blockchain *Ballot Box*. A permisioned (consortium) blockchain is proposed, with a possible implementation being the Hyperledger Fabric. The actual votes as well as the Voting Status records for an election are stored on nationally-located blockchain nodes. For auditing purposes, additional nodes at third party locations are recommended to be utilized, effectively creating a consortium blockchain with external electoral monitoring nodes. Potential placement of the external auditing nodes include the country's election oversight committee, the Office for Democratic Institutions and Human Rights (ODIHR - EU countries) and the EU Election Observation Missions organization (EUEOMs).

The Voting Status record has already being discussed. The second type of record supported in *TeV* framework is the *Vote* record. It includes, among others, the actual vote that an eligible voter cast along with the corresponding *AV-ID*, both encrypted with the appropriate district public key (see Fig. 4). After the election, the two quantities are decrypted for vote tallying and cast vote checking.

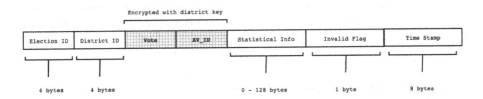

**Fig. 4.** Vote record

One of the design choices made in the framework is related to the number of blockchains used to store the various records. Two blockchain instances (*Cast Vote Register, Voting Status Register*) running on the same node are maintained. In this way, the actual votes and the *VEL-ID*s are kept separated, maintaining voter anonymity but supporting post-election vote checking at the same time. It is essential that records are stored simultaneously; a cast vote should not be validated if there is no corresponding vote status record.

Figure 5 illustrates the network setup of a consortium blockchain, with 6 blockchain instances in polling stations and 2 outside of the government sphere of influence (third party).

### 3.4   Vote Tallying Module

Once the election is completed, vote tallying commences (see Fig. 6). Only one blockchain instance is needed to determine the preliminary election results, which are stored in the *Election Results Register*. Verification of the results could be performed by repeating the vote tallying process using a different blockchain

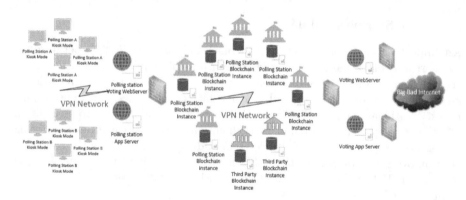

**Fig. 5.** Consortium blockchain network

node, with a minimum of 3 nodes to ensure the outcome correctness. The external nodes could verify the election results independently by following the same procedure. Any discrepancies would prompt for an investigation according to the national electoral legislation. An *Election Results Register* record has the same information as the *Vote* record, but in its decrypted format. In order to determine the final vote for a voter, the procedure shown in Algorithm 2 is followed.

---

**Algorithm 2.** Determine Final Vote

---

1: **function** DETERMINE FINAL VOTE(**AVID** $AV - ID$)
2:     Retrieve all records for $AV - ID$
3:     Check Retrieved Records Integrity
4:     Determine the latest added record based on the time stamp, and mark that vote as the final vote
5:     Check if the invalid flag is set. If the flag is set dismiss the record
6:     Determine the vote and add 1 to that candidate and or party, Invalid, Blank or any other predetermined election outcome
7: **end function**

---

One the strengths of *TeV* is that it leverages vote verification by allowing a voter to check his/her actual vote at a post-election time. This is done easily by generating locally his/her *AV-ID* and retrieving the final vote for the specific election from the *Election Results Register*. In this way, the average citizen who may not be fully aware of the technicalities of an electronic voting scheme, could still verify his/cast vote, something that is not possible in a paper-based voting scheme.

## 4   *TeV* Framework Use Cases

As mentioned earlier, a nationwide adoption of electronic voting is not anticipated to happen overnight. *TeV* supports three means of voting, namely

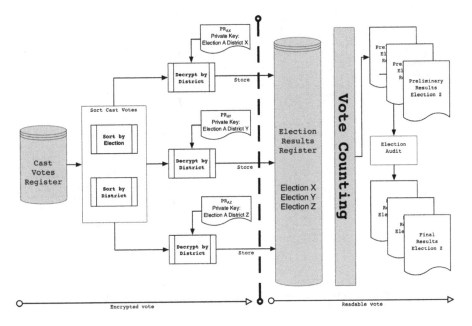

**Fig. 6.** Vote decrypting process

internet-based voting (i-Voting), paper voting (p-Voting), and a hybrid type of voting that allows a voter to cast multiple votes via i-Voting and still get the option to cast a vote at a traditional polling station.

### 4.1 i-Voting

Figure 7 illustrates the process flow of an i-Voting scenario, where a voter uses an Internet-enabled mobile device to cast his/her vote. It is assumed that $TeV$ is integrated with the national DGE and prior the election the voter indicated his/her preference regarding paper or electronic vote. Once authenticated via the DGE authentication module, an eligible voter accesses the two election tokens, $VEL\text{-}ID$ and $PR_v$, and initiates the voting process by entering the supplied $VEL\text{-}ID$ and his/her passcode. The first time the voter accesses the application for the specific election, a temporary passcode $tempPC$ is generated and sent via sms to the voter, who uses it to access the election application but he/she is required to supply a new passcode $PC$ before proceeding. The election id is checked to determine if the voter is eligible to vote. In this case, the voter casts the vote $v$. Meanwhile, a random number $RN$ gets generated and the anonymous voter id $AV\text{-}ID$ gets created. Both $AV\text{-}ID$ and $v$ are encrypted with the $PU_{District-ID}$, followed by a second encryption with $PR_v$. The latter serves as the voter's digital signature. The vote gets stored in the *Cast Votes Register* upon successful verification of the voter's signature. Note that at this point, the stored vote and $AV\text{-}ID$ are still encrypted with the district's public key. The *Voting Status Register* gets updated as well.

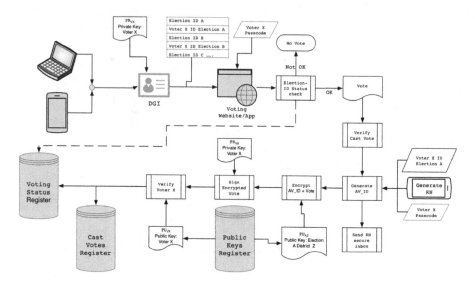

**Fig. 7.** Internet-enabled mobile device voting process flow

## 4.2    p-Voting

One of the considerations in p-Voting is the distribution of the $PR_v$ and the *VEL-ID*. Without loss of generality, paper-based voting is limited to the paper vote call, where a voter receives a call to vote via post mail. The paper vote call includes the QR codes for *VEL-ID* and $PR_v$. An example QR code is shown in Fig. 8, generated using [9].

**Fig. 8.** Voter election ID QR code

Figure 9 illustrates the paper-based voting. The actual voting is done electronically at a polling station, using a government device located at the station. The voter, upon his/her arrival at the physical location, presents his/her credentials along with a government-issued ID. Scanning of the QR codes allows the voter to cast the vote in pretty much the same way as with i-Voting, assuming first time access to the application, requiring him/her to choose a passcode *PC*. The *RN* token is printed so that the voter could check his/her vote after the election. Even though the election spans several days (usually two weeks), only on the last day of the election the physical polling stations are operational. The physical cast vote is always final.

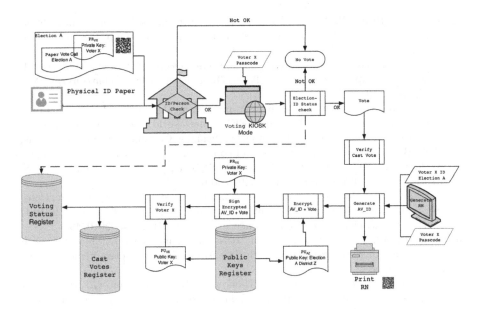

**Fig. 9.** Paper call vote process flow

## 5    Conclusion

In the era of Internet of Things, the political process of voting is going to be evolved as a digital service, an integral part of the electronic government ecosystem. There are concerns regarding the digital approach of the voting process, especially when it comes to provide guarantees for the integrity of the election procedure, and thus the election results themselves. A discrepancy between cast votes and votes counted towards the final election results would have a negative impact on the public confidence and trust on the system.

This paper proposes *TeV*, a novel e-Voting framework based on a permissioned blockchain platform, that provides guarantees for election votes and results integrity, voter anonymity, and post-election vote check by voter himself/herself. The latter feature leverages the accountability dimension of the e-Voting system, something that builds public confidence and helps election transparency.

The future directions of *TeV* are twofold: first, is the design of the *TeV* privacy framework that will ensure that the system complies with privacy directives (e.g. GDPR) and second, the implementation of a privacy-by-design prototype e-Voting system based on *TeV*.

# References

1. Barnes, A., Brake, C., Perry, T.: Digital voting with the use of blockchain technology, September 2016. https://www.economist.com/sites/default/files/plymouth.pdf. Accessed Mar 2018
2. Ayed, A.B.: A conceptual secure blockchain based electronic voting system. Int. J. Netw. Secur. Appl. *IJNSA* **9**(3), 1–9 (2017). http://aircconline.com/ijnsa/V9N3/9317ijnsa01.pdf
3. Bao, Z., Wang, B., Shi, W.: A privacy-preserving, decentralized and functional bitcoin e-voting protocol. In: 2018 IEEE SmartWorld, Ubiquitous Intelligence Computing, Advanced Trusted Computing, Scalable Computing Communications, Cloud Big Data Computing, Internet of People and Smart City Innovation (SmartWorld/SCALCOM/UIC/ATC/CBDCom/IOP/SCI), pp. 252–256, October 2018. https://doi.org/10.1109/SmartWorld.2018.00078
4. Gritzalis, D.A.: Principles and requirements for a secure e-voting system. Comput. Secur. **21**(6), 539–556 (2002). https://doi.org/10.1016/S0167-4048(02)01014-3. http://www.sciencedirect.com/science/article/pii/S0167404802010143
5. Hardwick, F.S., Gioulis, A., Akram, R.N., Markantonakis, K.: E-voting with blockchain: An e-voting protocol with decentralisation and voter privacy (2018). working Paper
6. Hjalmarsson, F., Hreidarsson, G.K., Hamdaqa, M., Hjalmtysson, G.: Blockchain-based e-voting system. In: 2018 IEEE 11th International Conference on Cloud Computing (CLOUD), pp. 983–986, July 2018. https://doi.org/10.1109/CLOUD.2018.00151
7. Kshetri, N., Voas, J.: Blockchain-enabled e-voting. IEEE Softw. **35**(4), 95–99 (2018). https://doi.org/10.1109/MS.2018.2801546
8. Kubjas, I., Pikma, T., Willemson, J.: Estonian voting verification mechanism revisited again. In: Krimmer, R., Volkamer, M., Braun Binder, N., Kersting, N., Pereira, O., Schürmann, C. (eds.) E-Vote-ID 2017. LNCS, vol. 10615, pp. 306–317. Springer, Cham (2017). https://doi.org/10.1007/978-3-319-68687-5_19
9. Brown, M.: QR Code Generator (2019). https://digid.nl/en/inloggen_basis. Accessed to generate QR codes: April 2019. https://www.theqrcodegenerator.com
10. Verwer, M.: Prev framework: a practical e-voting frameowrk (2019), masterThesis, Department of Computer Science, University of Nicosia
11. Nakamoto, S.: Bitcoin: A peer-to-peer electronic cash system. http://bitcoin.org/bitcoin.pdf (2008). Accessed Apr 2019
12. Nogaj, M., Poptcheva, E.M.: The Reform of the Electoral Law of the European Union. The European Parliament, September 2015. http://www.europarl.eu/thinktank, https://doi.org/10.2861/26011
13. Solvak, M., Vassil, K.: E-voting in Estonia: Technological diffusion and other developments over ten years (2005–2015). http://skytte.ut.ee/. Accessed Apr 2018
14. Swisspost: E-voting website, April 2019. https://www.evoting.ch/en. Accessed Mar 2019

15. Tarasov, P., Tewari, H.: Internet voting using zcash. In: Proceedings of the IADIS International Conference on WWW/Internet, pp. 159–170 (2017)
16. The European Commission: Special Eurobarometer 477: Democracy and Elections. The European Commission (2018). http://ec.europa.eu/commfrontoffice/publicopinion. Accessed Jan 2019
17. Wang, B., Sun, J., He, Y., Pang, D., Lu, N.: Large-scale election based on blockchain. Proc. Comput. Sci. **129** 234–237 (2018). 2017 International Conference on Identification, Information and Knowledge in the Internet of Things, https://doi.org/10.1016/j.procs.2018.03.063, http://www.sciencedirect.com/science/article/pii/S1877050918302874,
18. Lai, W.-J., Hsieh, Y., Hsueh, C.W., Wu, J.L.: Date: a decentralized, anonymous, and transparent e-voting system. In: 2018 1st IEEE International Conference on Hot Information-Centric Networking (HotICN), 2018 1st IEEE International Conference on Hot Information-Centric Networking (HotICN), p. 24 (2018)
19. Yavuz, E., Koç, A.K., Çabuk, U.C., Dalkiliç, G.: Towards secure e-voting using ethereum blockchain. In: 2018 6th International Symposium on Digital Forensic and Security (ISDFS). pp. 1–7, March 2018. https://doi.org/10.1109/ISDFS.2018.8355340
20. Yu, B., et al.: Platform-independent secure blockchain-based voting system. In: Chen, L., Manulis, M., Schneider, S. (eds.) ISC 2018. LNCS, vol. 11060, pp. 369–386. Springer, Cham (2018). https://doi.org/10.1007/978-3-319-99136-8_20

# Attitudes of Polish Voters Towards Introduction of e-Voting in the Context of Political Factors

Magdalena Musiał-Karg[1]([✉]) [iD] and Izabela Kapsa[2]([✉]) [iD]

[1] Adam Mickiewicz University, Poznań, Poland
magdalena.musial-karg@amu.edu.pl
[2] Kazimierz Wielki University, Bydgoszcz, Poland
izabela.kapsa@ukw.edu.pl

**Abstract.** Despite the lack of legal basis, electronic voting has been present in the public discourse in Poland for over ten years. This can be seen in particular before parliamentary, presidential, local or European elections. Then, political parties, while trying to raise their election capital, declare their willingness to implement innovative methods of voting (e.g. i-voting) in elections to make the election process more convenient for those entitled to vote. Parties assume that this can mobilize the part of the electorate which typically does not utilize their universal suffrage.

The main objective of this article is to analyze and explain to what degree (and to what extent) political preferences may affect the choice made by voters, provided it is possible to have electronic voting as a method of their participation in elections. We ask the question: if the voters' opinion on e-voting correlates with the opinions of the political parties for which they are voting. While looking for the answer to this question, the authors have assumed that there is a relationship between the political variable such as the preference and opinions on the use of modern forms of voting. To verify this diagnosis, we make a statistical analysis of the data coming from a survey implemented between March and May 2018 in Poland. Research findings lead to a general conclusion that political preferences are a statistically significant predicator for voters' attitudes towards the introduction and use of voting over the Internet.

**Keywords:** Electronic voting · E-Voting · Internet voting · Polish voters · Political preferences

This article has been written as a part of a research project: E-voting as an alternative way of voting procedures in national elections. Experiences of selected countries and prospects for implementation e-voting in Poland (E-voting jako alternatywna procedura głosowania w elekcjach państwowych. Doświadczenia wybranych państw a perspektywy wdrożenia e-głosowania w Polsce) funded by the National Science Center in Poland UMO-2014/15/B/HS5/01358.

S. Katsikas and V. Zorkadis (Eds.): e-Democracy 2019, CCIS 1111, pp. 144–160, 2020.
https://doi.org/10.1007/978-3-030-37545-4_10

# 1 Introduction

In the past several years, we have witnessed a rapid civilization development promoted, among other things, by major information and communication technology advancement in practically every field of life, including the political space.

The impact of the ICT on political processes and the relationship between the state and the citizen can be defined by such terms as the *Internet democracy*, *digital democracy*, *cyber democracy*, *virtual democracy*, or most often *electronic democracy*. According to Lewis A. Friedland the "concept of e-democracy means a radically new form of democratic practices modified by new information technologies". Regardless its name and scope of the definition, a common feature of these concepts is the conviction that with new technologies (which ensure interactive dimension, faster transfer of information and feedback) it is possible to influence democratic mechanisms [1, 2]. Apart from the paradigm shift [3, 4] and the concept of e-democracy, another consequence of the ICT impact on democracy is the introduction of e-participation, a term which stems from the use of modern technologies in civic decision-making procedures [5, 6]. The growing role of the Internet (as most rapidly developing ICT tool) in the broad area of politics and increasingly important impact on society and democracy provide major motivation for further studies.

One of the tools in the new form of governance is the so-called electronic voting which attracts a growing interest among political scientists, sociologists, psychologists or IT specialists, as well as politicians, experts, practitioners and representatives of NGOs dealing, for instance, with social participation.

By definition, *e-voting* involves the use of electronic means. Literature distinguishes two types of such voting: electronic voting (*e-voting*) and online voting (*i-voting*). E-voting is a wider concept and contains in itself the voting over the Internet. Electronic voting in practice refers to the use of voting techniques, such as digital TV platforms, telephones, and the Internet [7]. Internet voting can be divided into two categories: *Internet Voting at a polling station*[1] and *Remote Internet Voting*[2].

The popularity of electronic voting has been growing primarily because it is new, potentially beneficial and convenient for hundreds of millions of people around the world. Many voters prefer e-voting (in particular voting online) than traditional methods. This group includes the youngest voters in particular [8].

It should be emphasized that electronic voting does not aim at replacing traditional participation in elections with a new procedure. Supporters of *e-voting* assume that once an additional method of participation is added, it will make voting available to a wider range of citizens, including disabled people and people living or working abroad.

One of the most prominent examples of countries in which online voting was introduced is Estonia. According to the Estonian government, the *Remote Internet*

---

[1] *Internet Voting at the polling station*: voters cast their votes in a designated location using the Internet.

[2] *Remote Internet Voting* is a remote method of casting a vote whereby voters cast votes using "election kiosks", or from a desktop computer connected to the Internet. The Internet is used to transfer data to the central database from both types of voting posts.

*Voting* has been accepted as a voting method by the society. It is very important from the point of view of the electorate engagement [9]. This has been confirmed by figures announced by the Estonian Election Commission. They show an increasing proportion of i-votes (votes cast online) in the structure of all votes cast in an election. It confirms a high level of confidence the Estonian society puts to new election methods.

It needs to be pointed out that "Estonia was the first country in the world to implement i-voting in their national elections. Effective electronic voting has been in use in Estonia since 2005. I-voting is popular primarily due to its efficiency and convenience. Today, about one third of votes cast votes via the Internet. The i-voting system was first used in the 2017 local elections, and since then it has been developed according to the new electronic voting framework" [10]. It is worth mentioning that in the last parliamentary election in March 2019, 43.8% of voters cast their votes over the Internet. I-voters accounted for 27.9% of all eligible citizens.

It has been no surprise that voters who have chosen to vote online had at least basic knowledge of PC and Internet operation. According to a Canadian report titled *A Comparative Assessment of Electronic Voting* [11], in 2005, 20% of i-voters stated that if it had not been for the possibility of voting over the Internet, they would not have participated in the election at all. In 2007, 11% of voters declared that probably or certainly they would not have voted, if there had been no i-voting available. This shows that the possibility of voting over the Internet may influence the election turnout, especially among those who usually do not participate [9].

The main research problem discussed in the article concerns attitudes among Poles towards e-voting in the context of their political preferences. The main objective is to analyze and explain to what degree (and to what extent) political preferences may affect the choice made by voters, provided it is possible to have electronic voting as a method of their participation in elections. We have asked the following research question: Does voters' attitude to e-voting converges with the opinion of the political party they vote for? While looking for the answer to the question, the authors have assumed that there is a relationship between the political variable such as the preference and opinions on the use of modern forms of voting (hypothesis no. 1). Moreover, the political preferences are a statistically significant predicator for voters' attitudes towards the introduction and use of voting over the Internet (hypothesis no. 2). To verify the statement, we have provided a statistical analysis of data from a survey implemented between March and May 2018 in Poland.

## 2 The Use of IT in Elections and Views of Political Parties on e-Voting

The first use of an IT system to support the election in Poland was during 1993 parliamentary elections. The Internet, however, was used for the first time in the 2000 presidential election to transfer data. IT systems were used on a larger scale (in 10% of constituencies) during local elections of 2002. As a part of a pilot program, for the first time, encrypted data were sent directly from polling stations to the central database of the National Election Bureau (NEB) confirmed with the electronic signature. Voters could follow results over the Internet. Since then, the system has changed several times and played a role of an IT tool supporting Election Committees answerable to the National Election Bureau [12]. It should be mentioned that the 2014 local elections noted certain problems with the IT system which prevent vote counting and regional committees had to count votes manually. Problems also occurred while producing election reports [13]. Finally, in consecutive local elections, the use of the system was auxiliary only. Instead of counting votes, the system "supported election authorities and was used to eliminate possible errors". The system supports election committees while preparing elections, e.g. storage of data regarding voting, candidates and composition of election committees in particular constituencies. During voting, the system helps to collect information about the turnout and afterwards examine the arithmetical compliance of data in reports and accuracy of results. The platform is used to transfer voting results, revised by election committees, from constituencies to the State Election Committee. It also enables voters to check results over the Internet [12].

Despite the lack of the legal basis and shortage of experience in Poland, electronic voting is a topic that has been present in the public discourse for over 10 years. It is particularly vivid before consecutive parliamentary, presidential, local or European elections. Then, political parties, while trying to raise their election capital, declare their willingness to implement innovative methods of voting (e.g. i-voting) in elections to make the election process more convenient for those entitled to vote, assuming that this can mobilize the part of the electorate which typically does not utilize their universal suffrage.

As mentioned earlier, in Poland, there is no legal grounds to introduce e-voting. However, certain political parties show their interest in the topic, which is expressed in more intensive discussions on the issue concerned.

The following Polish political parties (included in survey) support e-voting:

- Platforma Obywatelska (PO) expressed their interest in e-voting during pre-term 2007 elections with the hope that once a new election code becomes effective, voting over the Internet will also be used during the 2011 parliamentary election. The assumption was that the solution could boost the turnout and mobilize the youngest generation of Poles eligible to vote. While casting an e-vote, the voter would no longer face the dilemma of choosing between "BBQ and voting", since he/she will not be assigned to any particular committee in his/her domicile. It is worth noting that before the 2010 presidential elections, the PO held a primary election and people could vote on their candidates (Radosław Sikorski and Bronisław Komorowski) over the Internet[3].

- One of postulates put forward by Kukiz' 15 is to simplify the election procedure and make Internet voting possible. Representatives of Kukiz' 15 believe that the system

---

[3] "There were two methods of voting available - via the Internet or by sending a special form via regular post (...). 21246 out of 44759 members of the party had voted in the primary elections. Turnout in presidential primary election in the PO was 47.47%. PO voters definitely preferred the Internet. Over 17 thousand votes were cast in this way. Four thousands of party members sent their votes by post": M. Musiał-Karg, Electronic Voting as an Additional Method of Participating in Elections? Opinions of Poles, First International Joint Conference, E-Vote-ID 2016, Bregenz, Austria, October 18-21, 2016, Proceedings, eds. R. Krimmer, M. Volkamer, J. Barrat, J. Benaloh, N. Goodman, P. Y. A. Ryan, V. Teague, Springer 2017.

can facilitate the organization of elections and vote counting, as well as simplify the participation of citizens, since the solution is easy to use and more efficient than the traditional voting [15]; It is worth noting that during the upcoming parliamentary campaign of October 13, 2019 - KUKIZ has entered into a coalition with PSL. Among the main program postulates, Paweł Kukiz proposed to the PSL among other things: e-voting, possibility of dismissal of a deputy during their term of office, reduction of a minimum voter turnout in referendums (no voting thresholds for the referendums to be valid), introduction of Single-Mandate Electoral Districts.
– Janusz Korwin-Mikke Party [16].

Only one political party expressed their objection to e-voting:
– PIS; In 2008, in one interview, Jarosław Kaczyński, PIS leader, expressed his opinion that "voting should not take place over the Internet, since it requires a more serious consideration that just a click". Kaczyński stated that he could not see any reason why "we should tell young people that participation in public life is something involving a mere click of a button". "If this is the price of engaging and changing attitudes among young people, we are not willing to pay it, sine public life must be something serious" [17]. Since that time, PiS rarely expresses any opinions on e-voting. It is worth noting, however, that in June 2017, after meeting Paweł Kukiz, Andrzej Duda, the Polish President, did not exclude the possibility of e-voting during the constitutional referendum [18].

Although e-voting is not the main topic of the campaign, it should be noted that thanks to throwing this thread into the campaign, e-voting is becoming more popular among the electorate. A kind of confirmation that electronic voting is increasingly raised in public debate in Poland is also the fact that the introduction of an electronic referendum appeared in the postulates of the Social Contract Incubator (Inkubator Imowy Społecznej – IUS; https://zdecentralizowanarp.pl/) association, which (with the support of local government officials, activists, scientists, people of culture, opinion leaders) public, innovators and entrepreneurs) promotes the idea of decentralization of Poland, aiming at developing new systemic solutions. One of the postulates of IUS is to put the citizen in the center and change the citizen-power relationship so that citizens have a real impact on the distribution of public goods in their commune, county, city and province. Electronic referendums are to give the citizen a sense of effectiveness and facilitate supervision of local authorities.

Thus, the analysis is based on an assumption that opinions among political parties on e-voting can be reflected by survey results. It is worth referring to results of the survey made by the author in 2014. The survey showed that the percentage distribution of answers to the question of introducing e-voting pointed that the largest number of PO supporters are for Internet voting (65.6%), next comes the Janusz Korwin-Mikke Party (total of 64.4%), and there were many supporters of the voting among SLD supporters. Groups with the lowest support for voting over the Internet are found among the supporters of PIS and PSL (49.5% and 45.6% respectively). Supporters of these two parties were also the most likely to oppose this voting mode (33.4% of PIS supporters and 30.4% of PSL supporters) [14].

## 3  E-voting in the Opinion of Poles of Different Party Preferences

The research results originate from the 2018 survey which covered a sample of 1717 Poles. The sampling was based on quota and demographic features of the population. Although most of respondents filled out a paper questionnaire, they could also use its electronic version available for all web users. The questionnaire included respondent's particulars and questions referring to the participation in elections, political preferences, use of the Internet, as well as electronic voting and electronic administration. The article presents findings based on answers given to the following statements:

1. *Poland should introduce Internet voting as an additional form of participation in elections*
2. *I would use the possibility of Internet voting in elections*

Answers to the statements are expressed using the Likert scale, and respondents could choose one out of five possible answers: definitely yes, rather yes, yes, hard to say, rather no, definitely no. While processing results, each option was expressed in numbers as follows: definitely yes – 5 points, rather yes – 4 points, hard to say – 3 points, rather no – 2 points, definitely no - 1 point.

Moreover, the article presents *opinions on i-voting* and *e-voting as an alternative voting methods.*

Political preferences were tested by the following question: *If the parliamentary election was held today, who would you vote for*...). The respondents could choose the following answers: (a) Sojusz Lewicy Demokratycznej (Democratic Left Alliance); (b) Wolność Janusza Korwin-Mikke (KORWIN); (c) Kukiz '15; (d) Nowoczesna (Modern); (e) Partia Razem (Together); (f) Platforma Obywatelska RP (Civic Platform); (g) Polskie Stronnictwo Ludowe (Polish People's Party); (h) Prawo i Sprawiedliwość (Law and Justice); (i) another party, which...?; (j) hard to say; (k) I would not vote.

The following analysis is based on an assumption of a relationship between party preferences and opinions voters have about the possible use of i-voting in elections. The main goal is to diagnose the degree (and scope) of political preferences and their influence on the probable use of electronic voting (if available) as an election participation method.

The analysis of results has examined election preferences expressed by voters and their decisions as if elections had been held at the time of the survey. Various answers were given about the use of the Internet and other methods of voting. A series of analyses was performed using the Kruskal-Wallis, $\chi^2$ and Fisher tests. Due to a large number of groups compared, results are shown in charts. In the case the use of a chart was not possible, results were included in tables. It is worth mentioning that in the case of qualitative data the analysis based on the Fisher Test comparison between groups may be very general only.

*Post-hoc* comparisons are shown to provide the name of a political party, i.e. when PiS (Law and Justice) is listed, data refer to a declaration by PiS supporters.

Before analyzing the results for individual statements, we present descriptive statistics related to them. As described in the table below (Table 1), the highest results regarding *"Poland should introduce Internet voting as an additional form of participation in elections"*[4] have been achieved in the group of voters ho support Partia Razem (Together), a political party interested in promoting e-voting. The lowest results are noted in the group of voters supporting PiS (Law and Justice), the only political party which was against introducing e-voting in Poland. Interestingly, PiS voters had even a lower average score than respondents who declared their will not to vote. As regards the second statement: *I would use the possibility of Internet voting in elections* – which is more of an individual declaration than a general opinion – respondents indicated similar answers to those to the first statement. The arithmetic average was 3.92. KORWIN voters had the highest score, whereas the score for those who would not vote was the lowest. It is worth to notice that among respondents who indicated their party preferences, PiS voters had the lowest score. The same applies to the third and fourth statements. In both instances (*Internet voting promotes turnout* and *Internet voting reduces probability of error while counting votes*), Partia Razem (Together) voters had the highest score. Interestingly, the same voters scored the lowest in the sixth statement: *Internet voting increases election turnout.* This may indicate their realistic opinion, and the same may apply to all respondents, since the average was the lowest – only 3.47). Although i-voting is not popular, we hardly observe any increase in the turnout with the introduction of this voting method. The situation regarding the fifth statement (*Electronic voting is much more convenient than voting in polling station)* was different. For the first time, Kukiz'15 voters had the highest score (they had quite high scores also in other statements, since it converges with political proposition of the party). Respondents who would not vote had the lowest score, and among respondents who indicated their party preferences, for the first time, SLD (Democratic Left Alliance) voters had the same score, whereas PiS voters has a very similar score.

1. Answers to the statement: **Poland should introduce Internet voting as an additional form of participation in elections** have been examined. The Kruskal-Wallis test was statistically significant, $H(10) = 98.43$; $p < 0.001$. *Post-hoc* tests showed statistically significant or nearly statistically significant differences between people who decided not to vote and PO (Civic Platform) ($p = 0.001$), Nowoczesna (Modern) ($p < 0.001$), people who would vote for other parties than listed in the questionnaire ($p = 0.009$), Kukiz'15 ($p = 0.003$) and Razem (Together) ($p < 0.001$);

---

[4] It is worth to notice that results regarding the statement: *Poland should introduce Internet voting as an additional form of participation in elections* are quite high: 40.91% of respondents answered "definitely yes"; 28.64% chose "rather yes"; 14.8% "hard to say"; 7.2% "rather no"; and 4.39% "definitely no". The arithmetical average for the statement is 3.98. For more results see: M. Musiał-Karg, I. Kapsa, Citizen e-Participation as an Important Factor for Sustainable Development, European Journal of Sustainable Development, vol. 8, no 4, 2019.

**Table 1.** Answers to statements with breakdown by political parties

| Political party voted for | Arithmetic average | | | | | |
| --- | --- | --- | --- | --- | --- | --- |
| | *Poland should introduce Internet voting as an additional form of participation in elections* | *I would use the possibility of Internet voting in elections* | *Internet voting promotes turnout* | *Internet voting reduces probability of error while counting votes* | *Electronic voting is much more convenient than voting in polling station* | *Internet voting increases election turnout* |
| SLD (Democratic Left Alliance) | 4,02 | 3,79 | 4,29 | 3,87 | 3,94 | 3,3 |
| KORWIN | 4,24 | 4,49 | 4,82 | 4,45 | 4,47 | 3,14 |
| Kukiz'15 | 4,25 | 4,33 | 4,72 | 4,38 | 4,56 | 3,66 |
| Nowoczesna (Modern) | 4,38 | 4,4 | 4,8 | 4,44 | 4,47 | 3,83 |
| Partia Razem (Together) | 4,52 | 4,38 | 4,83 | 4,5 | 4,41 | 2,84 |
| PO (Civic Platform) | 4,16 | 4,11 | 4,63 | 4,26 | 4,43 | 3,53 |
| PSL (Polish People's Party) | 3,82 | 3,54 | 4,29 | 3,76 | 4,18 | 3,29 |
| PIS (Law and Justice) | 3,55 | 3,46 | 4,14 | 3,85 | 3,96 | 3,48 |
| Other | 4,14 | 4,3 | 4,69 | 4,49 | 4,32 | 2,81 |
| Hard to say | 3,91 | 3,8 | 4,41 | 3,79 | 4,27 | 3,84 |
| I would not vote | 3,56 | 3,15 | 3,95 | 3,42 | 3,85 | 3,79 |

- PiS and people who would vote for other parties than listed in the questionnaire ($p < 0.001$), PO ($p < 0.001$), Kukiz'15 ($p < 0.001$), KORWIN ($p = 0.053$), Nowoczesna ($p < 0.001$) and Razem ($p < 0.001$);
- PSL (Polish People's Party) and Nowoczesna ($p = 0.009$) and Razem ($p = 0.002$)
- "hard to say" and PO ($p = 0.012$), Nowoczesna ($p = 0.001$) and Razem ($p < 0.001$).

Results are shown in Fig. 1.

2. Answers to statement *I would use the possibility of Internet voting in elections* have been examined. The Kruskal-Wallis test was statistically significant, $H(10) = 147.71$; $p < 0.001$. *Post-hoc* tests showed statistically significant differences at the level of a statistical tendency between

- people who decided not to vote and "hard to say" voters ($p = 0.014$), SLD ($p = 0.023$), PO ($p = 0.001$), Nowoczesna ($p < 0.001$), people who would vote for other parties than listed in the questionnaire ($p < 0.001$), Kukiz'15 ($p = 0.001$), KORWIN ($p < 0.001$) and Razem ($p < 0.001$);
- PSL and PO ($p < 0.001$), Nowoczesna ($p < 0.001$), people who would vote for other parties than listed in the questionnaire ($p < 0.001$), Kukiz'15 ($p = 0.001$), KORWIN ($p < 0.001$) and Razem ($p < 0.001$);
- undecided voters and people who would vote for other parties than listed in the questionnaire ($p < 0.001$), PO ($p = 0.003$), Kukiz'15 ($p = 0.002$), KORWIN ($p = 0.053$), Nowoczesna ($p < 0.001$), KORWIN ($p = 0,003$) and Razem ($p < 0.001$);
- SLD and Razem ($p = 0.064$).

Results are shown in Fig. 2.

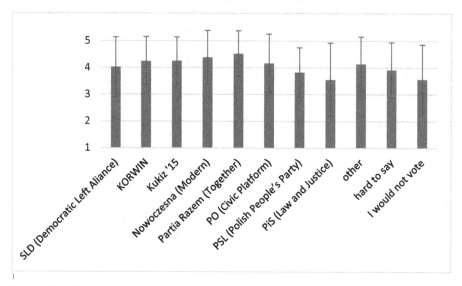

**Fig. 1.** Compliance with statement *Poland should introduce Internet voting as an additional form of participation in elections* and a decision to vote for a particular political party.

3. Then, the analysis focused on **preferred methods of voting.** The respondents answered the following question: *If you had a choice, how would you prefer to vote in elections?* In the questionnaire, they could choose one or more answers from the following list: in a polling station; electronic (over Internet); at home, with members of election committee visiting me with a portable ballot box; by correspondence; by proxy; never participate in voting; hard to say. The analysis below, indicates "yes" when an answer has been chosen and "no" when no answer is selected.

As indicated in Table 2, there were statistically significant or nearly statistically significant results for all variables examined. In the case of "I never vote" a moderate effect was recorded. However, the result was quite obvious – "I never

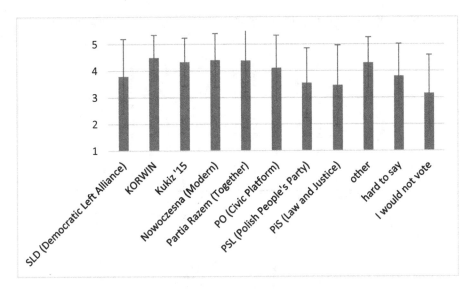

**Fig. 2.** Compliance with question *I would use the possibility of Internet voting in elections* and a decision to vote for a particular political party.

vote" was declared primarily by people who decided not to vote at the time of the survey. As regards other variables, the strength of the effect was low or very low. The largest percentage of people who declared their will to vote in the polling station supported SLD, Kukiz'15, PSL and PiS, whereas the lowest applied to people who decided not to vote. The strongest preference of electronic voting was expressed by supporters of Razem, whereas the lowest was among people who decided not to vote and supporters of PiS.

4. Next, the opinions on i-voting were examined. There were eight statements regarding benefits and risks of i-voting. Respondents indicated their opinions by choosing answers from the Likert scale. Below, we present results for four statements regarding advantages of i-voting. Firstly, the analysis focused on answers to the following statement: *Internet voting promotes turnout*.

The Kruskal-Wallis test was statistically significant, $H(10) = 147.35$; $p < 0.001$. *Post-hoc* test showed differences at the level of a statistical tendency or differences at the level of statistical tendency between:

− people who decided not to vote and undecided voters ($p = 0.035$), PO ($p < 0.001$), people who voted on other parties than those listed in the questionnaire ($p < 0.001$), Kukiz '15 ($p < 0.001$), Nowoczesna ($p < 0.001$), Razem ($p < 0.001$) and KORWIN ($p < 0.001$);

− PiS and PO ($p < 0.001$), people who voted on other parties than those listed in the questionnaire ($p < 0.001$), Kukiz '15 ($p < 0.001$), Nowoczesna ($p < 0.001$), Razem ($p < 0.001$) and KORWIN ($p < 0.001$);

− PSL and Kukiz '15 ($p = 0.077$), Nowoczesna ($p = 0.008$), Razem ($p = 0.019$) and KORWIN ($p = 0.019$);

**Table 2.** Votes cast during the survey and preferences regarding voting methods

| | In polling station | | | | Electronic (over Internet) | | | | At home, with members of election committee visiting me with portable ballot box | | | | By correspondence | | | | By proxy | | | | Never participate in voting | | | | Hard to say | | | |
| | Yes | | No | | Yes | | No | | Yes | | No | | Yes | | No | | Yes | | No | | Yes | | No | | Yes | | No | |
| | % | N | % | N | % | N | % | N | % | N | % | N | % | N | % | N | % | N | % | N | % | N | % | N | % | N | % | N |
| SLD | 86.90% | 86 | 13.10% | 13 | 65.70% | 65 | 34.30% | 34 | 9.10% | 9 | 90.90% | 90 | 10.10% | 10 | 89.90% | 89 | 2.00% | 2 | 98.00% | 97 | 0.00% | 0 | 100.00% | 99 | 4.00% | 4 | 96.00% | 95 |
| KORWIN | 70.60% | 36 | 2.40% | 15 | 80.40% | 41 | 19.60% | 10 | 5.90% | 3 | 94.10% | 48 | 9.80% | 5 | 90.20% | 46 | 7.80% | 4 | 92.20% | 47 | 0.00% | 0 | 100.00% | 51 | 2.00% | 1 | 98.00% | 50 |
| Kukiz15 | 85.00% | 108 | 15.00% | 19 | 83.50% | 106 | 16.50% | 21 | 1.60% | 2 | 98.40% | 125 | 6.30% | 8 | 93.70% | 119 | 0.80% | 1 | 99.20% | 126 | 0.00% | 0 | 100.00% | 127 | 4.70% | 6 | 95.30% | 121 |
| Nowoczesna | 71.60% | 63 | 28.40% | 25 | 81.80% | 72 | 18.20% | 16 | 6.80% | 6 | 93.20% | 82 | 9.10% | 8 | 90.90% | 80 | 4.50% | 4 | 95.50% | 84 | 1.10% | 1 | 98.90% | 87 | 3.40% | 3 | 96.60% | 85 |
| Razem | 73.40% | 47 | 26.60% | 17 | 90.60% | 58 | 9.40% | 6 | 0.00% | 0 | 100.00% | 64 | 9.40% | 6 | 90.60% | 58 | 4.70% | 3 | 95.30% | 61 | 0.00% | 0 | 100.00% | 64 | 1.60% | 1 | 98.40% | 63 |
| PO | 73.90% | 209 | 26.10% | 74 | 77.40% | 219 | 22.60% | 64 | 8.10% | 23 | 91.90% | 260 | 6.70% | 19 | 93.30% | 264 | 2.50% | 7 | 97.50% | 276 | 0.00% | 0 | 100.00% | 283 | 5.30% | 15 | 94.70% | 268 |
| PSL | 87.80% | 43 | 12.20% | 6 | 49.00% | 24 | 51.00% | 25 | 14.30% | 7 | 85.70% | 42 | 20.40% | 10 | 79.60% | 39 | 4.10% | 2 | 95.90% | 47 | 0.00% | 0 | 100.00% | 49 | 10.20% | 5 | 89.80% | 44 |
| PiS | 86.10% | 254 | 13.90% | 41 | 58.30% | 172 | 41.70% | 123 | 14.20% | 42 | 85.80% | 253 | 7.10% | 21 | 92.90% | 274 | 6.10% | 18 | 93.90% | 277 | 0.70% | 2 | 99.30% | 293 | 9.20% | 27 | 90.80% | 268 |
| Other | 74.20% | 161 | 25.80% | 56 | 81.10% | 176 | 18.90% | 41 | 2.30% | 5 | 97.70% | 212 | 8.80% | 19 | 91.20% | 198 | 0.90% | 2 | 99.10% | 215 | 0.90% | 2 | 99.10% | 215 | 5.10% | 11 | 94.90% | 206 |
| Hard to say | 83.10% | 286 | 16.90% | 58 | 73.80% | 254 | 26.20% | 90 | 5.80% | 20 | 94.20% | 324 | 5.80% | 20 | 94.20% | 324 | 3.50% | 12 | 96.50% | 332 | 1.70% | 6 | 98.30% | 338 | 8.40% | 29 | 91.60% | 315 |
| I would not vote | 62.90% | 61 | 37.10% | 36 | 47.40% | 46 | 52.60% | 51 | 6.20% | 6 | 93.80% | 91 | 11.30% | 11 | 88.70% | 86 | 6.20% | 6 | 93.80% | 91 | 19.60% | 19 | 80.40% | 78 | 15.50% | 15 | 84.50% | 82 |
| | $V=0.17$ | $p<0.001$ | $\chi^2(10)=$ 50.27 | | $V=0.25$ | $p<0.001$ | $\chi^2(10)=$ 110.06 | | $V=0.17$ | $p<0.001$ | $\chi^2(10)=$ 46.64 | | $V=0.10$ | $p=0.082$ | $\chi^2(10)=$ 16.71 | | $V=0.11$ | $p=0.015$ | Exact Fisher Test | | $V=0.34$ | $p<0.001$ | Exact Fisher Test | | $V=0.13$ | $p=0.003$ | $\chi^2(10)=$ 26.64 | |

Source: own conclusions based on survey findings.

- SLD and PO ($p = 0.084$), people who voted on other parties than those listed in the questionnaire ($p = 0.096$), Kukiz '15 ($p = 0.054$), Nowoczesna ($p = 0.004$), Razem ($p = 0.015$) and KORWIN ($p = 0.017$);
- undecided voters and PO ($p < 0.001$), people who voted on other parties than those listed in the questionnaire ($p = 0.001$), Kukiz '15 ($p = 0.002$), Nowoczesna ($p < 0.004$), Razem ($p = 0.001$) and KORWIN ($p = 0.002$).

Results are shown in Fig. 3.

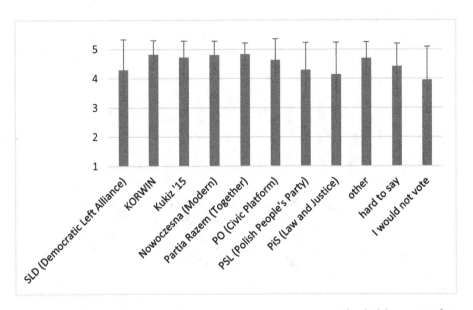

**Fig. 3.** Compliance with question *Internet voting promotes turnout* and a decision to vote for a particular political party.

In the next step, the analysis covered answers to ***Internet voting reduces probability of error while counting votes*** and ***Precision of internet voting is much larger than in the case of manual counting***.

The Kruskal-Wallis test was statistically significant, $H(10) = 173.13$; $p < 0.001$. *Post-hoc* tests showed differences at the level of statistical tendencies or differences at the level of a statistical tendency between:

- people who decided not to vote and PiS ($p = 0.043$), PO ($p < 0.001$), people who voted on other parties than those listed in the questionnaire ($p < 0.001$), Kukiz '15 ($p < 0.001$), Nowoczesna ($p < 0.001$), Razem ($p < 0.001$) and KORWIN ($p < 0.001$);
- undecided voters and PO ($p < 0.001$), people who voted on other parties than those listed in the questionnaire ($p < 0.001$), Kukiz '15 ($p < 0.001$), Nowoczesna ($p < 0.001$), Razem ($p < 0.001$) and KORWIN ($p < 0.001$);

- PSL and PO ($p = 0.086$), people who voted on other parties than those listed in the questionnaire ($p = 0.001$), Kukiz '15 ($p = 0.045$), Nowoczesna ($p = 0.008$), Razem ($p = 0.007$) and KORWIN ($p = 0.030$);
- PiS and PO ($p < 0.001$), people who voted on other parties than those listed in the questionnaire ($p < 0.001$), Kukiz '15 ($p = 0.001$), Nowoczesna ($p < 0.001$), Razem ($p < 0.001$) and KORWIN ($p = 0.005$);
- SLD and people who voted on other parties than those listed in the questionnaire ($p < 0.001$), Kukiz '15 ($p = 0.074$), Nowoczesna ($p = 0.012$), Razem ($p = 0.012$) and KORWIN ($p = 0.065$).

Results shown in Fig. 4.

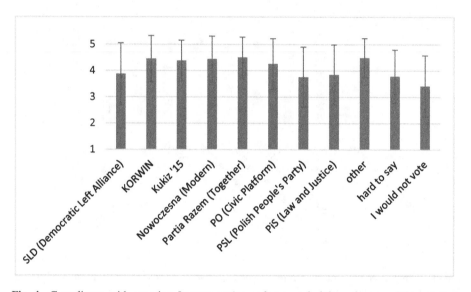

**Fig. 4.** Compliance with question *Internet voting reduces probability of error while counting votes. Precision of internet voting is much larger than in the case of manual counting* and a decision to vote for a particular political party.

Then, the analysis focused on answers to ***Electronic voting is much more convenient than voting in polling station***.

The Kruskal-Wallis test was statistically significant, $H(10) = 76.00$; $p < 0.001$. *Post-hoc* tests showed differences at the level of statistical tendencies or differences in statistical tendencies between:

- people who decided not to vote and undecided voters ($p = 0.026$), PO ($p < 0.001$), people who voted on other parties than those listed in the questionnaire ($p = 0.008$), Kukiz '15 ($p < 0.001$), Nowoczesna ($p = 0.001$), Razem ($p = 0.011$) and KORWIN ($p = 0.006$);

- PiS and undecided voters ($p = 0.093$), PO ($p < 0.001$), people who voted on other parties than those listed in the questionnaire ($p = 0.028$), Kukiz '15 ($p < 0.001$), Nowoczesna ($p = 0.006$), Razem ($p = 0.069$) and KORWIN ($p = 0.035$);
- SLD and PO ($p = 0.011$) and Kukiz '15 ($p = 0.003$).

Results are shown in Fig. 5.

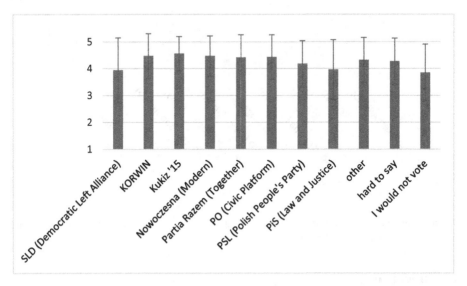

**Fig. 5.** Compliance with question *Electronic voting is much more convenient than voting in polling station* and a decision to vote for a particular political party.

Next, answers to **Internet voting increases election turnout** were examined.

The Kruskal-Wallis test was statistically significant, $H(10) = 126,06$; $p < 0,001$. Post-hoc tests showed statistically significant or nearly statistically significant differences between:

- people supporting other parties than listed in the questionnaire, who declared that they would not vote for any party ($p < 0.001$), undecided voters ($p < 0.001$), Nowoczesna ($p < 0.001$), PiS ($p < 0.001$), Kukiz '15 ($p < 0.001$) and PO ($p < 0.001$);
- Razem and people who declared that they would not vote for any party ($p = 0.001$), undecided voters ($p < 0.001$), Nowoczesna ($p < 0.001$), PiS ($p = 0.039$), Kukiz '15 ($p = 0.001$) and PO ($p = 0.009$);
- KORWIN and Nowoczesna ($p = 0,038$) and undecided voters ($p = 0.016$);
- SLD and Nowoczesna ($p = 0.008$) and undecided voters ($p = 0.048$);
- PiS and undecided voters ($p = 0.022$).

Results are shown in Fig. 6.

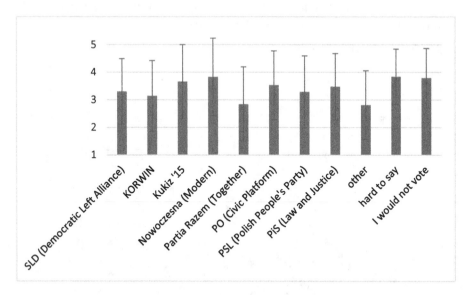

**Fig. 6.** Compliance with question *Internet voting increases election turnout* and a decision to vote for a particular political party.

## 4 Conclusions

The relationship between political preferences and support for e-voting in Poland is a considerably new and not yet explored research area. It is most certainly the result of the fact that from the legal and infrastructure points of view, Poland is not ready to implement such voting procedures.

For several years, together with rapid development of new technologies and experience of other countries, such as Estonia and Switzerland, we have observed an increasingly heated debate on e-voting and growing popularity of the idea. The analyses presented in the article, based on the data from the 2018 survey implemented in Poland, lead to the following conclusions. Poles declare that Poland should introduce Internet voting as an additional form of participation in elections and they would use the possibility of i-voting (median in both statements was 4 in scale 1–5). In their opinion, Internet voting promotes turnout (arithmetic average was 4.47), it is much more convenient than the voting in a polling station (arithmetic average 4.25) and it reduces probability of an error while counting votes (arithmetic average 4.07). As regards benefits of i-voting they rated "Internet voting increases election turnout" the lowest (arithmetic average of 3.47) which may reflect their realistic opinion. The i-voting practice is not popular, and we do not observe an increase of turnout due to the introduction of this voting method. Therefore, the more realistic approach they show to i-voting, the more optimistic is their high assessment of the benefits of this form of voting.

While examining the research question: if the voter's opinion on e-voting converged with the opinion of political parties for which they vote, we assume that there is a relationship between the political variable such as the preference and opinions on the use of modern forms of voting. The empirical study enabled to verify hypothesis no 1. Descriptive statistics, resented in the article, indicate that the lowest level of support for i-voting is typical for PiS (Law and Justice) voters. This is the only political party in Poland that has expressed their objection to e-voting. The situation is not so obvious with the highest scores. The analysis of opinions on i-voting shows that the highest results are achieved in the group of Razem (Together) and KORWIN (promoting e-voting), whereas the highest score was achieved by Kukiz'15 voters (party which also promotes e-voting). They had quite high scores also in the other statements, so it converges with the political proposition of the party. In the case of PO (Civic Platform) voters, we do not observe such positive opinions on i-voting, but it is worth to notice that they always scored higher than the population average. Similar conclusions can be drawn from the analysis of preferred methods of voting. The lowest preference of electronic voting was expressed by people who decided not to vote and supporters of PiS, whereas the strongest was among supporters of Razem (Kukiz voters scored second highest result; however, PO's sore was fifth).

The analysis above supports hypothesis no. 2: the political preferences are a statistically significant predicator for voters' attitudes towards the introduction and use of voting over the Internet. According to the survey, opinions among voters are convergent with their support to political parties. Results of the statistical analysis lead to a general conclusion that political preferences are a statistically significant predicator for voters' attitudes towards the introduction and use of voting over the Internet. Supporters of parties promoting the introduction of online voting are reserved in declaring their support to such solutions, since they recognize certain threats to a lager extent that supporters of other political parties.

# References

1. Friedland, L.A.: Electronic democracy and the new citizenship. Media Cult. Soc. **18**(2), 185–212 (1996)
2. Hagen, M.: A Typology of Electronic Democracy (1997). http://martin-hagen.net/publikationen/elektronische-demokratie/typology-of-electronic-democracy/
3. Hague, B.N., Loader, B.: Digital Democracy: Discourse and Decision-Making in the Information Age. Psychology Press, New York (1999)
4. Becker, T.: Governance and electronic innovation: a clash of paradigms. Inf. Commun. Soc. **1**(3), 339–343 (1998)
5. Krimmer, R.: The Evolution of E-voting: Why Voting Technology is Used and How it Affects Democracy. Tallinn University of Technology, TUT Press, Tallinn (2012)
6. Kersting, N.: Online participation: from'invited'to'invented'spaces. Int. J. Electron. Govern. **6**(4), 270–280 (2013)
7. Nowina-Konopka, M.: Elektroniczna urna. http://www.rpo.gov.pl/pliki/12066058070.pdf
8. The I's Have It. http://www.everyonecounts.com/index.php/

9. Goodman, N., Pammett, J.H., DeBardeleben, J., Freeland, J.: A Comparative Assessment of Electronic Voting, Strategic Knowledge Cluster Canada-Europe Transatlantic Dialogue, Carlton University, p. 3, February 2010. http://www.carleton.ca/europecluster/events/2010-01-26-InternetVotingMaterials/AComparativeAssessmentofInternetVotingFINALFeb19-a.pdf
10. Estonian National Electoral Committee
11. A Comparative Assessment of Electronic Voting. http://www.elections.ca/content.aspx?section=res&dir=rec/tech/ivote/comp&document=description&lang=e#fg1
12. Dlaczego w Polsce wciąż nie głosujemy przez internet? https://www.forbes.pl/technologie/glosowanie-przez-internet-w-polsce/egw4rj1. Accessed 2 Nov 2018
13. Wybory samorządowe 2014: awaria systemu informatycznego. https://wiadomosci.onet.pl/kraj/wybory-samorzadowe-2014-awaria-systemu-informatycznego/3n764. Accessed 17 Nov 2018
14. Musiał-Karg, M.: Electronic voting as an additional method of participating in elections. opinions of poles. In: Krimmer, R., et al. (eds.) E-Vote-ID 2016. LNCS, vol. 10141, pp. 218–232. Springer, Cham (2017). https://doi.org/10.1007/978-3-319-52240-1_14
15. Pozwólmy Obywatelom głosować przez internet! http://ruchkukiza.pl/pozwolmy-obywatelom-glosowac-internet/. Accessed 30 Aug 2017
16. Popieram wprowadzenie e-voting! https://www.facebook.com/watch/?v=566177850548239
17. J. Kaczyński: głosowanie to coś więcej niż kliknięcie, 12.03.2008, WPROST, https://www.wprost.pl/125517/J-Kaczynski-glosowanie-to-cos-wiecej-niz-klikniecie
18. E-głosowanie w referendum? "Prezydent nie wykluczył". https://www.tvn24.pl/wiadomosci-z-kraju,3/spotkanie-kukiza-z-prezydentem-duda-ws-referendum-konstytucyjnego,748291.html. Accessed 17 June 2017

# A Revised Forensic Process for Aligning the Investigation Process with the Design of Forensic-Enabled Cloud Services

Stavros Simou[1](✉), Christos Kalloniatis[1], Stefanos Gritzalis[2], and Vasilis Katos[3]

[1] Privacy Engineering and Social Informatics Laboratory,
Department of Cultural Technology and Communication,
University of the Aegean, University Hill, 81100 Mytilene, Greece
ssimou@aegean.gr
[2] Laboratory of Systems Security, Department of Digital Systems,
University of Piraeus, 18534 Piraeus, Greece
[3] Department of Computing and Informatics, Bournemouth University,
Poole House, Fern Barrow, Bournemouth BH12 5BB, UK

**Abstract.** The design and implementation of cloud services, without taking under consideration the forensic requirements and the investigation process, makes the acquisition and examination of data, complex and demanding. The evidence gathered from the cloud may not become acceptable and admissible in the court. A literature gap in supporting software engineers so as to elicit and model forensic-related requirements exists. In order to fill the gap, software engineers should develop cloud services in a forensically sound manner. In this paper, a brief description of the cloud forensic-enabled framework is presented (adding some new elements) so as to understand the role of the design of forensic-enabled cloud services in a cloud forensic investigation. A validation of the forensic requirements is also produced by aligning the stages of cloud forensic investigation process with the framework's forensic requirements. In this way, on one hand, a strong relationship is built between these two elements and emphasis is given to the role of the forensic requirements and their necessity in supporting the investigation process. On the other hand, the alignment assists towards the identification of the degree of the forensic readiness of a cloud service against a forensic investigation.

**Keywords:** Cloud forensics · Forensic requirements · Cloud forensic investigation process · Forensic readiness · Forensic constraints

## 1 Introduction

Since the early days of Cloud Forensics discipline, introduced by Ruan [1], both software engineers and investigators have put a lot of effort to identify the issues of the new discipline and find appropriate solutions. There are many issues associated with legal matters, multi-tenancy, flexibility of deleting instances, data replication, location transparency and dependence on Cloud Service Providers (CSPs) that are unique to

© Springer Nature Switzerland AG 2020
S. Katsikas and V. Zorkadis (Eds.): e-Democracy 2019, CCIS 1111, pp. 161–177, 2020.
https://doi.org/10.1007/978-3-030-37545-4_11

cloud forensics and makes the investigation even more complex than in the traditional environments [1–5]. Investigators' main objective is to conduct an investigation in the cloud in a forensically sound manner and present evidence that can be admissible in a court of law. In order to achieve these goals, investigators should be able to rely both on cloud services that are designed and implemented by software engineers and on the investigation process. Therefore, a strong cooperation between software engineers and investigators is necessary. Software engineers should be able to design and implement forensic-enabled cloud services so as to assist investigators in case of an incident.

Thus, the aim of the specific paper is to examine how the design and implementation of a service can assist investigators in a cloud forensic investigation. Cloud Service Providers are responsible for providing cloud services to consumers. According to a report, 96% of small, medium business and enterprises are using cloud services [6]. A cloud incident may exploit possible vulnerabilities of the cloud services and gain access or harm sensible data. Hence, the cloud service concept plays an important role in a cloud forensic investigation. A great challenge for software engineers is to identify the forensic requirements and design cloud services in a forensically sound manner. To accomplish this, they need to understand the cloud forensic investigation process and how it is conducted.

NAS report (page 181) states that "some agencies still treat the examination of digital evidence as an investigative rather than a forensic activity" [7]. The proposed framework introduced in a way to eliminate the burden of an investigation. It introduces the activities to implement a service so as in case of an incident the outcome of the investigation should be in accordance to the forensic guidelines and principles. All the incidents should be investigated either forensically or not. In this paper the proposed framework achieves the first.

Within this work, an alignment of the design of cloud forensic-enabled services is introduced after an explanation of the forensic requirements, in order first to describe how cloud services can become forensic-enabled and second to understand the role of the design of forensic-enabled cloud services in a cloud forensic investigation. The paper also extends our previous work [8] in the direction of adding a new stage in the process that software engineers may follow for eliciting, modeling, implementing and validating forensic requirements in cloud services. The proposed process is at high level thus, it can be applied in any digital forensic with appropriate adjustments.

The rest of the paper is organized as follows. Section 2 presents the work that has been done so far in relation to cloud forensic investigation and the different processes or models introduced by researchers. Section 3 presents a cloud forensic analysis consisting of the cloud forensic high level requirements that a service need to include in its design and implementation stages as well as the framework for reasoning about cloud forensics so as to make the specific cloud service forensic-enabled. Section 4 aligns the different stages of the cloud investigation process with the forensic constraints in order to validate the forensic requirements. Section 4.1 presents a validation approach of the work, while Sect. 5 concludes the paper by raising future research on this innovative research field.

## 2 Cloud Forensic Investigation

One of the most important aspect of implementing a cloud forensic-enabled service is to actually understand how a cloud investigation is conducted. Therefore, a research had to be made in order to design the cloud investigation process. Cloud forensics introduces processes for resolving incidents occurring in cloud computing environments. However, designing cloud services capable to assist a cloud investigation process is of vital importance and various research efforts concentrate on these directions [8, 9]. In addition, digital forensics methods cannot support an investigation in cloud environments since the particular environments introduce many differences compared to traditional IT environments [1, 10].

### 2.1  Related Work

In the past years, a number of researchers introduced methodologies and frameworks in relation to the cloud investigation process. In 2012, Martini et al. [11] proposed the Integrated Conceptual Digital Forensic Framework for Cloud Computing, which is based on McKemmish [12] and Scarfone et al. [13]. The framework emphasizes on the differences in the preservation of forensic data and the collection of cloud computing data for forensic purposes. It includes four stages, identification and preservation, collection, examination and analysis, and reporting and presentation. According to Agarwal et al. [14], the iteration of the framework demonstrates one of the key differences in the identification and analysis of evidence sources.

The same year Ruan et al. [15] presented the Cloud Forensic Maturity Model (CFMM). It is a reference model for evaluating and improving cloud forensic maturity. The model is composed of a Cloud Forensic Investigative Architecture (CFIA) and a Cloud Forensic Capability Matrix (CFCM). The CFIA introduces four main sections: pre-investigative readiness, core-forensic process, supportive processes and investigative interfaces. The CFCM is a capability maturity model that consists of six maturity levels. The model is a step forward towards an acceptable solution for cloud forensic investigation.

In 2015, Open Cloud Forensics (OCF) model was introduced by Zawoad et al. [16]. It proposes a cloud forensic process, which consists of the preservation stage, which runs throughout the process and the stages of identification, collection, organization, presentation and verification. Examination and analysis is included in the organization stage. During the verification stage, the court authority verifies the cloud-based evidence provided by the investigators. Considering the important role of CSPs, the proposed model can support reliable forensics in a realistic scenario. As stated by the authors, cloud architects can use the model to design clouds that support trustworthy cloud forensics investigations.

There are also some other proposed models concerning cloud forensics such as Adams et al. [17] and Guo et al. [18] but there are limitations mostly in relation to the later stages. Both models do not include any actions or stages after the evidence collection and acquisition. Therefore, the stages of examination, analysis and presentation are out of the scope of the researchers.

## 2.2    Proposed Cloud Forensic Investigation Process

Simou et al. [9] presented a comparison framework to merge same or similar stages of the previous proposed frameworks and models that produce the same outcome into one stage. The comparison framework consists of the following four sequential stages: identification, preservation-collection, examination-analysis, and presentation and two concurrent stages, the chain of custody and documentation. Authors stated that the preservation stage should also run concurrently with the other two stages or should be included in the chain of custody. Based on the comparison framework and the literature review conducted in [10], Simou et al. [9] proposed a generic process for cloud-forensic investigation including the steps of Incident Confirmation, Incident Identification, Collection-Acquisition, Examination-Analysis, and Presentation. They were stating that understanding the cloud forensic investigation process is of vital importance in order to design and implement cloud forensic-enabled services. The proposed process is illustrated in Fig. 1.

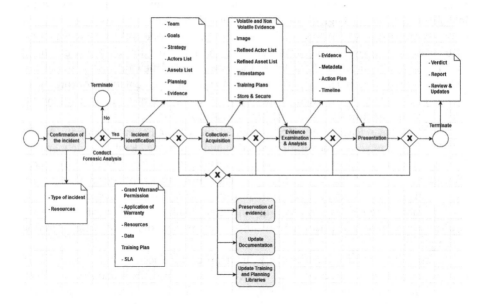

**Fig. 1.** Process for cloud forensic investigation.

Beside the five sequential steps presented in Fig. 1 there are three more steps running throughout the investigation process. They are parallel activities/steps running concurrently with the four steps after the confirmation of the incident. These are: preservation of evidence, documentation, and training and planning.

Even though incident confirmation is not an actual step of the investigation process, it has to be included since it is the stage where the administrator of the Information Technology (IT) department and the stakeholders come together to decide whether the cloud investigation will start or not, depending on the type and the nature of the incident. It also depends on the organization's available resources. During the incident identification stage, all relevant assets (software, hardware and data) that may contain potential evidence should be identified.

In the collection-acquisition stage, the main goal is to obtain the data and the potential evidence in a forensically sound manner. The acquired assets should be securely stored for further analysis. The examination and analysis stage includes the data extraction from the previous stage and the process to analyse the results in order to find any useful evidence. Finally, in the presentation stage experts should be prepared to confront the jury who lacks knowledge of cloud computing and try to present the evidence collected in a language that anyone can understand. The outcome of a trial depends on the weight of the evidence (how concrete they are).

The three concurrent stages are needed in the investigation process since they are the most important and crucial parts of the process. If the evidence are not preserved, anyone from the opposite side can challenge them. The same applies for the documentation since the chain of custody will not be maintained. As far as the training and planning stage concerns, it prepares and ensures that personnel, operations and infrastructures are able to support an investigation.

## 3 Cloud Forensic Analysis

Since cloud forensics is relative newly developed research area, our main and primary focus was to conduct a thorough analysis of the respective literature in order to identify and present a set of forensic constraints that can be the first step towards the creation of a set of forensic requirements. A reason of this analysis is to examine how the forensic constraints involve in the investigation process.

In [19, 20] a thorough literature review was conducted based on the most cited papers presented in respective scientific journals, conferences, books and industrial reports. Based on the specific analysis, the cloud characteristics, and forensic properties, a set of forensic constraints were proposed and presented in [8]. The findings of this analysis constitute an initial but robust set of constraints that designers and software engineers need to consider when designing information systems or individual services in the cloud.

### 3.1 Cloud Forensic High Level Requirements

Frameworks, models and methodologies in cloud forensics, identify the necessary steps, methods, concepts or activities and produce useful information. This information can be used to specific cases to explain and resolve these cases. Beside the methodologies and models, the forensic requirements need to be clarified to specify capabilities and functions that a cloud service must be able to perform. The identified forensic requirements introduced as forensic constraints since their implementation forces the mandatory use of specific technologies in addition to the existing functionality of the services, to eliminate the existing gap in the cloud environments. Forensic constraints are requirements related to system forensicability (the term forensicability is used as a service that can be forensic-enabled; can be developed in a forensically sound manner) and specify a service's quality attributes. The seven identified forensic constraints are listed as follow.

*Internal disciplinary procedure:* process through which a CSP or a third party deals with its employees in order to ensure that they follow certain norms of discipline.

*Accountability:* CSP's obligation to protect and use consumer's data with responsibility for its actions and liability in case of an issue.

*Transparency:* condition where an entity can have full access to manage and control its own data at any given time and allow feedback from the entities that accommodate it.

*Legal matters (Regulatory):* procedures and actions that need to be undertaken related to jurisdiction issues, international law, contractual terms, legislative frameworks and constitutional issues.

*Access rights (Policies)* is the permissions that are assigned by an administrator to grand users and applications access to specific operations. Security (data protection) mechanisms for authentication, authorization, access controls, and auditing are parts of this concept.

*Isolation* is the mechanism to ensure that each consumers' data is sealed and cannot be seen by other tenants.

*Traceability* is the ability, for the data to be traced or not by the user [21] and the capability of keeping track of the actions taken at any given point. It also refers to the ability to trace the activities of a consumer in order to lead to him/her.

### 3.2   Framework for Reasoning About Cloud Forensics

It is indeed true that designing cloud services capable of assisting investigators to solve an incident is a huge challenge. A thorough analysis of the respective literature revealed that there is a literature gap in supporting software engineers so as to identify forensic-related requirements for information systems [10]. Thus, to fill the aforementioned gap, a presentation of a requirements engineering framework is introduced in [8], to support software engineers in the elicitation of forensic requirements and the design of forensic-enabled cloud services. The framework supports cloud services by implementing a number of steps to make the services cloud forensic-enabled. It consists of a set of cloud forensic feature diagrams (one for each forensic constraint), a modelling language expressed through a conceptual meta-model and a process based on the concepts identified and presented in the meta-model.

**Feature Diagrams.** The initial step of our research framework was the design of a set of feature diagrams based on the identified forensic constraints. For every proposed forensic constraint a feature diagram has been introduced for expressing the basic tasks that need to be realized. These diagrams are used to describe the necessary tasks a cloud provider need to consider in order to make a cloud service forensic-enabled. Each feature diagram consists of a set of tasks/nodes that implement a specific forensic constraint. A detailed description of all the feature diagrams and their tasks has been presented in [8]. Also, in Sect. 4, a table (Table 1) is introduced illustrating the different tasks for each forensic constraint. To understand how the feature diagrams of the seven forensic constraints work, one of them, the internal disciplinary procedures feature diagram is illustrated in Fig. 2 and explained as follow.

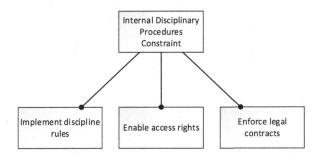

**Fig. 2.** Internal disciplinary procedures feature diagram

The feature diagram for internal disciplinary procedures constraint presents the tasks that need to be fulfilled to ensure that the constraint is successfully implemented. Cloud providers should implement discipline rules and in case of any deviations, CSP should be able to discipline the responsible party without harming its interests. Access rights, both physical and digital should be categorized and their allowance should be granted accordingly. Contracts between the CSP and its personnel should be signed, stating all the details about misuse of information and the penalties. In the case that one or more of the previous tasks have not been fulfilled, the provider should seek or implement techniques that resolve the issue. The same applies for all the constraints listed in the paper. The rest of the feature diagrams have been illustrated and can be viewed in [8].

In order for a cloud service to be characterized as forensic-enabled, all the afore-mentioned seven cloud forensic constraints should be realized at the same time. The implementation of a service consists of numerous actions that need to be carefully examined to prevent malicious activities. These actions can be implemented using one or more forensic constraints. In the case that a forensic constraint is not satisfied, the investigation does not meet the forensic requirements and cannot be characterized as 100% satisfactory.

**Meta-model.** The second step of the framework was to propose a common modelling language in order to support the elicitation and modelling of the aforementioned forensic constraints. The modelling language is presented in terms of a meta-model, based on the concepts and the forensic constraints identified for designing a cloud forensic-enabled system [8]. Figure 3 presents the meta-model, which consists both the concepts of making a system or a service forensic-enabled and the concepts that form a cloud forensic investigation process. The two groups of concepts are separated with each other with the dotted lines. The one inside the dotted lines is the investigation process group, while the other outside of the lines is the forensic-enabled group. All relationships among critical components are illustrated in Fig. 3.

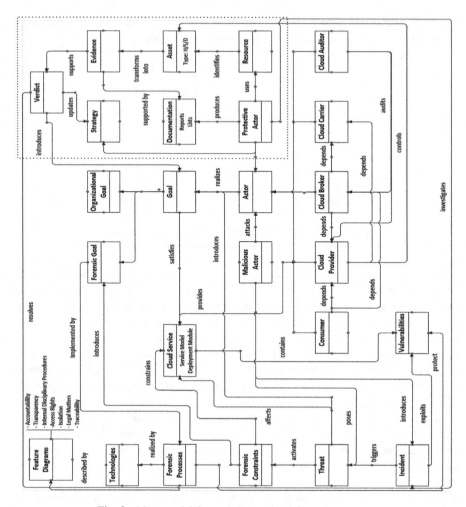

**Fig. 3.** Meta-model for assisting a cloud forensic process

**Framework Process.** The last step to the completion of the framework was the development of a process based on the concepts identified and presented in the meta-model. The process provides the necessary steps towards the design of a cloud forensic-enabled service, based on the potential vulnerabilities of the service and the systematic analysis of forensic requirements.

On one hand, it assists in the identification of the organizational strategy and needs and on the other, it analyses in depth the various organizational cloud services in order to provide the necessary requirements for well-structured cloud forensic-enabled services. The revised process consists of four main stages: Organizational Analysis, Cloud Forensic Requirements Analysis, Evaluation-Assessment and Forensic Investigation Validation. The first three stages have been introduced and explained in [8], while the fourth one will be presented and detailed described in Sect. 4 of this paper. Figure 4 illustrates the stages and sub-stages of the process.

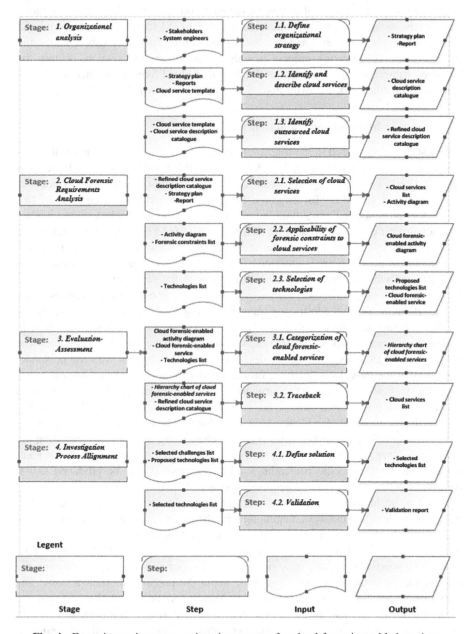

**Fig. 4.** Forensic requirements engineering process for cloud forensic-enabled services

# 4    Cloud Forensic Requirements and Their Support in the Investigation Process

In order to align the design of forensic-enabled cloud services with the investigation process, the seven forensic constraints introduced in [8] have been considered and used. The forensic constraints and their tasks need to fulfil specific stages or inputs and outputs of the investigation process in order to assist the investigators. Within the following paragraphs, an alignment of the design of cloud forensic-enabled services is introduced together with the extension of our previous work [8].

## 4.1    Forensic Investigation Validation

A new stage is introduced in the forensic requirements engineering process that has to deal with the validation of the selected forensic enabled services against the investigation process. This new stage is placed at the end of the process after the "Evaluation-Assessment". It is called "Investigation Process Alignment" and it consists of two steps: "Define Solutions" and "Validation". In order to assist the investigators when conducting an investigation following the process described in Sect. 4.1, an analysis of the seven forensic constraints and the identification of their relation to the proposed forensic investigation stages is presented. This has to be explained and understood, so as to proceed with the description of the two steps of the new stage.

The first forensic constraint, the internal disciplinary procedures contributes to the investigation process in the following ways. Enforcing legal contracts task assists to the incident identification stage with the use of the SLAs. All the contracts should be read in order to prepare the line of defence and the strategy. On the other hand, the team that will be formed to investigate the incident will be in co-operation with the personnel who work in the provider's facilities. Implement discipline rules should be realized at the same stage so as to exclude the providers' personnel, especially those who work in the investigation team and handle the evidence. The access right of the constraint realizes the preservation of evidence stage. Only the personnel that has the proper rights can access specific parts of the infrastructures, eliminating the danger of handling the evidence by unwanted users, aiming to narrow access immediately when an incident occurs. Due to the specific constraint a refined actors list will be produced that it contributes to the collection and acquisition stage.

Both the accountability and transparency constraints contributes to the investigation process in three different stages, beginning with the evidence examination and analysis stage. With the use of special tools, the examination of data takes place. Metadata and evidence are produced concerning the actions of a specific person or different persons. This information will be used in a court, so the provider and the people accessing the data should be transparent and accountable about the process and their actions. The next two stages are the preservation of evidence and documentation. During the investigation, all data and potential evidence should be preserved in order to maintain the chain of custody. At the same time, personnel actions, assets used and resources provided should be clear documented, so no one can challenge the outcome of the process. In order the investigator's team working on the incident to succeed on this, they should be transparent and accountable for their actions at all times. Besides the above contribution, the accountability constraint also assists to confirmation of the incident by providing attributability. In other words, to reveal the system element or the actor, responsible for a deviation from the expected behavior. On the other hand, the task monitor action is realized in the incident identification stage by monitoring all the actions of the team.

As far as the legal matters constraint is concerned, it assists a wider range of stages in the investigation process. In particular, it realizes the incident identification stage with two of its tasks, the SLAs and jurisdiction. From the SLAs point of view, all contracts and agreements should be read and reviewed to understand all the legal and technical aspects - rights and obligations. This will help to determine the strategy the investigators will take to fulfil the goals. From the jurisdiction point of view, depending on the contracts, application of warranty should be produced to grant permissions to different stages of the investigation. The next stage that the specific constraint is applied to is the preservation of evidence with the maintained trained personnel task. The organization's persons that will assist in the investigation need to be trained in laws and legislations in relation to the Information Technology. By providing the appropriate trained personnel, the constraint fulfils the concurrent stage, training and planning of the investigation process, at the same time. This is because the personnel will be trained to be able to manage any issues that arise and update strategy and plans in accordance. Another point is that the preservation of evidence is exclusively related to legal matters due to the legal frameworks. There are specific rules, policies and regulations on how to preserve the evidence and what processes should be followed. The last stage that the legal matters constraint is applied to is in the presentation. It provides the testimony and the documentation of the evidence. In order for a cloud service to be forensic-enabled, investigators should take under consideration all the legal aspects and present them in a court.

The forensic constraint of access rights is very important in the evidence examination and analysis stage. Depending on the access rights given to the consumers, investigators can put the bits and pieces stored in the log files together. Log files include timestamps with the users' movements, date and time of all authentication and authorization access to the cloud services and accessed files. During the examination of logs, a timeline with the reconstruction of events of the incident can be produced and metadata can be provided. However, access rights constraint also assists to the preservation of evidence stage. It provides the documentation of how the evidence were identified, collected and acquired by investigators, providers and external users, during the investigation process.

The isolation constraint besides the ability of separating the users with one another, reflecting the difficulty of the perpetrator to contaminate the rest of the consumers, also assists to the cloud forensic investigation process in the following way. During the collection and acquisition stage, it provides confidentiality and privacy to the consumers sharing the same resources by not allowing access to their sensitive data since they are isolated from the rest of the users. In that way, people responsible for collecting potential evidence can move forward without worrying about privacy violation.

Finally, the traceability constraint fits into the investigation process in two different stages. On one hand, at the confirmation of the incident, where the detection of the incident occurs by different sources such as personnel, detection systems, etc. Monitoring users' activities and data logs (two of the tasks of the traceability constraint) can allow systems to capture an incident by detecting any malfunctions or abnormal activities. After the detection, it is up to the organization will to decide whether the incident imposes an immediate threat or not. On the other hand, all four tasks of the traceability constraint can fulfil the examination and analysis stage. Since data is monitored and recorded in log files, investigators can search for these log files during the examination stage and find evidence such as timestamps, metadata or any other information. Log files are also responsible for providing correct timelines and reconstruction of the events, as a result to link users with their data. Besides the two main stages, traceability assists also in the concurrent activities of preservation of evidence and documentation. By storing and securing the log files in restricted areas and taking back-up on a daily basis, investigators can be almost certain that the chain of custody can be preserved and the integrity of the evidence will be maintained at all times. Reports and lists can be also produced from the log files in order to proper document the investigation process.

Now that the seven forensic constraints have been presented in relation to the proposed forensic investigation stages, it is clear their contribution to the investigation process. Thus, the next step is a detailed description of the two steps of the last stage of the proposed process in order to understand its importance.

**Define Solutions.** This step of the process concerns the selection of the solutions. In stage 2 of the framework process, a selection of the technologies for the implementation of forensic constraints took place based on specific criteria. A number of different technologies/solutions have been presented for each task that fulfills the implementation of the constraint. At this point, software engineers should choose the most appropriate solution out of the selected ones that fits into their organization. The selected solution for each forensic constraint will be summarized in the cloud service template [8] introduced in the first stage of the process.

Table 1 presents the seven forensic constraints and their tasks in relation to the cloud investigation process and the stage or stages they apply to. It specifies which task of the constraint fulfils and fits to a specific stage or stages of the process. The first two columns illustrate the forensic constraints and their tasks. The third column illustrates the different stages of the investigation that the constraint/tasks fulfils, while the last one, presents the existing solutions for the specific challenge of the forensic constraint's task. Observing Table 1 someone can notice that all seven forensic constraints contribute to the cloud forensic investigation process. All the stages of the process are aligned to the seven constraints. This validates that the proposed seven forensic constraints interfere/influence the cloud forensic investigation and they take under consideration the investigation process.

**Validation.** The last step of the framework process is the validation where software engineers validate the selected solution against the investigation process based on the input of Table 1. The selected solution is tested using a scenario in order to investigate if it is capable to overcome the problems. An incident is initiated and software engineers follow all the investigation process steps in a forensically sound manner to validate the technology/solution chosen and the framework itself.

**Table 1.** Forensic requirements contribution to cloud investigation process

| Constraint | Task | Fulfillment | Indicative solutions |
|---|---|---|---|
| Internal disciplinary procedures | Implement discipline rules | Incident identification – Collection and acquisition | Define SLA parameters and objectives - Robust SLAs |
| | Enable access rights | Preservation of evidence – Collection and acquisition | Organizational policies and SLAs |
| | Enforce legal contracts | Incident identification – Collection and acquisition | Well and clear-written terms - Robust SLAs |
| Accountability | Ensure agreements | Incident identification – Evidence examination & analysis – Documentation | Define SLA parameters and objectives - Robust SLAs |
| | Provide assurance | Evidence examination & analysis – Documentation | Accountable cloud - External auditors |
| | Monitor actions | Preservation of evidence – Evidence examination & analysis – Documentation | Detailed documentation from start to end - Distributed signature detection framework - Unified time system |
| | Provide attributability | Confirmation of the incident – Evidence examination & analysis – Documentation | Accountable cloud - Define SLA parameters and objectives |
| Transparency | Ensure visibility | Evidence examination & analysis – Documentation | Accountable cloud - TrustCloud framework |
| | Provide procedures and policies of treating data | Evidence examination & analysis – Documentation | Define SLA parameters and objectives - Robust SLAs |
| | Provide notification on policy violation | Evidence examination & analysis – Documentation | Accountable cloud - Robust SLAs |
| Legal matters | Define SLAs | Incident identification – Presentation | Define SLA parameters and objectives - Robust SLAs |
| | Ensure jurisdiction | Incident identification – Presentation | Faster compliance with court orders - International laws |
| | Maintain trained personnel | Preservation of evidence – Update training & planning libraries – Presentation | Team collaboration with wide range of skills - Trained and qualified personnel |

(*continued*)

**Table 1.** (*continued*)

| Constraint | Task | Fulfillment | Indicative solutions |
|---|---|---|---|
| Access rights | Ensure registration and validation control | Preservation of evidence – Evidence examination & analysis | Logging mechanism - Secure-Logging-as-a-service - Digital signature |
| | Enable authentication and authorization control | Preservation of evidence – Evidence examination & analysis | Logging framework - Digital forensic readiness model |
| | Enable access control | Preservation of evidence – Evidence examination & analysis | Level of access - Organizational policies and SLAs |
| Isolation | Ensure users do not have access to each other | Collection and acquisition | Proofs Of Retrievability - Identity and access management in future internet architecture |
| | Prevent contamination of other users | Collection and acquisition | Compartmentalization - Intrusion Detection Systems |
| | Provide confidentiality | Collection and acquisition | Multi-tenancy model - Digital forensic readiness model - DAC-MACS |
| Traceability | Monitor user activities | Confirmation of the incident – Evidence examination & analysis | Log-based model - Log management architecture |
| | Monitor data logs | Confirmation of the incident – Evidence examination & analysis | SecLaas - Log management architecture |
| | Store and secure logs | Evidence examination & analysis | SecLaas-RW - Log management |
| | Link users to data | Evidence examination & analysis | Identity management - Identity governance |

## 4.2 Digital Forensic Readiness

The main purpose of the proposed alignment is the identification of the degree of the forensic readiness of a specific cloud service against a forensic investigation. A number of researchers introduced various definitions for cloud forensic readiness [22–24]. In [25] cloud forensic readiness has been defined as "The organization's preparations to minimize the impact of an incident in a cloud forensic investigation, while identifying and acquiring the maximum amount of digital evidence".

Cloud forensic readiness is a subset of digital forensics readiness and it designates the need for digital forensic readiness in cloud environments. DFR is important due to the fact that organizations can fortify behind activities and processes that can predict and assist investigators in case of an incident. ISO/IEC 27043: 2015 [26] deals with investigative readiness and the steps that need to be taken prior to an incident occurring. ISO/IEC 27043: 2015 is the only international standard that includes detailed guidelines on the implementation of DFR as a process [27]. The readiness process class is shown outside of the dotted lines since it is a precautionary measure or proactive process that does not have to be involved (an optional process) in the reactive Digital Forensic Investigation (DFI) process [28].

## 5  Conclusion

Cloud Service Providers bring services to consumers on demand through the internet. In order to provide these services in a forensically sound manner, CSPs should be able to design and implement the services taking under consideration specific forensic requirements. This will assist investigators to acquire and examine evidence in accordance to the forensic investigation rules and procedures and produce admissible evidence in a court. The research community should bend over the specific field and produce reliable solutions towards this direction. In this paper, an alignment between the forensic requirements that are included in the design of forensic-enabled cloud services and the cloud forensic investigation process took place providing a form of validation to our previous work regarding the design of a framework for designing forensic-enabled cloud services. The results of the validation are encouraging since all the different stages of the investigation process align with the proposed forensic requirements.

## References

1. Ruan, K., Carthy, J., Kechadi, T., Crosbie, M.: Cloud forensics. In: Peterson, G., Shenoi, S. (eds.) DigitalForensics 2011. IFIPAICT, vol. 361, pp. 35–46. Springer, Heidelberg (2011). https://doi.org/10.1007/978-3-642-24212-0_3
2. Thethi, N., Keane, A.: Digital forensics investigations in the cloud. In: Proceedings of the IEEE International Advance Computing Conference, IACC 2014, Gurgaon, Harayana, India, 21–22 February 2014, pp. 1475–1480. IEEE, New York (2014)
3. Orton, I., Alva, A., Endicott-Popovsky, B.: Legal process and requirements for cloud forensic investigations. In: Ruan, K. (ed.) Cybercrime and Cloud Forensics: Applications for Investigation Processes, pp. 186–229. IGI Global, Hershey (2013). https://doi.org/10.4018/978-1-4666-2662-1.ch008
4. Freet, D., Agrawal, R., John, S., Walker, J.J.: Cloud forensics challenges from a service model standpoint: IaaS, PaaS and SaaS. In: Proceedings of the 7th International Conference on Management of Computational and Collective intElligence in Digital EcoSystems, MEDES 2015, Caraguatatuba, Brazil, 25–29 October 2015, pp. 148–155. ACM (2015)
5. Almulla, S., Iaqi, Y., Jones, A.: Cloud forensics: a research perspective. In: 2013 9th International Conference on Innovations in Information Technology (IIT), pp. 66–71. IEEE (2013)
6. RightScale. State of the Cloud Report 2018: Data to Navigate your Multi-Cloud Strategy. https://www.rightscale.com/lp/state-of-the-cloud. Accessed Feb 2019

7. National Research Council: Strengthening Forensic Science in the United States: A Path Forward. National Academies Press, Washington, D.C. (2009)

8. Simou, S., Kalloniatis, C., Gritzalis, S., Katos, V.: A framework for designing cloud forensic-enabled services (CFeS). Requir. Eng. **2018**, 1–28 (2018). https://doi.org/10.1007/s00766-018-0289-y

9. Simou, S., Kalloniatis, C., Mouratidis, H., Gritzalis, S.: Towards a model-based framework for forensic-enabled cloud information systems. In: Katsikas, S., Lambrinoudakis, C., Furnell, S. (eds.) TrustBus 2016. LNCS, vol. 9830, pp. 35–47. Springer, Cham (2016). https://doi.org/10.1007/978-3-319-44341-6_3

10. Simou, S., Kalloniatis, C., Mouratidis, H., Gritzalis, S.: A survey on cloud forensics challenges and solutions. Secur. Commun. Netw. **9**, 6285–6314 (2016). https://doi.org/10.1002/sec.1688

11. Martini, B., Choo, K.-K.R.: An integrated conceptual digital forensic framework for cloud computing. Digit. Invest. **9**, 71–80 (2012). https://doi.org/10.1016/j.diin.2012.07.001

12. McKemmish, R.: What is Forensic Computing?. Australian Institute of Criminology, Canberra (1999)

13. Scarfone, K.K., Chevalier, S., Grance, T., Dang, H.: Guide to integrating forensic techniques into incident response. NIST Special Publication, SP 800–86, 121 p (2006)

14. Agarwal, R., Kothari, S.: Review of digital forensic investigation frameworks. In: Kim, K. (ed.) Information Science and Applications. LNEE, vol. 339, pp. 561–571. Springer, Heidelberg (2015). https://doi.org/10.1007/978-3-662-46578-3_66

15. Ruan, K., Carthy, J.: Cloud forensic maturity model. In: Rogers, M., Seigfried-Spellar, K.C. (eds.) ICDF2C 2012. LNICST, vol. 114, pp. 22–41. Springer, Heidelberg (2013). https://doi.org/10.1007/978-3-642-39891-9_2

16. Zawoad, S., Hasan, R., Skjellum, A.: OCF: an open cloud forensics model for reliable digital forensics. In: Proceedings of the IEEE 8th International Conference on Cloud Computing, CLOUD 2015, p. 437–444. IEEE, New York (2015)

17. Adams, R.: The emergence of cloud storage and the need for a new digital forensic process model. In: Ruan, K. (ed.) Cybercrime and Cloud Forensics: Applications for Investigation Processes, pp. 79–104. IGI Global, Hershey (2013). https://doi.org/10.4018/978-1-4666-2662-1.ch004

18. Guo, H., Jin, B., Shang, T.: Forensic investigations in cloud environments. In: Proceedings of the 2012 International Conference on Computer Science and Information Processing (CSIP), Xi'an, Shaanxi, China, 24–26 August 2012, pp. 248–251. IEEE, New York (2012)

19. Simou, S., Kalloniatis, C., Kavakli, E., Gritzalis, S.: Cloud forensics: identifying the major issues and challenges. In: Jarke, M., et al. (eds.) CAiSE 2014. LNCS, vol. 8484, pp. 271–284. Springer, Cham (2014). https://doi.org/10.1007/978-3-319-07881-6_19

20. Simou, S., Kalloniatis, C., Kavakli, E., Gritzalis, S.: Cloud forensics solutions: a review. In: Iliadis, L., Papazoglou, M., Pohl, K. (eds.) CAiSE 2014. LNBIP, vol. 178, pp. 299–309. Springer, Cham (2014). https://doi.org/10.1007/978-3-319-07869-4_28

21. Kalloniatis, C., Mouratidis, H., Vassilis, M., Islam, S., Gritzalis, S., Kavakli, E.: Towards the design of secure and privacy-oriented information systems in the cloud: Identifying the major concepts. Comput. Stand. Interf. **36**, 759–775 (2014). https://doi.org/10.1016/j.csi.2013.12.010

22. Alenezi, A., Hussein, R.K., Walters, R.J., Wills, G.B.: A framework for cloud forensic readiness in organizations. In: 2017 5th IEEE International Conference on Mobile Cloud Computing, Services, and Engineering (MobileCloud), San Francisco, USA, pp. 199–204. IEEE (2017)

23. De Marco, L., Kechadi, M.-T., Ferrucci, F.: Cloud forensic readiness: foundations. In: Gladyshev, P., Marrington, A., Baggili, I. (eds.) ICDF2C 2013. LNICST, vol. 132, pp. 237–244. Springer, Cham (2014). https://doi.org/10.1007/978-3-319-14289-0_16
24. Kebande, V., Ntsamo, H.S., Venter, H.S.: Towards a prototype for achieving digital forensic readiness in the cloud using a distributed NMB solution. In: Rodosek, G., Koch, R. (eds.) 15th European Conference on Cyber Warfare and Security, ECCWS 2016, Munich, Germany, pp. 369–378. Academic Conferences International Limited (2016)
25. Simou, S., Troumpis, I., Kalloniatis, C., Kavroudakis, D., Gritzalis, S.: A decision-making approach for improving organizations' cloud forensic readiness. In: Furnell, S., Mouratidis, H., Pernul, G. (eds.) TrustBus 2018. LNCS, vol. 11033, pp. 150–164. Springer, Cham (2018). https://doi.org/10.1007/978-3-319-98385-1_11
26. ISO. ISO/IEC 27043:2015: Information Technology - Security techniques - Incident investigation principles and processes (2015)
27. Kigwana, I., Venter, H.S.: A digital forensic readiness architecture for online examinations. South Afr. Comput. J. 30(1), 1–39 (2018)
28. Kebande, V.R., Karie, N.M., Venter, H.S.: A generic digital forensic readiness model for BYOD using honeypot technology. In: 2016 IST-Africa Week Conference, pp. 1–12. IEEE (2016)

# Online Social Networks and "Fake News"

# Towards Designing a Knowledge Graph-Based Framework for Investigating and Preventing Crime on Online Social Networks

Ogerta Elezaj[1(⊠)], Sule Yildirim Yayilgan[1(⊠)], Edlira Kalemi[2(⊠)],
Linda Wendelberg[1(⊠)], Mohamed Abomhara[1(⊠)], and Javed Ahmed[1(⊠)]

[1] Department of Information Security and Communication Technology,
Norwegian University of Science and Technology (NTNU), Gjøvik, Norway
{ogerta.elezaj,sule.yildirim,mohamed.abomhara,javed.ahmed}@ntnu.no,
lindawen@stud.ntnu.no
[2] University of Tirana, Tirana, Albania
edlira.kalemi@unitir.edu.al

**Abstract.** Online Social Networks (OSNs) have fundamentally and permanently altered the arena of digital and classical crime. Recently, law enforcement agencies (LEAs) have been using OSNs as a data source to collect Open Source Intelligence for fighting and preventing crime. However, most existing technological developments for LEAs to fight and prevent crime rely on conventional database technology, which poses problems. As social network usage is increasing rapidly, storing and querying data for information retrieval is critical because of the characteristics of social networks, such as unstructured nature, high volumes, velocity, and data interconnectivity. This paper presents a knowledge graph-based framework, an outline of a framework designed to support crime investigators solve and prevent crime, from data collection to inferring digital evidence admissible in court. The main component of the proposed framework is a hybrid ontology linked to a graph database, which provides LEAs with the possibility to process unstructured data and identify hidden patterns and relationships in the interconnected data of OSNs.

**Keywords:** Crime · Ontology · Online social networks · Digital evidence · Knowledge graph · Biometrics · Security

## 1 Introduction

Over the last years, social networking – the most recent innovation in communication – has become an integral part of daily life for many people of all ages. It has changed the behavior and perception people have about the information shared online [22]. The influence of social networking sites, such as Facebook, LinkedIn, Twitter, Google Plus, etc. has exploded in a relatively short amount

S. Katsikas and V. Zorkadis (Eds.): e-Democracy 2019, CCIS 1111, pp. 181–195, 2020.
https://doi.org/10.1007/978-3-030-37545-4_12

of time. The number of worldwide users is expected to reach some 3.02 billion by 2021[1], around a third of the Earth's entire population. As of March 31, 2019, Facebook claims to have 2.38 billion monthly active users worldwide[2]. This expansion in connectedness among people on digital platforms has created a vast repository of information with potential value for LEAs in to use more efficiently for making informed decisions. OSNs have fundamentally and permanently altered the arena of detecting, preventing and solving of digital and classical crimes changing the field of crime investigations [1,18].

Different types of digital crime evidence can be collected by OSNs. For example, digital evidence may come in the form of public posts, private messages, pictures, videos, tweets, geo-tagged content and, location-based data. Such open source of intelligence can be a reliable mine of evidence that can alter the outcome of a trial. LEAs can data mine social networking sites to identify victims, witnesses and perpetrators. Photographs, videos and other information that witnesses to crime post on social networks intentionally or unintentionally can be used as evidence later in an investigation. In general, a variety of information coming from OSNs can be utilized to solve many types of crime cases. Some instance of crime through open sources include cyberbullying and offenses primarily on Facebook and Twitter [26,32], terrorism and burglars using social media to find targets [41].

Initially, LEAs started using social media as a communication channel for citizens to offer feedback and to participate in virtual consultations, thus building an online presence on main platforms to increase their legitimacy, transparency and trustworthiness. Nowadays, social media has expanded opportunities for surveillance by providing adequate tools for systematically gathering information from different digital platforms to track people's activities from the prospect of both suspects and victims [33]. Ericson and Haggerty [17] view police officers as "knowledge workers" rather than "crime fighters". LEAs conduct online surveillance to reconstruct events using knowledge management technologies and the corresponding knowledge about crime detection and prevention to assist with identifying crime trends. In legal proceedings, it may be considered good practice for police departments to successfully involve social media as an invaluable tool in their investigations.

The process of criminal investigation involves very high volumes of information that must be handled in a time-critical environment [12]. The success of investigation consequently depends on how the information is turned into evidence [15]. The information and knowledge obtained by OSNs is material that counts as potential evidence. Such material must be properly authenticated in order to be admitted into evidence. There are numerous examples of different courts of law having accepted social media content as digital evidence, leading to convictions and sometimes prison sentences [7,29,39].

---

[1] https://www.statista.com/topics/1164/social-networks/.

[2] https://www.statista.com/statistics/264810/number-of-monthly-active-facebook-users-worldwide/.

However, despite the noticeable power of social media as evidence in legal proceedings, LEAs are always scrambling to keep up with new technologies and use intelligent systems to sift through massive amounts of raw social media content. Technically it is challenging handeling the flow of massively voluminous, heterogeneous, unstructured and multimedia content on OSNs. Also, to integrate, process and transform multimedia content on OSNs into intelligence used to identify suspects, locate witnesses and convict defendants. Monitoring social networks and transforming these vast amounts of unstructured data into actionable intelligence can be a daunting task. This overwhelming number of OSNs that serve as potential evidence are in high demand and deplete LEAs. Manual analysis, and keyword-based flagging are impractical, therefore an integrated system is needed to respond to the requirements of OSNs in the crime domain. Such system is required to handle massive volumes of data by supporting simplified automation and interoperability.

Existing solutions to meet requirements in the field of crime investigation are currently limited [7]. There is no exhaustive tool to support crime analysis and prevention on multiple social networks and that is capable of analyzing extremely high volumes of online content relating to chain of custody of digital evidence and their validation using biometric features. The existing approaches are narrow in terms of the integrating different data sources and hence fall short of providing solutions to larger-scale, more complex crime like organized crime and terrorism. Many of the existing digital forensics tools are in the form of individual tools that can only deal with partial aspects of crime investigation and offer limited features for investigations in complex environments [25]. Among the issues to be addressed is the development of automatic tools and techniques for analyzing vast amounts of data that have capability to gather digital evidence. Such solutions should provide visualization features and unified standards [11]. Furthermore, none of the previous frameworks for OSNs take account of the biometric aspect which is significant to the quality of the digital evidence collected. Biometrics technology plays a key role for LEAs during the investigation process stage of narrowing down the persons suspected of a crime. It is an important part of the digital evidence admitted in the court of law.

The contribution of this paper is twofold. In order to identify the research gap, we survey existing frameworks used for crime investigation in the context of OSNs content. Based on the discovered gap, we introduce an intelligent framework, which is a knowledge graph-based framework that is suitable for gathering digital evidence from OSNs, which may help LEAs to increase their analytical capabilities. The main components of the proposed framework are a hybrid ontology for collecting and integrating the unstructured social media content and a graph database used as a storage back-end to store the semantic data and perform efficient querying and storage. This hybrid ontology is an improved version of SMONT [23], which is a semantic-based ontology model originally developed by the authors with the main purpose of enriching an ontology with social media content.

The remaining part of the paper is organized as follows. Section 2 presents a review of literature relevant to existing frameworks used by LEAs to gather intelligence from online social networks to provide to legal bodies. In Sect. 3 discusses main challenges and solutions in order to build a knowledge graph-based framework. Section 4 introduces the proposed framework architecture and its main components. The conclusion and future work are presented in Sect. 5.

## 2   Related Work

Based on the meta-analysis and literature review, a summary of existing frameworks for crime investigation based on OSN content is presented in Table 1. We conducted a keyword search in scientific databases of the keywords crime, ontology, biometrics, digital evidence and framework. Articles were filtered by title and abstract while articles that do not cover OSNs were discarded. Focus was on analyzing frameworks capable of handling social media content. The frameworks were evaluated based on the following criteria: - data sources used, type of crime, detection capabilities, prevention capabilities, biometric capacities, support for the collection of digital evidence, support for visual analysis, and methods used for crime detection and prevention.

According to our analysis, few semantic solutions exist that are specifically designed for investigating crime on social media. Moreover, no solution is sufficiently detailed to cover important aspect of crime investigation such as digital evidences and biometrics that have a crucial role in investigations.

Arshad et al. [7] introduced a multilayer semantic framework for OSNs that is based on a methodology of mapping multiple ontologies into a global one capable of integrating unstructured data drawn from different data sources. This framework lacks the required level of details about digital evidence gathering. Furthermore, the framework was not developed for processing biometric data.

The criminal ontology presented by Kastrati [24], SEMCON, is a simple ontology developed to identifying if a Facebook user is a possible suspect or not. The proposed model uses Facebook API to retrieve user' data and exploits it semantically and contextually. However, SEMCON does not cover all perspectives necessary to meet the complexity in criminal cases. To be usable, it needs to be extended to deal with all crime investigation aspects.

In [30] is presented a computational framework that focuses on physical evidence from a crime scene. This framework has three main components: - a physical biometrics ontology, a law enforcement ontology and several supporting stubs. The framework is interesting but does not emphasize crime investigation by OSNs. However, it must be mentioned that this is the only framework that cover biometric aspects of a crime scene in a semantic context. There is a lack of evaluation of the proposed framework.

Nouh et al. [34] presented an outline of a multipurpose cybercrime intelligence framework that helps LEAs investigate criminal cases and prevent crime. The proposed framework is composed of five layers: - data-handling, analysis, front-end, users and data-sources. It integrates different data analyses, such as Social

Network Analysis (SNA), time series, content and sentinel analyses. The top-down approach is used for prevention based on various hypotheses of some event incidents and to detect and solve different crime cases. This solution does not address digital evidence and biometric aspects. The concept of connected data in OSNs and modeling with graph technologies is not addressed either.

In [10] authors built a predictive model pertaining to reactions on Twitter in order to analyze the Woolwich, London terrorist attack that took place in 2013. The model use statistical methods and machine learning to predict the size and survival of information flow related to the terrorist attack. It lacks semantic capability and is limited to predictive capacity.

Cosic et al. [14] developed an ontology to manage the digital chain of custody of digital evidences. This ontology based on the top-down methodology deals with the management of the chain of custody of digital evidence. Furthermore, it may serve as a method to expand on our ontology related to the digital evidence.

**Table 1.** Review of existing frameworks in crime investigation.

| Authors | Framework description | Data Sources | Type of crimes | Detection | Prevention | Semantic Analyses | Biometric | Digital Evidence | Visual Analyses | Methods | Technology |
|---|---|---|---|---|---|---|---|---|---|---|---|
| [27] | Criminal network prediction model | UCINET cocaine smuggling | Drug Trafficking | X | ✓ | X | X | X | ✓ | Deep Learning | Graph |
| [7] | Semantic framework for social media | Social Media | General | ✓ | X | ✓ | X | X | ✓ | Frequency analysis and clustering | Ontology, Graph |
| [23] | Ontology for crime solving | Social media | General | ✓ | ✓ | ✓ | X | X | X | Ontology Reasoning | Ontology |
| [24] | Analysis of OSNs Posts to investigate | Facebook | General | ✓ | X | ✓ | X | X | X | Semantic and contextual data-mining | Ontology |
| [30] | Situation-Based Ontologies Focusing on Crime Scenes | | Cybercrime | ✓ | X | ✓ | ✓ | ✓ | X | Situation Management | Ontology |
| [3] | Analysis and detection of microblogging spam | Twitter | Cybercrime | ✓ | X | X | X | X | X | Machine learning | Graph |
| [37] | Criminal Network Analysis Using Big Data | - | General | ✓ | ✓ | X | ✓ | X | X | Machine Learning | Hadoop, Graph |
| [34] | Cybercrime Intelligence Framework | OSN | General | ✓ | ✓ | X | X | ✓ | ✓ | SNA, Space and Behavior Analyses | Relational Database |
| [10] | Modelling the Social Media Reaction | Twitter | Terrorism | X | X | X | X | X | X | Regression Machine learning | - |
| [2] | Surveillance of Instant Messages | Social Media | General | ✓ | X | ✓ | X | X | X | Association Rule Mining | Ontology, knowledge database |
| [14] | Ontology DEMF | - | General | X | X | ✓ | X | ✓ | X | - | Ontology |

According to this review and to the best of our knowledge, it is concluded that none of the existing frameworks cover digital evidence collection, biometric data and elaboration of data from OSNs simultaneously. The previous frameworks are mostly not generalized but are platform based, meaning they are capable of handling data sourced from one specific social network platform. Moreover, among all frameworks analyzed, only one is graph-based, which is a requirement when OSNs are to be used in criminal cases investigation. Utilizing of graph-based technology is important in analyzing the characteristics and behaviors of suspects or criminals as well as the structure of communities or sometimes an overall network. The graph representation helps LEAs understand a criminal network structure, and identify the cliques, groups and key players in a network [31].

## 3   Identified Major Challenges and Solutions

In this section, we identify the main challenges and proposed solutions that facilitate LEAs investigating crimes happening in OSNs.

**Challenge 1:** Developing an appropriate model to organize and integrate the massive volume and different data types obtained from OSNs.

OSNs contain massive volumes of content and linkage data, which can be utilized by LEAs in crime investigation. Generally, the data can be divided into structured and unstructured data. Unstructured data is a textual content, known as User Generate Content (UGC) for a particular user. UGC is often in the form of text, but it can contain images, videos or other type of data. On the other hand, structured data are modeled by graph data models, where the entities are presented as vertices (e.g., people or things) and edges (i.e., relationships of vertices). The OSNs data is heterogeneous and also accompanied with different properties, such as the time stamp and the location related to a specific user activity, which means that processing and managing this kind of data is a bigger challenge compared to other data sources such as web pages or blogs. It is foreseen that 80% of worldwide data will be unstructured by 2025[3]. If LEAs are struggling to manage their unstructured data now, they are going to find it difficult to cope with the increasing volume of unstructured data over time, to turn it into a more structured format.

Previous studies observed that Semantic web frameworks provide a graph model (RDF), a query language (SPARQL) and definition systems (OWL) to efficiently represent and manage heterogeneity of OSNs data [40]. Semantic Web technology uses ontology to model an abstract view of a specific real domain. Only few studies have concentrated on using semantic technologies to integrated data coming from OSNs and mostly offer general solutions not related to crime investigation [8].

In 1995, Gruber [19] originally defined the notion of an ontology as knowledge engineering that use explicit specification of conceptualization. The advantages of ontologies are: (a) use of common language; (b) manage of unstructured data; (c) enable reuse of domain knowledge and (d) use of inference steps utilizing ontology reasoning [40]. The most significant advantage that ontologies might

---

[3] https://www.idc.com/.

bring to the domain of crime investigation is the ability to support the integration and processing of unstructured data received from OSNs.

The Web Ontology Language (OWL) is one of the most commonly used language to formalize ontologies of different domains and to describe their relation by converting to descriptive logic. In the proposed framework, the crime domain ontology is developed using an OWL editor tool developed by Stanford University, named Protégé [38]. This tool is a JAVA-based open source ontology editor which is compatible with different platforms. OWL uses the Resource Description Framework (RDF) of classes and properties. The framework contains a hierarchical description of conceptual things in the crime domain. Individuals are instances of predefined classes, and properties of each class describe attributes of the concepts.

According to literature, there exists different methods used for developing ontologies. These methods are divided into two main groups: evaluation prototype models and experience-based methods [9]. In the proposed solution, we adopted the 101 method which contains seven defined steps to develop an ontology for a specific domain [35]. First, we develop a conceptual ontology – which is an abstract view of classes – defined and arranged in a taxonomic presentation with sub-classes and super-classes, properties and facts of properties. In the second stage, the physical ontology is developed by using Protégé. Based on the data collected in the acquisition layer, we create instances of each class to model the crime domain. The crime ontology covers classes, data properties, object properties, individuals and relationships.

**Challenge 2:** Developing an appropriate storage technology to handle complex and dynamic relationships in highly connected OSNs to generate new knowledge for LEAs.

While the use of ontologies in the crime domain give big advantages related to knowledge representation and extraction, it also poses problems. The main key challenge is related to the storage of the data and searching for the relevant information in a big data environment [16]. To solve these problems, nowadays, graph databases are being widely and intensively used for storing and querying data for OSNs. The graph databases overcome the limits of traditional databases for storing and managing data represented as graph-like data. As the usage of social networks is increasing rapidly, storing and querying data for information retrieval by LEAS is critical. This due to the characteristics of social networks like dynamic structure, highly volume, velocity and interconnectivity of data. Relational databases struggle to handle the volume and velocity of data generated in big data environment [5]. Also, an other reason that graph databases are used to store OSNs data is the fact that social networks are modeled as graphs.

Moreover, Not only SQL (NoSQL) is one of the main solutions for storing and processing OSNs data [6]. Its main characteristics is that it is schema-free. Different open-sources NoSQL are available as low-cost solutions. NoSQL is more efficient in comparison to relational databases because it ensures efficient big data storage, provide high performance, high volume, high velocity and can handle complex data structure [20]. NoSQL databases are divided into four types: - graph database, key-value store, column store and document database. As our scope is to model the data received from OSNs, we employed graph databases, as the most popular storage technology used for analyzing data from OSNs [6], assuring natural modeling of their networks.

We employed a NoSQL open source graph database, named Neo4j, released in 2007 [13]. Neo4j is known as "world leading graph database" and is one of the most popular graph databases, characterized by robustness and high performance [42]. It scales billions of nodes and relationship in a network. Therefore, the entire interconnected data obtained from OSNs, needed by LEAs for investigation, can be stored and managed using Neo4j.

The aim of the proposed framework is to extend the SMONT ontology developed by Kalemi et al. [23]. The top-level classes identified in the framework ontology are: Agent, Crimes, Crime Case Solving, Social Networks, Biometric Artifacts and Institutions as shown in Fig. 1. Agent class represents information about persons, groups or organizations whose data are collected by police reports/evidence streams and from OSNs.

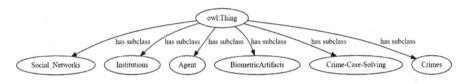

**Fig. 1.** Top hierarchy classes of crime ontology

Crime class describes the types of crimes based on widely accepted classification by law and jurisprudence. Social Networks represents all data collected by OSNs used for investigation. Biometric artifacts class represents physical biometric features (e.g., fingerprint, iris) about persons that committed a crime or anyone who is suspected. Institutions represent a class that contains information about institutions involve in crime investigations like LEAs, banks, courts, insurance companies etc. Crime-Case-Solving contains information about cases that have not been solved. Using reasoning rules, machine learning and SNAs the information of all the classes of ontology is contributing to provide instances in the Digital Evidence that is a sub-class of Crime-Case-Solving. Class dependencies are as shown in Fig. 2.

**Challenge 3:** Developing an appropriate method to automatically extract and visualize the relevant knowledge.

The increase demand for structured knowledge in investigating crimes has created considerable interest for LEAs in crime analytical techniques in order to provide LEAs better insights into criminal networks. As most of the social networks are big graphs with unpredicted volume, velocity and variety, LEAs face challenges related to effective information search and crime analysis. LEAs require to deploy automatic procedures for analysis related to detection and prediction of crime incidents.

To enhance national security, LEAs and intelligent agencies collect massive amount of data which must be transformed into information, knowledge and

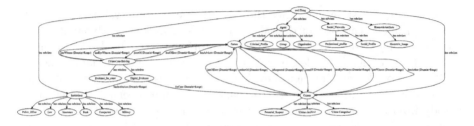

**Fig. 2.** Class dependencies of crime ontology

intelligence. As LEAs struggle to manage and process this enormous volume of data by traditional methods, the use of machine learning (ML) discipline offers efficient solutions for crime detection and prevention in large crime datasets [36]. Based on ML, LEAs can develop and deploy models to classify crimes, investigate hidden crime patterns or predict future crime patterns. Different classification algorithms are nominated for crime analysis, crime prediction, and to get insight into potential crime hotspot areas [4].

A common problem for LEAs during investigation is to analyze groups of people involved in organized crime and dark networks. In order to analyze the dynamic structure of criminal networks, LEAs must employ quantitative measurements of SNA, which provides models and techniques to analyze OSNs based on graph theory and visualization tools. SNA methods has the ability to find out leaders of the networks, observe network changes over time and model diffusion processes. Also, SNA methods can be used to discover the leaders of a criminal network based on centrality and prestige measures of direct relations. The centrality and prestige are linked with the members that are extensively linked or involved with other members. Finding these leaders in such networks and removing them may defragment the criminal network or disrupt it.

The proposed framework based on machine learning methods, deep learning and SNA can provide information to LEAs in order to predict different crime categories including whether a person or organization will or motivated to commit a crime, crime target, time that a new crime might be committed, the crime location and type of crimes etc. Thus, combining machine learning techniques, SNA analyses and ontologies reasoning inferences, the solution aims to improve prediction performance helping LEAs to predict different types of crime that might occur in a particular geographical location and in a given time period.

**Challenge 4:** Developing an appropriate method for preservation of digital evidence.

In crime investigation process, LEAs must collect and infer digital evidence that require authenticity and non-repudiation properties to rely on in the court. Digital evidence gathering and analyses requires special procedures and techniques to be used and accepted as evidences in the court. The goals of the systems that produce digital evidence is the maintenance of the chain of custody, which in legal context is the documentation of the order of handled items of evidence during a crime investigation. Since the process of collection, validation, preservation and documentation of digital evidences is complex and dynamic, chain of custody should be kept. Some common problems faced by LEAs in maintaining the integrity of evidence with chain of custody include data integrity, modification of elements of digital evidences and access control for the storage.

The proposed framework aims to ensure the management of the chain of custody from the starting point of a new criminal case. To maintain the chain of custody, in our framework, we are based on the 5W+H investigative model (Who, What, When, Where, Why and How) [21]. In the crime ontology (top-down methodology), we have created sub-classes under class of Digital Evidence. The elements of the sub-class Digital Evidence can respond to the 5W+H aspects of the chain of custody. Combining two classes (Digital Evidence and Biometric), the integrity of chain of custody is strength and the framework can produce biometric digital evidence which are admissible in court for prosecution of offenders and attackers.

**Challenge 5:** Developing an appropriate method to acquire data from social networks.

In general, there are three different data types that can be retrieved from OSNs. The first, content data includes user profiles, photos, videos etc., which are mostly unstructured data. The second is behavior data which is classified into three different categories: user-user behavior – interaction between two individuals such as following or sending a private message; user-entity behavior – interaction between a user and an OSNs entity such as liking or writing a post in Instagram and user-community behavior – interaction between a user and an online community such as participating in community discussions. The third type is network structure data that consists of explicit hyperlinks between users and their content.

Social network like Facebook provides application program interface (API) and query languages which are key part for researchers in academia and enterprises too [26]. Recently OSNs platform have clearly restricted the access on data that developers can retrieve. For example, Facebook, after the Cambridge Analytica scandal, changed several APIs in order to protect user data. A string called Facebook access token that identifies a user, or an application is used to make API calls and now based on the new rules. All these requests must be reviewed and approved by Facebook. Also, Twitter hands down new strict rules restricting the volume of data that third-party developers can get access to. For example, as for June 2018, the Twitter API can return only the most recent 3200 tweets and during a single request only 200 tweets are return.

To overcome these limitations, the proposed framework combines API and web crawlers to feed real time data and to optimize quality for each data sources. Crawlers are used to extract the information that cannot be collected automatically by API. Also, the framework must address the issue of metadata, which are fundamental important to be collected along with respective data.

## 4   Knowledge Graph-Based Framework Architecture

Aimed at addressing the main challenges in gathering intelligence from OSNs in the crime domain, this paper presents a knowledge graph-based framework incorporating semantic web and graph database. The architecture of the proposed framework is given in Fig. 3. It is composed of 4 layers, data acquisition, knowledge creation and semantic enrichment, knowledge extraction and application layer.

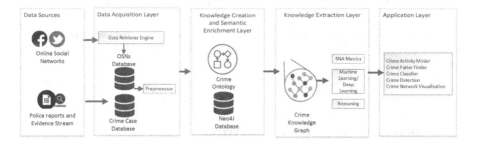

**Fig. 3.** The architecture of the knowledge graph-based framework

Two data sources have been identified for crime investigation, reports and evidence streams that exist in LEAs repositories and OSNs data. The data acquisition layer contains a data retriever engine capable to feed real time data from OSNs combining API and developed crawlers. For different social networks, different API plugin are included in the engine. To deal with rate limits of API request per hour and per user, crawlers are used. This layer includes data preprocessing focused on removing errors and inconsistency from the data, imputing missing data, and data integration. As data coming from OSNs are user generated data and their quality varies from valuable data to rubbish, data preprocessing is a crucial process. Having good quality of data is more important than having in place efficient machine learning algorithms that run in poor datasets. The framework should be capable to automatically extract information from multimedia content taken from OSNs and format it. This process includes different tasks related to audio and video segmentation and transcriptions, image processing to extract logos, weapons, biometric features etc. The framework can process files of diffrent formats such as audio file, image file, video file, text files, that are stored locally in LEAs repositories or can optionally be extracted by specific OSNs.

The next layer is the knowledge creation and semantic enrichment, where the data are modeled based on the developed crime ontology and are stored in a Neo4j graph database. A mapping schema of the Neo4j data model and the crime ontology that is an RDF directed graph is required in order to preserve the details. The RDF graph triples are composed by a subject, a predicate and an object, where the subject and predictor are resources and the object can be a resource or a literal. Each resource is identified by a Uniform Resource Identifier (URI). All subjects of triples are mapped to nodes in the Neo4j graph. If the object is literal, predicates are mapped to node properties, otherwise if the object is a resource, predicates are mapped to relationships.

Knowledge extraction layer covers application of machine leaning techniques, SNA and ontology reasoning to analyze the graph data to extract the required knowledge. Using machine learning algorithms, criminal behavior is modeled. Based on anomaly detection, the system alert LEAs for unusual patterns or behaviors. All the methods applied at this layer will be tuned to avoid false positive alarms (FP). If the system has a high FP alarms rate, it makes it very challenging for LEAs due to the high workload required. Thus, it is necessary to train appropriate algorithms in order to obtain high detection rate and to ensure a low FP rate. SNA metrics are used to discover strategic members who belong to criminal networks.

The last layer, the application layer is the dashboard supporting user to customize different processes related to crime investigation and prediction.

## 5  Conclusions and Further Work

We have conducted a review of the literature on the use of OSNs data in crime detection and prevention. The aim of this review was to analyze existing intelligent crime solving frameworks and to identify various challenging factors that restrict the use of OSNs by LEAs in the preventive policing of criminal activities. Lack of efficient models to organize and integrate the massive volume and different data types coming from OSNs and the increased demand for structured knowledge in investigating crimes, were found to impede the implementation of efficient intelligent crime frameworks for LEAs.

Existing crime frameworks do not consider digital evidence collection, biometric data and elaboration of data from OSNs simultaneously such that existing solution remain unsuitable to meet LEAs requirements in the process of crime investigation. Solutions that can efficiently collect, store and query the unstructured, high volume, velocity and inter-connected data and guarantee LEAS deeper insight into the criminal activities are demanded. Based on the identified challenges and the requirements of LEAs we have introduced our initial design of a knowledge graph -based framework for investigation and preventing of crime on OSNs. This framework is a hybrid ontology linked to a graph database, which provides LEAs with the possibility to process unstructured data and identify hidden patterns and relationships in the interconnected data of OSNs with the focus on crime investigation and prevention.

Future work will consist in fully implementation of this framework. We aim in developing real use cases obtained from police crime cases and real data of OSNs and to evaluate the whole system and the performance of prediction methods covering a broader range of crimes.

**Acknowledgements.** This work was carried out during the tenure of an ERCIM "Alain Bensoussan" Fellowship Programme.

# References

1. Abdalla, A., Yayilgan, S.Y.: A review of using online social networks for investigative activities. In: Meiselwitz, G. (ed.) SCSM 2014. LNCS, vol. 8531, pp. 3–12. Springer, Cham (2014). https://doi.org/10.1007/978-3-319-07632-4_1

2. Ali, M.M., Mohammed, K.M., Rajamani, L.: Framework for surveillance of instant messages in instant messengers and social networking sites using data mining and ontology. In: Proceedings of the 2014 IEEE Students Technology Symposium (2014)

3. Almaatouq, A., et al.: If it looks like a spammer and behaves like a spammer, it must be a spammer: analysis and detection of microblogging spam accounts. Int. J. Inf. Secur. **15**, 1–17 (2016)

4. Almanie, T., Mirza, R., Lor, E.: Crime prediction based on crime types and using spatial and temporal criminal hotspots. Int. J. Data Min. Knowl. Manag. Process **5**(4), 01–19 (2015)

5. Alsubaiee, S., Carey, M.J., Li, C.: LSM-based storage and indexing: an old idea with timely benefits. In: ACM Workshop on Managing and Mining Enriched Geo-Spatial Data - GeoRich 2015, pp. 1–6 (2015)

6. Appel, A.P., Moyano, L.G.: Link and graph mining in the big data era. In: Zomaya, A., Sakr, S. (eds.) Handbook of Big Data Technologies, pp. 583–616. Springer, Cham (2017). https://doi.org/10.1007/978-3-319-49340-4_17

7. Arshad, H., Jantan, A., Hoon, G., Butt, A.: A multilayered semantic framework for integrated forensic acquisition on social media. Digit. Invest. **29**, 147–158 (2019)

8. Breslin, J., Bojars, U., Passant, A., Fernandez, S., Decker, S.: SIOC: content exchange and semantic interoperability between social networks. In: W3C Workshop on the Future of Social Networking, pp. 15–16 (2009)

9. Brusa, G., Caliusco, M.L., Chiotti, O.: A process for building a domain ontology: an experience in developing a government budgetary ontology. In: 2nd Australasian Workshop on Advances in Ontologies, Hobart, TAS, Australia, 72, pp. 7–15 (2006)

10. Burnap, P., et al.: Tweeting the terror: modelling the social media reaction to the Woolwich terrorist attack. Soc. Netw. Anal. Min. **4**, 206 (2014)

11. Caviglione, L., Wendzel, S., Mazurczyk, W.: The future of digital forensics: challenges and the road ahead. In: IEEE Security and Privacy, vol. 6, pp. 12–17 (2017). Investigation, vol. 29, pp. 147–158 (2019)

12. Chen, H., Schroeder, J., Hauck, R.V., et al.: COPLINK connect: information and knowledge management for law enforcement. Decis. Support Syst. **34**(3), 271–285 (2003)

13. Chen, Y., Chen, Y.: Decomposing DAGs into spanning trees: a new way to compress transitive closures. In: 2011 IEEE 27th International Conference on Data Engineering, Hannover, pp. 1007–1018 (2011)

14. Cosic, J., Baca, M.: Leveraging DEMF to ensure and represent 5ws&1h in digital forensic domain. Int. J. Comput. Sci. Inf. Secur. **13**(2), 7 (2015)

15. Dean, G., Fahsing, I.A., Gottschalk, P.: Profiling police investigative thinking: a study of police officers in Norway. Int. J. Sociol. Law **34**, 221–228 (2006)

16. Elbattah, M., Roushdy, M., Aref, M., Salem, A.M.: Large-scale ontology storage and query using graph database-oriented approach: the case of freebase, pp. 39–43 (2015)

17. Ericson, R.V., Haggerty, K.: Policing the Risk Society. University of Toronto Press, Toronto (1997)

18. Europol. Crime in the age of technology, Europol unclassified - Basic protection level, The Hague 12.10.207, EDOC#924156v7 (2017)
19. Gruber, T.R.: Toward principles for the design of ontologies used for knowledge sharing. Int. J. Hum Comput. Stud. **43**(5–6), 907–928 (1995)
20. Gupta, A., Tyagi, S., Panwar, N., Sachdeva, S., Saxena, U.: NoSQL databases: critical analysis and comparison. In: 2017 International Conference on Computing and Communication Technologies for Smart Nation (IC3TSN) (2017)
21. Hart, G.: The five W's: an old tool for the new task of task analysis. Tech. Commun. **43**(2), 139–145 (1996)
22. Imran, M., Castillo, C., Diaz, F., Vieweg, S.: Processing social media messages in mass emergency: a survey. ACM Comput. Surv. **47**(4), 67 (2015)
23. Kalemi, E., Yildirim, S., Domnori, E., Elezaj, O.: SMONT: an ontology for crime solving through social media. Int. J. Metadata Semant. Ontol. **12**(2/3), 71–81 (2017)
24. Kastrati, Z., Imran, A.S., Yildirim-Yayilgan, S., Dalipi, F.: Analysis of online social networks posts to investigate suspects using SEMCON. In: Meiselwitz, G. (ed.) SCSM 2015. LNCS, vol. 9182, pp. 148–157. Springer, Cham (2015). https://doi.org/10.1007/978-3-319-20367-6_16
25. Khan, S., Gani, A., Wahab, A.W., Shiraz, M., Ahmad, I.: Network forensics: review, taxonomy, and open challenges. J. Netw. Comput. Appl. **66**, 214–235 (2016)
26. Kokkinos, C.M., Baltzidis, E., Xynogala, D.: Prevalence and personality correlates of Facebook bullying among university undergraduates. Comput. Hum. Behav. **55**, 840–850 (2016)
27. Lim, M., Abdullah, A., Jhanjhi, N., Supramaniam, M.: Hidden link prediction in criminal networks using the deep reinforcement learning technique. Computers **8**(1), 8 (2019)
28. Lomborg, S., Bechmann, A.: Using APIs for data collection on social media. Inf. Soc. **30**(4), 256–265 (2014)
29. Mason, S., et al.: Electronic Evidence, Elsevier (UK) Ltd. (2012). Currie, R.J., Coughlan, S.: Chapter 9, Canada, p. 293 (2012)
30. Mcdaniel, M., Sloan, E., Nick, W., Mayes, J., Esterline, A.: Ontologies for situation-based crime scene identities. In: SoutheastCon 2017, pp. 1–8 (2017)
31. Mena, J.: Investigative Data Mining for Security and Criminal Detection. Butterworth-Heinemann, Amsterdam (2003)
32. Moore, K.: Social media 'at least half' of calls passed to front-line police. BBC Radio 4's Law in Action. (2014). http://www.bbc.co.uk/news/uk-27949674
33. Murphy, J., Fontecilla, A.: Social media evidence in government investigations and criminal proceedings: a frontier of new legal issues. Rich JL Tech. **XIX**, 1–30 (2013)
34. Nouh, M., Nurse, J.R., Goldsmith, M.: Towards designing a multipurpose cyber-crime intelligence framework. In: 2016 European Intelligence and Security Informatics Conference (EISIC) (2016)
35. Noy, N., McGuinness, D.: Ontology development 101: a guide to creating your first ontology. Stanford University (2000)
36. Oludare, A.I., Jantan, A., Omolara, A.E., Singh, M.M., Anbar, M., Zaaba, Z.F.: Forensic DNA profiling for identifying an individual crime. Int. J. Civil Eng. Technol. **9**, 755–765 (2018)
37. Pramanik, M.I., Zhang, W., Lau, R.Y., Li, C.: A framework for criminal network analysis using big data. In: e-Business Engineering (ICEBE), pp. 17–23 (2016)
38. Protégé 5.5.0. https://protege.stanford.edu/. Accessed June 2019
39. Recchia, M.: Court of Appeals Declares Facebook "Private Data" and Other Social Media Subject to Discovery, New York Law Journal. www.law.com

40. Turnbull, B., Randhawa, S.: Automated event and social network extraction from digital evidence sources with ontological mapping. Digit. Invest. **13**, 94–106 (2015)
41. Weimann, G.: New Terrorism and New Media. Commons Lab of the Woodrow Wilson International Center for Scholars, Washington, DC (2014)
42. Williams, D.W., Huan, J., Wang, W.: Graph database indexing using structured graph decomposition. In: IEEE 23rd International Conference on Data Engineering, pp. 976–985 (2007)

# A Prototype Framework for Assessing Information Provenance in Decentralised Social Media: The EUNOMIA Concept

Lazaros Toumanidis[1]([✉]), Ryan Heartfield[2][iD], Panagiotis Kasnesis[1][iD],
George Loukas[2][iD], and Charalampos Patrikakis[1][iD]

[1] University of West Attica, Aigaleo, Attiki, Greece
{laztoum,pkasnesis,bpatr}@uniwa.gr
[2] University of Greenwich, London, London, UK
{R.Heartfield,G.Loukas}@greenwich.ac.uk
https://www.uniwa.gr, https://www.gre.ac.uk

**Abstract.** Users of traditional centralised social media networks have limited knowledge about the original source of information and even less about its trustworthiness and how this information has spread and been modified. Existing media verification tools include websites or browser add-ons that are closed-source or centralised, or they do not include user involvement in the information verification process. In this paper, we introduce EUNOMIA, an open source, decentralised framework that aims at providing information about social media content and context in an intermediary-free approach and in a way that assists users in deriving their own conclusions regarding a social media post's trustworthiness. We present its components, how they interact with each other and how user contribution is key to its concept.

**Keywords:** Decentralised social media · Trustworthiness · Fake news · Human-as-a-trust-sensor

## 1 Introduction

Traditional Social Media has rapidly become a dominant, direct and highly effective form of news generation and sharing at a global scale, in a manner that influences, enhances, but also challenges and often antagonizes traditional media corporations. However, paradoxically, it has led to the further accumulation of power to a relatively short list of central intermediaries, such as Facebook, Twitter, Instagram and other large companies, whose practices are seen as increasingly invasive of users' privacy. Many users get the bulk of their daily news from social media. As news passes to users, the news passes through the hands of actors whose credibility and goals are unknown. Even less is known about the credibility and quality of the information cascades they trigger.

© Springer Nature Switzerland AG 2020
S. Katsikas and V. Zorkadis (Eds.): e-Democracy 2019, CCIS 1111, pp. 196–208, 2020.
https://doi.org/10.1007/978-3-030-37545-4_13

Ironically, "the most effective forms of censorship today involve meddling with trust and attention, not muzzling speech itself" [6], and it is already evident that deliberate misinformation, as exemplified by fake news, is not being tackled effectively by large intermediaries. Relying on large-scale detection of disinformation on third party professional curators (as in, OpenSources, Snopes.com, and politifact.com) would effectively introduce a new type of intermediary, while relying solely on static machine learning (as in, Truthnest and Fakebox), is unsuitable for the dynamic and extremely fast-paced information cascades of social media, especially as fake news adapts and spreads much faster than real news [7]. There is a need for an intermediary-free and democratic approach, where what is true and what is false is not left to third party experts or entirely on computer algorithms.

In addition, a series of new decentralised social media networks show that transition away from centralised big companies and other intermediaries to peer-to-peer (P2P) federated social networks is highly practical. For instance, the fast-growing Mastodon platform[1] has similar utility to Twitter, but is open-source and decentralised, and user communities are encouraged to set up their own server domains. Similarly, the Diaspora* platform[2] has a utility akin to Facebook, but is also open-source and decentralised, and the users can choose which server to connect to depending on each country's security and privacy policies, as well as setup their own. Intermediary-free solutions, such as these, are promising in addressing the concerns of users regarding ownership of data and visibility of processes but are not by themselves able to address disinformation. EUNOMIA adopts the same ethos with an intermediary-free decentralised solution, that will help users establish the source of information and the associated information cascade, and evaluate its trustworthiness themselves.

In this paper, we present the architecture and data workflows of the EUNO-MIA (User-oriented, secure, trustful & decentralised social media) project[3]. EUNOMIA will employ a decentralised architecture and a digital companion providing the user with intuitive indications of the content and context of the sources for defining user-specific trust criteria, and determination of the nodes (users and posts) along an information cascade derived by a machine learning approach.

Towards tackling the challenge of information provenance and veracity in social media, there are three primary questions that EUNOMIA aims to help users answer:

- Which social media user is the original source of a piece of information?
- How has this information had spread and been modified in an information cascade?
- How likely is it to be trustworthy?

---

[1] https://joinmastodon.org.

[2] https://diasporafoundation.org.

[3] The EUNOMIA acronym is after the Greek goddess of good order and lawful conduct, associated with the internal stability of a state, including the enactment of good laws and the maintenance of civil order.

At the heart of the EUNOMIA concept is the objective to provide users with the tools and necessary information to help answer these questions, where users are empowered to make informed decisions about whether they can trust a piece of information presented on a social media platform. Importantly, EUNOMIA does not aim to assess trustworthiness itself or to make centralised judgements on what pieces of information are more trustworthy than others. Instead, EUNO-MIA aims to enable users to conduct this task themselves, but more efficiently and effectively through the aggregation and formulation of existing information that can be collected or derived from social media platforms. Crucially, EUNO-MIA is strictly opt-in, which means that only posts of users that have explicitly opted in are considered. This is rendering the scarcity of information a key challenge in information cascade development.

## 2  Related Work

In this section, we introduce existing tools (primarily applications, browser add-ons and websites) that have been developed with the objective of providing answers to at least one of the aforementioned three questions. Human-as-Trust-Sensor (HaTS) is one of the paradigms employed in EUNOMIA, which involves leveraging human sensing capabilities for evaluating trustworthiness. HaTS typically requires two facilities: (1) a way to collect and structure data for human analysis and assessment, and (2) a way for users to respond to information visualised to them, for example by voting. Here, an information cascade provides data attributes for HaTS analysis to interpret and evaluate and attempt to answer the following aforementioned questions: what is the source of a post and importantly how its content might have changed. That is, providing post content metrics which users can assess to apply their own trustworthiness score to with respect to the information cascade as a whole, specific post content and the cascade source. In the scope of post content and reputation scoring, Web Of Trust is a tool that provides safety and security ratings for visited websites and search engine results. It is mostly based on user ratings, utilizing also some third-party trusted sources, such as phishing directories, and displays reputation icons next to search results, social media, and other popular sites to help users make informed decisions online. Moreover, Microsoft provides a plugin called NewsGuard for its Edge web browser, that uses "Green-Red" ratings to signal if a website is trying to get it right or instead has a hidden agenda or knowingly publishes falsehoods or propaganda, giving readers more context about their news online. To this end, NewsGuard relies on trained analysts, who are experienced journalists, research online news brands and check the validity of the produced news.

Media Bias/Fact Check is a large media bias resource that also provides Firefox and Chrome extensions which displays a color-coded icon denoting the bias of the page one is currently viewing, according to their analysis results. Existing platforms like Twitter are also working towards the use of crowdsourcing tools, as a part of the "battle against rampant abuse on its platform" [4]. Furthermore, WhatsApp provides a tip-line to which one can send forwards, rumors, and suspicious-sounding messages and have them verified [5].

Regarding text analysis and misinformation detection, TextBox and Fake-Box, are two tools created by MachineBox[4] that process text, perform natural language processing, sentiment analysis, entity and keyword extraction and try to assess whether news articles are likely to be real news or not. Users can interact with these services using a web browser, being able to provide the content they want to be analysed and view the results. In Table 1, we provide a high-level summary of the existing platforms and services which employ HaTS functionality to support the assessment of information trustworthiness. This summary evaluates HaTS state-of-the-art by assessing whether the capabilities implement source verification, information cascade discovery, and whether the system requires expert curation (or is crowdsourced) and if users are involved in the assessment of information trustworthiness.

**Table 1.** The current landscape of social media information verification market and where EUNOMIA sits

| Tool name | Type | Verifies source | Verifies cascade | Users are involved |
|---|---|---|---|---|
| https://fullfact.org | Website | ✓ | ✗ | ✗ |
| Truthnest[a] | Software | ✓ | ✗ | ✗ |
| https://africacheck.org http://politifact.com/ http://factscan.ca/scoring/ http://chequeado.com | Website | ✗ | ✗ | ✗ |
| aosfatos.org | Website | ✓ | ✗ | ✗ |
| B.S Detector[b] | Browser add-on | ✓ | ✗ | ✗ |
| OpenSources[c] | Database resource | ✗ | ✗ | ✗ |
| http://areyoufakenews.com | Website | ✓ | ✗ | ✗ |
| Check This by MetaCert[d] | Browser add-on | ✓ | ✗ | ✗ |
| FiB[e] | Browser add-on | ✓ | ✓ | ✗ |
| Official Media Bias Fact Check Icon[f] | Browser add-on | ✓ | ✗ | ✓ |
| Hoaxy | Website | ✓ | ✓ | ✗ |
| Fakebox | Software | ✗ | ✗ | ✗ |
| **EUNOMIA**[g] | **P2P plat. & digital comp.** | ✓ | ✓ | ✓ |

[a]http://www.truthnest.com/.
[b]http://bsdetector.tech/.
[c]http://opensources.co.
[d]https://chrome.google.com/webstore/detail/felmjclcjadopolhjmlbemfekjaojfbn/.
[e]https://devpost.com/software/fib.
[f]https://chrome.google.com/webstore/detail/official-media-bias-fact/hdcpibgmmcnpjmmenengjgkkfohahegk.
[g]https://eunomia.social.

Beyond the current state-of-the-art, EUNOMIA addresses a key gap in the landscape of the social media information verification market. Current offerings

---

[4] https://machinebox.io/.

cover only a small subset of the requirements that EUNOMIA is addressing. The vast majority are websites, where expert curators analyse a variety of sources to establish the veracity of claims posted on social media, in a manner that is not scalable and generates one more intermediary (the group of expert curators employed). The only alternatives that are available today are browser add-on FiB and software Truthnest, that are not open-source, decentralised or able to involve the users in the information verification challenge.

## 3    The EUNOMIA Concept

EUNOMIA's concept is based on a circular data-driven "**user involvement** → **provenance identification** →**trustworthiness indicators** →**visualisation**" approach. Data will be collected and shared in accordance with a security and privacy framework, relating to data analytics and the HaTS component, and then will be utilised in a reasoning phase in near real-time evaluation of information trustworthiness supported by machine learning information cascade learning and a user-driven assessment mechanism. Reasoning may be performed locally (on the users' devices) or remotely (on EUNOMIA servers), in a P2P form and in line with the philosophy of Blockchain, avoiding entirely the dependence on third-party centralised cloud servers. A digital companion provides both visualisation

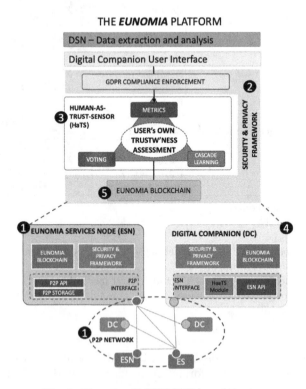

**Fig. 1.** The overall EUNOMIA architecture

of possible indicators of information trustworthiness and a facility for allowing the user to be involved, e.g., by voting or other means.

**Decentralised Platform Architecture.** EUNOMIA is planned to operate as a system of systems (Fig. 1) integrated with existing open-source distributed social networks by extending their application and server software, effectively creating a EUNOMIA-enhanced Mastodon instance and a EUNOMIA-enhanced Diaspora* pod.

The EUNOMIA architecture consists of five core components running in a decentralized manner: the first (1) is a peer-to-peer network between EUNOMIA Services Nodes (ESN) which support and synchronise data and service components across EUNOMIA (and act as service nodes to users' Digital Companion clients). The ESN P2P network enforces (2) a security and privacy framework which supervises a strict GDPR-compliant opt-in post data extraction policy for EUNOMIA users. The security and privacy framework directly enables (3) a Human-as-Trust-sensor mechanism with an integrated collection and extraction toolkit for analysis of social media post content and context, feeding output into a visualisation interface on (4) the EUNOMIA digital companion, where users are enabled to make their own trustworthiness assessment for post content and metrics. Finally, an immutable record of EUNOMIA user trustworthiness votes (relating to a users own trustworthiness scoring criteria) is stored and tracked in (5) a Blockchain infrastructure, supported and synchronised across the ESN P2P network.

## Architecture Components

*EUNOMIA Peer to Peer Infrastructure*
The EUNOMIA infrastructure will be supported by a decentralised P2P overlay network providing access to EUNOMIA services and distributed storage and peer-to-peer communication for two types of peers: service providers (EUNOMIA services) and users (EUNOMIA digital companion). The users will contribute with a tiny part of their storage to the network (i.e. EUNOMIA storage infrastructure). The P2P network will provide:

- **Open decentralised access** – any user will be able to participate in the EUNOMIA P2P network without requiring any central controlling organization
- **Scalability** – as the number of users increases, more users are contributing with their resources, consequently shared resources will be available for the EUNOMIA community
- **Resilience** – due to its highly distributed architecture it is possible to avoid the existence of single points of failure, mitigate and quickly recover from denial of service attacks

Third party EUNOMIA services can run as parallel instances of existing open-source P2P technology (e.g. IPFS). IPv4 and IPv6 internet connections will be the low-level support for the P2P Layer, which will provide:

- **Distributed Storage:** Allows to efficiently and in a distributed way store all the data about media and users. It supports the blockchain as an off-blockchain database, and benefits from its tractability and integrity controls. It manages EUNOMIA data objects inside the P2P network ensuring their isolation.
- **Messaging:** this service provides peer-to-peer messaging, will be used by the Digital Companion peers to access the EUNOMIA services residing on the EUNOMIA Services peers.
- **Network Management:** Will support the management of peers in the EUNOMIA P2P network, providing functions for joining, routing functions, locating, accessing and publishing services.

*EUNOMIA Blockchain Infrastructure*

The Blockchain infrastructure is able to cryptographically link the user posts to a Blockchain and create Blockchain-based signatures that can be used for verification purposes. It includes:

- **Data aggregator:** Collects and stores all posts meant to be published on the Blockchain.
- **Data formatter:** Each post is appropriately formatted. The formatting encodes two basic types of data: (i) the actual content of the post, (ii) any metadata associated with the post (e.g., author, timestamp, assessment labels, etc.).
- **Publisher:** Publishes posts in the Blockchain - this is the permanent storage solution being in accordance with one of the main features of blockchains. Considers a set of formatted posts for creating a single Blockchain transaction. Specifically, the posts are hashed and a single hash code (Merkle tree root) is created. This code can be regarded as cryptographic "summary" of all posts, which is published on the Blockchain. Also Publishes posts in Off-Blockchain storage - this can be regarded as a temporary storage solution that precedes the previous one. For this, the EUNOMIA P2P infrastructure will be utilised.
- **Logger:** Maintains records for each Blockchain transaction.
- **Transaction controller:** Controls the above modules focusing on the number of posts to be included in a single Blockchain transaction, and the frequency of transactions in terms of time.
- **Verifier:** Performs "proof-of-existence" for a given post (i.e., checks if the respective record exists in the Blockchain). In case of successful verification, it returns the associated metadata. This operation is supported for any storage solution (i.e., Blockchain or Off-Blockchain).

*Security and Privacy Component*

The starting point for the development of the security and privacy modules will be the privacy and security requirements that will result from the Privacy, social and ethical Impact Assessment (PIA+) and will ensure General Data Protection Regulation (GDPR) compliance. This will be complemented by the security and privacy requirements that should be derived from the overall operational model and exploitation operation model. These security and privacy components will provide the following high-level security properties:

- **Authentication of Users and Devices:** will provide user and device authentication on the decentralised peer-to-peer network, implementing key derivation mechanisms in order to allow a single user to hold multiple related devices and mitigate risks of the hijacking of the "user account".
- **Anonymization and minimization:** functions will be provided to support anonymised, but yet verifiable, voting, and minimization of data recorded on the long-term ledger to the strictly required to achieve the project objectives and in compliance with privacy and security requirements;
- **Confidentiality:** to avoid interception of voting and other user related information
- **Integrity checking:** recording of relevant information and ensuring the transparency of the voting process including integrity forcing mechanisms.

*Human-as-Trust-Sensor (HaTS) Mechanism*
EUNOMIA allows the active involvement of social media users, who can act in a Human-as-Trust-Sensor capacity: this is feasible through the use of the digital companion visualization component. A EUNOMIA user can create one or more unique IDs (and do so in an anonymous way or with a public name).

*Content and Context Data Collection and Analysis*
This component focuses on user-oriented and content-oriented analytics. The former relates to information on each user as a unique node of a network exhibiting particular activity, while the latter constitutes a user-agnostic computational analysis dealing with the processing of the posted content. In relation to content, EUNOMIA will focus on the text modality because of the availability of powerful analytic techniques that can be leveraged for trustworthiness evaluation. Yet, the platform will maintain a link between a user and the analytics extracted from the respective content so as to consider other modalities (such as image, video and audio) when similarly powerful techniques become available. Examples include encoding the user's activity in terms of posts-related metrics (number of posts/re-posts/comments, ratio of posts to re-posts, etc.).

The content-oriented analytics will be automatically extracted through the employment of several computational tools, focusing on the processing of textual posts. For this purpose, we aim to incorporate a series of well-established natural language processing and information extraction classifiers for shallow linguistic analysis (language detection, named entity recognition: recognition of main entities mentioned), semantic analysis (categorisation of posts as factual vs. opinionated) and detection of socially deviant language (e.g., offensive statements, hate speech).

*Digital Companion*
The Digital Companion is conceptualised as an application which will be able to be deployed on all types of devices, (desktop/tablets and personal) and featuring

a responsive web-based and a personal (mobile/wearable) app version, allowing for the active involvement of social media users.

**Data Workflows**

Here we provide early examples of three core data workflows which illustrate the user-driven functionality of EUNOMIA. Specifically, we describe diagrammatically three user functions which EUNOMIA will implement: (1) Creating a new post "EUNOMIA-enriched" post, (2) Information Cascade Query and (3) Trustworthiness Voting.

*Creating a new "EUNOMIA-enriched" Post*

Figure 2 depicts the sequence of actions that occur when a user creates a new post to one of the linked Decentralised Social Networks(DSN), using EUNOMIA Digital Companion (DC). The client, having been authenticated on the DSN, and using its' own Restful API services, forwards the new post to one of the Digital Companion servers (1). Through the Authentication Authorization and Accounting (AAA) Service, this post is added to a cluster group (based on cotent similarity) in the P2P database service (2). At the information cascade module, all the related posts with the same cluster ID are sub-sampled from the P2P service (3) and the results are forwarded, along with the original post, to the paraphrase detection service; it relies on BERT model [2] fine-tuned on the MRPC dataset [3]. The results may contain existing information cascade samples along with their corresponding bloom filters, or samples that do not currently belong to a cascade. In parallel with paraphrase detection, the post is

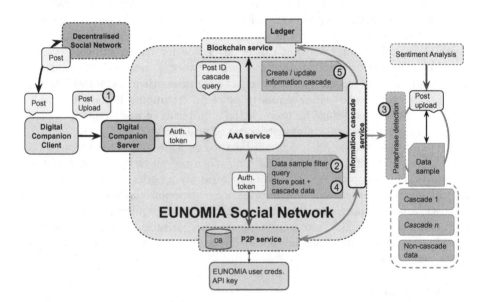

**Fig. 2.** Creating a new "EUNOMIA-enriched" post

also sentiment analysed, and the classification is added to the post meta-data. The overall result of paraphrase detection and sentiment analysis is stored back to the P2P database whether the post is added to a cascade or not (4). If the post is added to an information cascade, on the Blockchain ledger, a cascade ID is either updated or created if it did not already exist (5).

*Information Cascade Query*
Following a similar logic, one can retrieve the information cascade of an existing a post (Fig. 3). The user, using the DC client, makes a request to the digital companion server regarding a post from the DSN (1). The server, after authentication on the AAA service, forwards the request to the information cascade service. This time, a query on the Blockchain service is made (2) first, and the cascade information results are then used to retrieve the cascade details from the P2P database (3). The JSON representation of the results is sent back to the DC server and they are visualised on the DC client (5). It is worth noting that as EUNOMIA will implement a GDPR-compliant right to be forgotten (and right to privacy) policy, both information cacasde (and non-cascade) posts may be anonymised by users and also deleted. In the case of the latter, deleted posts will be removed from associated cascades, P2P databases and the EUNOMIA Blockchain ledger [1].

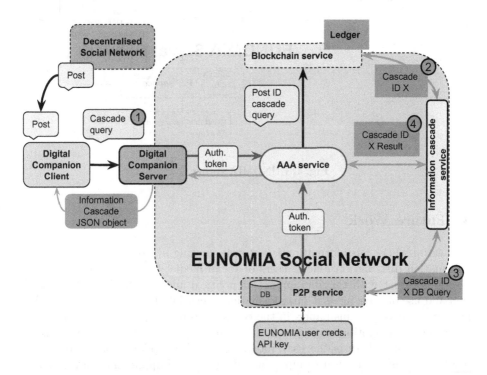

**Fig. 3.** Information cascade query

*Trustworthiness Voting*

Voting will be carried out in a fully decentralised way, where the request is forwarded to several peer nodes inside the EUNOMIA network. The vote results will be saved both on the P2P database and the Blockchain ledger before returning back to the DC client and presented to the user. This same information will be retrieved within an Information Cascade Query, alongside other collected metrics (Fig. 4).

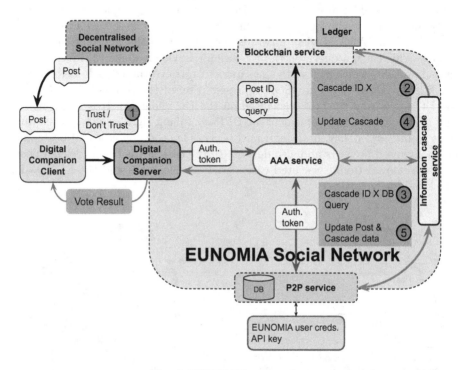

**Fig. 4.** EUNOMIA voting flow

## 4   Future Work

In a world where misinformation is not only causing a problem in the credible information distribution among users of social media, but is rapidly becoming a serious threat with tangible impact at political and societal level, the adoption and use of tools against misinformation is crucial. The work of EUNOMIA project presented in this paper, in the course of providing tools which can offer the arsenal for fighting misinformation, is at early research stage. What is of high importance here is the easy integration and compliance of the project's results such as the Digital Companion with tools and applications used by the social network users. The next steps in our research are in the direction of working with end users in order to identify the specifications which should define the implementation of these tools, in order to be able to extend the results of EUNOMIA to popular social networks, and provide the basis for implementation of similar tools, or porting of the EUNOMIA tools in these networks. At the same time, future proof design is of high priority for the research teams working in the project. In this course, a promising concept is the use of machine learning not for determining trustworthiness, but for assisting users in accessing information about a post that would not otherwise be available to them in a reasonable amount of time.

## 5 Conclusion

In this paper we have presented the concept of EUNOMIA, a Horizon 2020 Innovation Action project that aims at providing users information that may be find useful in assessing themselves the trustworthiness of content they access on social media. It mainly focuses on how information is spread in an information cascade. It is designed to be fully decentralized, utilizing P2P and Blockchain technologies, connecting with the existing open-source distributed social networks Mastodon and Diaspora*. We have provided the structure of the framework's components and the way they connect with each other to provide a modular system of systems. We have also shown the way information flows between these components allowing the end user not only be informed about the results, but also actively participate in the process.

**Acknowledgment.** Work presented in this paper has received funding from the European Union's H2020 research and innovation programme under EUNOMIA project, grant agreement No. 825171.

## References

1. Ateniese, G., Magri, B., Venturi, D., Andrade, E.: Redactable blockchain - or - rewriting history in bitcoin and friends. In: 2017 IEEE European Symposium on Security and Privacy (EuroS P), pp. 111–126. IEEE, April 2017. https://doi.org/10.1109/EuroSP.2017.37
2. Devlin, J., Chang, M.W., Lee, K., Toutanova, K.: Bert: pre-training of deep bidirectional transformers for language understanding. arXiv preprint arXiv:1810.04805 (2018)
3. Dolan, W.B., Brockett, C.: Automatically constructing a corpus of sentential paraphrases. In: Proceedings of the Third International Workshop on Paraphrasing (IWP2005) (2005)
4. Dwoskin, E.: Twitter is looking for ways to let users flag fake news, offensive content, June 2017. https://www.washingtonpost.com/news/the-switch/wp/2017/06/29/twitter-is-looking-for-ways-to-let-users-flag-fake-news. Accessed 6 Aug 2019

5. Ghoshal, A.: Whatsapp launches a tip line in India to battle fake news, April 2019. https://thenextweb.com/apps/2019/04/02/whatsapp-launches-a-tip-line-in-india-to-battle-fake-news-ahead-of-national-elections. Accessed 6 Aug 2019
6. Tufekci, Z.: It's the (democracy-poisoning) golden age of free speech, February 2018. https://www.wired.com/story/free-speech-issue-tech-turmoil-new-censorship/. Accessed 6 Aug 2019
7. Vosoughi, S., Roy, D., Aral, S.: The spread of true and false news online. Science **359**(6380), 1146–1151 (2018). https://doi.org/10.1126/science.aap9559

# Fighting Biased Online News: Lessons from Online Participation and Crowdsourcing

Himesha Wijekoon[1(✉)], Boris Schegolev[1], and Vojtěch Merunka[1,2]

[1] Department of Information Engineering, Faculty of Economics and Management, Czech University of Life Sciences Prague, Prague, Czech Republic
{wijekoon, shegolev, merunka}@pef.czu.cz
[2] Department of Software Engineering, Faculty of Nuclear Sciences and Engineering, Czech Technical University in Prague, Prague, Czech Republic
vojtech.merunka@fjfi.cvut.cz

**Abstract.** Online news has become a major source of news especially for younger generation. However, it is evident that certain media outlets report biased news. This bias can cause harmful effects on society thus democracy. There have been various attempts to identify and mitigate bias in news. At the same time various successful crowdsourcing platforms have emerged as many internet users are now active participants than passive readers. Some of these techniques have been already used related to online news sector. In this article we investigate how online participation techniques have been used in crowdsourcing and how lessons from crowdsourcing platforms can be used further to fight against biased news. New means to mitigate biased online news are proposed and discussed in the end.

**Keywords:** News bias · Online news · Crowdsourcing · Online participation · Media bias mitigation

## 1 Introduction

The same incident can be covered from different viewpoints by various news sources. This is quite natural. However, some sources can use this unethically to artificially plant viewpoints in the audience. This can be identified as media bias. Media bias is formally defined as follows.

*"By definition, the word bias refers to showing an unjustified favoritism toward something or someone. Thus, on a very simplistic level, media bias refers to the media exhibiting an unjustifiable favoritism as they cover the news. When the media transmit biased news reports, those reports present viewers with an inaccurate, unbalanced, and/or unfair view of the world around them."* [1]

There are various kinds of media bias identified by the scholars. *HonestReporting* has defined 8 categories of media bias as follows [2].

1. Misleading definitions
2. Imbalanced reporting
3. Opinions disguised as news
4. Lack of context

© Springer Nature Switzerland AG 2020
S. Katsikas and V. Zorkadis (Eds.): e-Democracy 2019, CCIS 1111, pp. 209–220, 2020.
https://doi.org/10.1007/978-3-030-37545-4_14

5. Selective omission
6. Using true facts to draw false conclusions
7. Distortion of facts
8. Lack of transparency

In another attempt, bias types are defined as follows [3].

1. Bias by source
2. Bias by placement
3. Bias by Headline or Story
4. Bias by Camera angles, photos and captions
5. Bias by labeling

However, bias exists in commercial media due to various reasons [4]. Media owners' political views and the demand for biased news are the main reasons as per the researchers [5, 6].

General audience is usually manipulated by media through biased news by employing above mentioned bias types. It is not easy for common readers to critically analyse and detect bias in news [7]. In their research DellaVigna et al. [8] present how *Fox News* affected the voters' behaviour in the United States of America. Hence democracy is directly affected by biased news. Biased news can spread in minutes to millions of people with the help of modern telecommunication technologies. Thus, biased news can bring great harm to people. For an example, biased news can make people agitated and trigger destructive events such as riots. Therefore, finding ways to mitigate the media bias is beneficial to the society as a whole.

Along with the success and popularity of Internet, online news gradually is becoming a major source for news [9, 10]. Recent study in United Kingdom has found out that online news shares same level of popularity as television news, while printed media has a huge decline of popularity [11]. For people below 35 years of age, online media has become the main source of news even surpassing television.

Researchers have proposed different approaches to tackle online news bias. However, in this paper we intend to discuss solutions based on online participation and crowdsourcing techniques. *Merriam-Webster* dictionary defines crowdsourcing as *"the practice of obtaining needed services, ideas, or content by soliciting contributions from a large group of people and especially from the online community rather than from traditional employees or suppliers"* [12]. As internet users have become more active and participative with Web 2.0, use of crowdsourcing platforms and techniques can be quite useful to fight against biased news.

This paper initially presents existing tools related to the mitigation of biased online news. Then online participation methods related to news sector is discussed. Next the lessons from crowdsourcing platforms are evaluated. New means to mitigate biased online news are proposed and discussed in the end.

## 2  Existing Tools

There are various approaches taken by scholars to mitigate news bias. Such attempts related to this study are discussed in this section.

*DiversiNews* is an innovative news surfing system which helps users to discover various viewpoints on a single news story, event, or issue [13]. News is aggregated real-time from different sources and then automatically clustered into stories. These stories are presented to the readers with interactive controls to filter and sort related news. Automatic sentiment analysis is also performed for each news article which calculates the polarity (positive, neutral or negative) and this figure is displayed in the user interface. This can be also taken as an indication about news bias.

In the same vein, *NewsBird* provides bias-aware news analysis using matrix-based news aggregation [14]. *NewsBird* is an opensource news aggregator which provides aggregated news on international topics. It gathers articles from *Europe Media Monitor* [15] and automatically group them into topics using Latent Dirichlet Allocation (LDA) technique. Then the articles are summarized and visualized in a matrix view. The main objective of *NewsBird*'s approach is to provide a broader view of the topics to the readers so that they can themselves identify the bias.

*NewsCube2.0* is another system developed to mitigate media bias [7]. It automatically creates topics based on contentious issues and then users can add news articles under these topical structures along with their framing metrics. So, the future users can get a diverse view about topics via many related news articles. As per the study, user participation and management of framing spectrum were the major issues they have faced.

Budak et al. have used machine learning and crowdsourcing techniques to measure media bias on political issues in major US news sources [16]. They have used *Mechanical Turk* crowdsourcing platform to classify news and identify bias in news. However major issue in this approach is that task doers in Mechanical Turk are not regular news readers with context awareness. Therefore, data quality is questionable.

A tool called *UnbiasedCrowd* is also built to mitigate visual news bias [17]. This tool supports visual bias identification, aggregation and representation of visual bias to users. It also enables activists to inform public, related to the identified biased news. The recruitment of activists for every biased news story is a problem and too much manual work is involved in this case.

*Blews* system provides a user interface with news articles and their emotional sentiment towards liberal or conservative [18]. They have utilized text processing and link analysis techniques.

*DisputeFinder* [19] is a browser extension which highlights disputed text in a web page a user is reading. This application uses a local database of disputed claims and run a text processing algorithm to identify the disputed text within a web page. This local database is prebuilt by crawling websites which maintain disputed claims.

Most of the researchers are in a view point that the effects of media bias can be minimized when the users are provided with more than one news article related to stories. In this case the user experience is enriched and individually perceived bias could be eliminated up to a certain extent. Scholars have also tried to quantify the media bias. The sentiment analysis and natural language processing techniques have been used in order to automate this, while in some cases expert knowledge is used. Even though this is a good place to utilize help of crowdsourcing, only few projects have used it.

## 3  Methods of Online Participation

There are various ways of online participation used in news sector. Main approaches are discussed in this section.

**Wiki Journalism (Opensource Journalism)**
Wiki journalism falls under the broad category of citizen journalism. Sometimes wiki journalism is also named as opensource journalism as it shares similar principles to opensource software. The main idea behind the wiki journalism is collaborative editing and sharing of news articles. Further the writers do not necessarily to be journalists but general public. Similar to opensource software, anybody can edit or improve a news article any number of times after its creation.

Ideally, wiki journalism provides a solid foundation to fight news bias. However major drawbacks of it are vandalism and authority [20]. However, wiki platforms have come up with ways to fight vandalism such as limiting features for newly registered users until they pass certain time period.

*Wikipedia* is the pioneer and the most successful in wiki journalism which was started in 2001. Then *Wikinews* has been launched by *Wikipedia* in 2004 with the objective of promoting citizen journalism [21]. Despite still been an active website, the popularity of *Wikinews* is questionable. Thus, the creator of *Wikipedia* Jimmy Wales started another website named *WikiTribune* with the aim of fighting against fake news in 2017. *WikiTribune* is not affiliated to *Wikipedia Foundation* and it is a for-profit site [22]. Further *WikiTribune* has also employed few reputed journalists as paid staff to keep up the quality of the submissions of its users. Therefore, articles edited by users must be approved/edited by the staff or reputed users before they become public.

In an interview with Seward, Lih [23] has mentioned that major challenge of *Wikinews* is the inability of general public to compile a news article quickly as par with qualified journalists with a strong lead and coherent narrative. Users do not get time to edit articles leisurely for near real time news and the style should be also appealing in contrast to the factual style used in *Wikipedia*.

But there seems to be also successful wiki journalism projects such as *Ushahidi* and *OhMyNews* [24, 25]. In both of these cases, paid staff members are utilized to verify news and finalize the publication. Therefore, to be successful wiki news site, it needs not only citizen reporters but citizen editors as well. Also, it is observed that special interest wiki news sites (focused on selected events or topics) have been successful such as *Ushahidi* as they could attract good set of contributors.

**Social News Aggregators**
General news aggregators fetch news from different sources and provide them in a systematic way. Some of such popular news aggregators are *Google News*, *Yahoo*

*News* and *Huffington Post*. In general, they automatically crawl news and utilize algorithms to group, summarize and visualize news for readers [14].

As a result of Web 2.0 (which is also known as Participative and Social Web), many social news aggregator sites have been emerged. Mainly, users of these sites can post stories (with links to news items) along with their comments and tags. Most of these websites are publicly accessible with a front page showing limited number of stories which are been selected by individual rankings. The ranking algorithm varies depending on the site. Also, it is common to classify and present stories under subtopics such as main, political, sports, business, technology etc. [26]. Some of the major successful social news web sites are listed below.

- Reddit
- Digg
- Fark
- Slashdot

*Reddit* is the most popular among the above with about 330 million users in 2018 [27]. *Digg* has enjoyed 12 million monthly users as per 2015 [28]. Large userbases of these sites enable them to deal with massive number of stories and utilize the labour of the crowd to filter and rank the stories to be summarized and presented [29].

News aggregators in general help readers to understand the bias of news stories by providing different sources [13, 14]. Social news sites further empower this with tagging, ranking and commenting news items.

### User Generated Content (UGC)

User-generated content is also known as user-created content. These can be images, videos, text and audio, that have been contributed by users on websites [30]. This also can be contributed to Web 2.0. Major news sources such as *BBC*, *CNN* and *TIMES Magazine* have already developed frameworks to support uploading of user generated content. However, verification of the content such as video/audio clips and documents is a difficult task. Furthermore, there are legal concerns over copyright and responsibility. Despite of these concerns, it is been widely used in mainstream media. The main advantage of UGC is they can be used to get ground level raw information and footage from places where journalists cannot enter. Therefore, UGC indirectly supports mitigation of biased news.

### User Comments

Another way of involving user participation is allowing users to comment on news items. Some time ago most of the popular news sites started facilitating user comments. But recently some of the major news companies started restricting or cutting off this feature [31]. One of the main reasons for this is the fact that users engage with uncivil and impolite comments on news sites which is very hard to moderate [32]. However, user commenting opens the door to readers to engage with the author and other interested readers and this can definitely help to resolve bias. Commenting facilitates a good platform for conversation and very useful for a democratic society. Unethical behaviour of commenting can be solved by utilizing best practices from crowdsourcing to a certain extent. Therefore, commenting can be encouraged than been restricted.

# 4 Lessons from Crowdsourcing Platforms

Two of the major successful crowdsourcing platforms *Wikipedia* and *Stack Overflow* are selected for this study as they resemble close relation with online news sector.

**Stack Overflow**
*Stack Overflow* is the most popular question and answer website which caters a wide range of computer programming topics. By 2019 number of registered users in *Stack Overflow* has reached 9.5 million with 205.2 million of monthly visits [33]. Therefore, it will be beneficial to learn lessons from this hugely successful crowdsourcing platform which could be applied for news sector.

A registered user in *Stack Overflow* can post questions and then the other members can answer or comment. Members also can tag and vote both questions and answers. Based on the contribution, user can earn reputation. And the level of reputation is used to allow more controls to the user. For an example, features like commenting is not available for novice users until they earn some reputation from their contribution [34].

A question in *Stack Overflow* projects easily to a news story submitted by a member in a social news website. Then the other members can tag, comment, reply and vote for this story. It is also quite similar to *Reddit*.

Tagging can be used to classify news stories into topics/subtopics with the help of crowd. It is possible to further extend tagging to mark the bias of the stories. Therefore, crowd can be utilized to identify the media bias.

Voting can be used to rank the news stories, so that in the end top news stories will be displayed in the website under subtopics. However, there is one challenge in this aspect. *Stack Overflow* does not have a time-value for questions and answers as similar to news stories. In contrary, popularity of news stories has a high correlation with the time. The algorithms should take this into consideration in their implementation. Searching, sorting and filtering features can also be provided to search for less popular or specific news stories.

Replies will enrich the user experience as it facilitates a dialog between interested parties and as it shares first hand experiences of affected parties. In *Stack Overflow*, members can comment on both questions and answers. Similarly, commenting on news story itself or on each reply can be facilitated. This will help to verify each activity (story or reply) separately by the help of crowd and consequently function as crowd-based moderation.

Nevertheless, moderation features are not available for every member in *Stack Overflow*. Moderation features also needed to be earned through contribution by the members. This helps to fight against vandalism and edit-wars. This is a key success factor of *Stack Overflow* as it could use crowd to successfully fight against junk, biased or false entries.

Even though only registered users can contribute, *Stack Overflow* content is publicly available for free access. This is another aspect of its popularity and success.

**Wikipedia**
*Wikipedia* is introduced in its own site as *"multilingual, web-based, free-content encyclopaedia project supported by the Wikimedia Foundation and based on a model*

*of openly editable content"* [35]. Currently it has 5,911,626 content articles and 48,358,579 pages in total. There are about 36.9 million registered users with 122,062 active users (users with at least one edit or other action in a certain month) and 1,149 administrators [35]. There is no doubt about its popularity as it is currently 10th most popular website in the *Alexa* rankings [36].

One of the major aspects of *Wikipedia* is having different language editions. Most of the scholars who wanted to come up with automatic bias detection could not achieve multilingual support. Therefore, *Wikipedia* model can be combined to overcome this barrier.

Another key success factor of *Wikipedia* is its very powerful underlying software named *MediaWiki*. It is a free and open-source wiki engine [37]. This software can be used by anyone who wants to try out wiki approach for journalism. Since it is an opensource software, customization is also possible to make it tailor-made to match the context where it is used.

Conceptually a *Wikipedia* article can be created and edited by any user. However, to fight against vandalism and content disputes *Wikipedia* has adopted a solid protection policy which sometimes limits user actions. This specifies a system of moderation and conflict resolution which also help against biased viewpoints.

Furthermore, *Wikipedia* has a comprehensive guide for addressing bias [38]. Readers can also complain about biased articles. Then the administrators can take necessary action to resolve the bias or temporarily flag the respective articles as biased until the issues are resolved. This community-based tagging of biased articles can be easily adopted into social news sites.

**Motivation to Contribute**

Success of any community driven website depends mainly on the user contribution [39]. Therefore, two main questions arise.

1. How to motivate the community to contribute?
2. How to ensure the quality of submissions?

Successful crowdsourcing platforms provide good means to answer these questions. In most of the cases such as *Stack Overflow, Wikipedia, Reddit, Slashdot* or *Digg* there is no financial incentive to the users for their contribution. Therefore, most of these platforms provide intrinsic motivation such as reputation, satisfaction and values for their contributors. Thus, most of crowdsourcing platforms engage user reputation systems where users are assigned with points/badges to value their contribution level. This provides the necessary motivation along with additional powers of control over the platform.

In the contrary, *Wikipedia* does not occupy such reputation system. Therefore, its success hugely depends on personal values. Figure 1 displays April 2011 *Wikipedia* Editor Survey with top reasons for continuing to contribute [40]. It is an interesting fact to reveal that 53% of users contribute to find articles that are biased/incomplete.

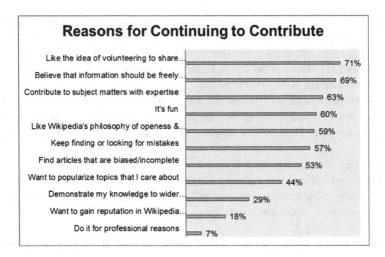

**Fig. 1.** Wikipedia Editor Survey – April 2011 [40].

## 5   Discussion

47% of online news viewers directly visit websites of broadcasters or newspapers while 20% find news via searching and 25% via social media [10]. Therefore, there is a huge chance that the online readers are to get affected with biased media. Hence providing readers with multiple news articles from various news sources related to an event can improve this situation. This has been already tested by some of the researchers [7, 13, 14].

Wiki journalism is a good candidate to provide multiple viewpoints on news stories. However, wiki journalism is not a feasible solution in this case as it has not been successful so far due to multiple reasons. Therefore, news aggregation is a good choice for this purpose. Social news aggregation is a well proven technique. However, crowd will not be exclusively enough to handle the large number of common news stories emerging. Automated news aggregation can be utilized to crawl news from selected sources to overcome this challenge. For an example *NewsFeed* crawling software has been already successfully used to crawl news for *NewsBird* [13, 41]. But in cases when specialized domains or topics are tackled, there can be situations that social news aggregation will only be enough for news gathering.

Identifying bias of news items and tagging them appropriately is another place where crowd can be helpful. The automated text analysis is not yet capable of identifying the complex scenarios of different kinds of media bias [42]. Ideally these techniques can only be used to identify specific kinds of bias such as framing but not all kinds. In contrast the crowd will need some time to act upon a news item. Therefore, in contrary to the automated approach of detecting bias, there will be a lag. Further if there is no user activity for a news item, there is no way of identifying the bias. This scenario still favours automated approach of bias detection. Hence, giving the users freedom to tag bias would be a good approach.

Vandalism and edit-wars can be moderated by involving proper good practices already proven in successful crowdsourcing systems. Giving users the opportunity to reply and comment will also create a good atmosphere to mitigate news bias. It will be possible to attach user generated content via replies to the stories.

Voting will facilitate presenting the top news as per the moment. So that the presentation of news items can be sorted according to the votes they receive. However, count of votes itself will not be enough to sort the news because the news stories have a time-value. Therefore, there must be a mechanism to incorporate this time-value when displaying the top news stories/items in the website. Finally, visualization of the news stories in the website is also an important aspect to consider. The usability of the platform will be a key success factor for community driven websites.

As a summary we propose a high-level design for a news crowdsourcing platform architecture with combining most of the above-mentioned techniques. The proposed new platform is illustrated in Fig. 2.

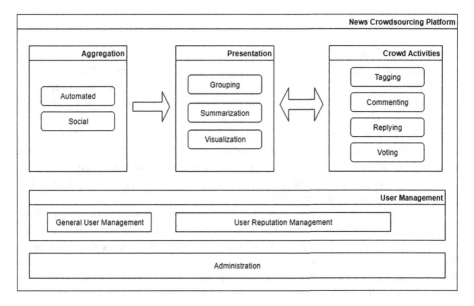

**Fig. 2.** News crowdsourcing platform architecture.

This architecture consists of five main modules namely Aggregation, Presentation, Crowd Activities, User Management and Administration. Social news aggregation in parallel with automated news crawling techniques is proposed for Aggregation phase. Gathered news items are then grouped, summarized and visualized for readers in the Presentation module. However, the tagging, commenting, replying and voting actions implemented in Crowd Activities module will dynamically affect the presentation of gathered news items to the users.

User Management and Administration modules are support modules of the whole news platform. User Management consists of two submodules General User

Management and User Reputation Management. General User Management should cover general maintenance of users of the news platform, while User Reputation Management should cover the mechanism of reputation handling of the registered users. Meantime Administration module should support the general maintenance activities of the news platform such as configurations, basic data etc.

This proposed architecture can be used for a generic news platform or a platform created for a specific domain/topic/event. Further research should be carried out in order to build a prototype news crowdsourcing platform using the provided architecture. It should be kept in mind that the success of crowdsourcing depends on user contribution; thus, attracting enough crowd is crucial. One way to improve the situation is to make the website freely accessible to general public.

If these crowdsourcing news platforms are successful, they will provide databases which can be used for data mining as well. As a side result this will provide opportunity to reveal interesting patterns related to news sector.

## 6    Conclusion

News can affect individual readers and then eventually society as whole. When readers are provided with biased news, the consequences can be even irrevocable. Therefore, biased news mitigation is important to preserve the values of a democratic society. This article provides insights in this regard from the best practices from online participation and crowdsourcing platforms.

Initially similar attempts to fight against biased news from other scholars were reviewed. Then methods of online participation in the context of news are discussed following an analysis of best practices from successful crowdsourcing platforms. Especially pioneering and popular crowdsourcing platforms such as *Stack Overflow* and *Wikipedia* were taken into consideration.

All the findings of this study were then reviewed and compiled in order to propose a novel news crowdsourcing platform architecture harnessing the strengths of online participation and crowdsourcing with special focus on online news bias mitigation. This high-level news crowdsourcing platform is yet to be realized. Thus, it is open for proof-of-concept. Major challenges of this approach are to tackle time value of news and getting a sufficient crowd base.

## References

1. Levasseur, D.G.: Media bias. In: Kaid, L.L. (ed.) Encyclopedia of Political Communication. Sage Publications (2008)
2. Benson, P.: The Eight Categories of Media Bias. https://honestreporting.com/news-literacy-the-eight-categories-of-media-bias/. Accessed 18 Aug 2019
3. Evaluating News: Bias News. https://uscupstate.libguides.com/news_aware/BiasNews. Accessed 18 Aug 2019
4. Herman, E.S.: The Propaganda Model: A Retrospective. Against All Reason 1, 1–14 (2003)

5. Gentzkow, M., Shapiro, J.M., Stone, D.F.: Media bias in the marketplace: theory. In: Anderson, S.P., Waldfogel, J., Stromberg, D. (eds.) Handbook of Media Economics, pp. 623–645. Elsevier, North Holland (2015)

6. Tully, M., Vraga, E., Smithson, A.: News media literacy, perceptions of bias, and interpretation of news. Journalism 146488491880526 (2018). https://doi.org/10.1177/1464884918805262

7. Park, S., Ko, M., Kim, J., Choi, H., Song, J.: NewsCube2.0: an exploratory design of a social news website for media bias mitigation. In: Paper presented at the 2nd International Workshop on Social Recommender Systems, Hangzhou, China, 19–23 March (2011)

8. DellaVigna, S., Kaplan, E.: The fox news effect: media bias and voting. Q. J. Econ. **122**(3), 1187–1234 (2007). https://doi.org/10.1162/qjec.122.3.1187

9. Kohut, A.P.R.: Pew Surveys of Audience Habits Suggest Perilous Future for News. Pew Research Center Survey Report. Pew Research Center, Washington, DC (2013)

10. Kennedy, P.J., Prat, A.: Where do people get their news? Econ. Pol. **34**(97), 5–47 (2019). https://doi.org/10.1093/epolic/eiy016

11. Oxford University: Where do people get their news? https://medium.com/oxford-university/where-do-people-get-their-news-8e850a0dea03. Accessed 16 Aug 2019

12. Merriam-Webster: Crowdsourcing. https://www.merriam-webster.com/dictionary/crowdsourcing. Accessed 18 Aug 2019

13. Trampuš, M., et al.: DiversiNews: surfacing diversity in online news. AI Mag. **36**(4), 87–104 (2015). https://doi.org/10.1609/aimag.v36i4.2528

14. Hamborg, F., Meuschke, N., Gipp, B.: Bias-aware news analysis using matrix-based news aggregation. Int. J. Digit. Lib. (2018). https://doi.org/10.1007/s00799-018-0239-9

15. Atkinson, M., der Goot, E.: Near real time information mining in multilingual news. In: Proceedings of the 18th international conference on World wide web, pp. 1153–1154 (2009)

16. Budak, C., Goel, S., Rao, J.M.: Fair and balanced? quantifying media bias through crowdsourced content analysis. Pub. Opin. Q. **80**, 250–271 (2016). https://doi.org/10.1093/poq/nfw007

17. Narwal, V., et al.: Automated assistants to identify and prompt action on visual news bias. In Proceedings of the 2017 CHI Conference Extended Abstracts on Human Factors in Computing Systems (CHI EA 2017), pp. 2796–2801. ACM, New York (2017). https://doi.org/10.1145/3027063.3053227

18. Gamon, M., Basu, S., Belenko, D., Fisher, D., Hurst, A., König, A.: BLEWS: using blogs to provide context for news articles (2008)

19. Ennals, R., Trushkowsky, B., Agosta, J.M.: Highlighting disputed claims on the web. In Proceedings of the 19th International Conference on World Wide Web (WWW 2010), pp. 341–350. ACM, New York (2010). http://dx.doi.org/10.1145/1772690.1772726

20. Lih, A.: Wikipedia as Participatory Journalism: Reliable Sources? Metrics for Evaluating Collaborative Media as a News Source. Nature **3**(1) (2004)

21. Bradshaw, P.: WIKI JOURNALISM Are wikis the new blogs? (2007)

22. Hern, A.: Wikipedia founder to fight fake news with new Wikitribune site. https://www.theguardian.com/technology/2017/apr/25/wikipedia-founder-jimmy-wales-to-fight-fake-news-with-new-wikitribune-site. Accessed 18 Aug 2019

23. Seward, Z.M.: Why Wikipedia beats Wikinews as a collaborative journalism project. https://www.niemanlab.org/2010/02/why-wikipedia-beats-wikinews-as-a-collaborative-journalism-project/. Accessed 16 Aug 2019

24. Okolloh, O.: Ushahidi, or 'testimony': Web 2.0 tools for crowdsourcing crisis information. In: Participatory Learning and Action, vol. 59, pp. 65–70 (2009)

25. Bentley, C.H.: Citizen journalism: back to the future. In: Discussion paper presented at the Carnegie Knight Conference on the Future of Journalism, Cambridge, MA (2008)

26. Steinbaur, T.: Information and Social Analysis of Reddit. http://snap.stanford.edu/class/cs224w-2011/proj/tbower_Finalwriteup_v1.pdf. Accessed 18 Aug 2019
27. McCormick, R.: Reddit overhauls its front page for new users and lurkers. https://www.theverge.com/2017/2/15/14632390/reddit-front-page-popular-change-new-users. Accessed 16 Aug 2019
28. Engel, K.: Digg: Its Rise and Fall and Rebirth. https://www.whoishostingthis.com/blog/2016/08/22/digg-rise-fall/. Accessed 18 Aug 2019
29. Bruns, A.: Gatewatching: Collaborative Online News Production (2005)
30. Berthon, P., Pitt, L., Kietzmann, J., McCarthy, I.P.: CGIP: managing consumer-generated intellectual property. California Manag. Rev. **57**(4), 43–62 (2015)
31. Green, M.: No Comment! Why More News Sites Are Dumping Their Comment Sections. https://www.kqed.org/lowdown/29720/no-comment-why-a-growing-number-of-news-sites-are-dumping-their-comment-sections. Accessed 18 Aug 2019
32. Naab, T., Kalch, A.: Replying, Evaluating, Flagging: How Users Engage With Uncivil and Impolite Comments on News Sites (2017)
33. Stack Exchange Inc.: About – Stack Exchange. https://stackexchange.com/about. Accessed 18 Aug 2019
34. Stack Exchange Inc.: Help Center – Stack Overflow. https://stackoverflow.com/help. Accessed 18 Aug 2019
35. Wikipedia: Wikipedia:About. https://en.wikipedia.org/wiki/Wikipedia:About. Accessed 18 Aug 2019
36. Alexa Internet, Inc.: The top 500 sites on the web. https://www.alexa.com/topsites. Accessed 18 Aug 2019
37. MediaWiki: MediaWiki. https://www.mediawiki.org/wiki/MediaWiki. Accessed 18 Aug 2019
38. Wikipedia: Wikipedia: Guide to addressing bias. https://en.wikipedia.org/wiki/Wikipedia:Guide_to_addressing_bias. Accessed 18 Aug 2019
39. Zhao, Y., Zhu, Q.: Evaluation on crowdsourcing research: Current status and future direction. Inf. Syst. Front. **16**(3), 417–434 (2012). https://doi.org/10.1007/s10796-012-9350-4
40. Wikipedia: Wikipedia community. https://en.wikipedia.org/wiki/Wikipedia_community. Accessed 18 Aug 2019
41. Trampuš, M., Novak, B.: Internals of an aggregated web news feed. In: Paper presented at the Fifteenth International Multiconference on Information Society, Ljubljana, Slovenia, 8–12 October 2012
42. Hamborg, F., Donnay, K., Gipp, B.: Automated identification of media bias in news articles: an interdisciplinary literature review. Int. J. Digit. Lib. (2018). https://doi.org/10.1007/s00799-018-0261-y

# Can EU Data Protection Legislation Help to Counter "Fake News" and Other Threats to Democracy?

Yordanka Ivanova(✉)

Law Faculty of Sofia University "St. Kliment Ohridski", Sofia, Bulgaria
d_mintcheva@abv.bg

**Abstract.** This paper examines how data protection can help to fight the root causes of "fake news", while supporting the exercise of other fundamental rights such as the right to free expression, non-discrimination, effective remedy and the right to vote. The General Data Protection Regulation (GDPR) and the draft e-Privacy Regulation are explored as legal instruments that could be applied against fake news, including during times of election. While privacy is by no means a magical solution to all problems in internet, this paper claims that proper enforcement of the EU data protection legislation provides a powerful instrument to address the root causes of fake news and reduce the extent to which personal data has been so far misused in the digital space, including for manipulation by spreading false information to improperly influence people's decisions or opinions.

**Keywords:** Threats to democracy · Fake news · Freedom of expression · Censorship · GDPR · Big data · Artificial intelligence

## 1 Introduction

Democracy in Europe, one of the fundamental values on which the Union is based, is at serious risk. Authoritarian regimes are rising in Eastern European countries such as Poland and Hungary, while Italy and other western countries face powerful Eurosceptic and populist movements, which are threatening liberal values in otherwise traditional democratic societies. The media freedom in Europe is estimated at its worst level ever [1] which hampers the ability of our societies to hold accountable the state and to provide a neutral ground for political debate and compromises.

These worrying tendencies are taking place in a global context where elaborate surveillance and profiling is performed by more and more states and by dominant private tech companies that provide the essential digital infrastructure in Europe and globally. From safe harbor for anonymity and freedom of expression, internet breeds now "surveillance capitalism" [2] where every digital trail people leave on internet is knowingly or unknowingly collected, analyzed and used to profile and open the internet users to microtargeted messages aimed at guiding their behavior or to take decisions that can significantly affect citizens' fundamental rights e.g. from rejecting job applications to predictive policing. On the other hand, the digitalization has also led

S. Katsikas and V. Zorkadis (Eds.): e-Democracy 2019, CCIS 1111, pp. 221–235, 2020.
https://doi.org/10.1007/978-3-030-37545-4_15

to profound societal changes with global platforms and social media becoming increasingly the public fora for our democratic processes such as news dissemination, public debates, self-expression, electoral campaigns. This has allowed not only privacy abuses in notorious scandals such as Cambridge Analytica, but also "fake news" dissemination at an unprecedented extent that have affected a number of national elections and other democratic debates [3]. Understood as all legal *"forms of false or misleading information designed, presented and promoted for profit or to intentionally deceive the public, and may cause public harm"* [4], fake news or online disinformation was recently recognized by the European Union as an *"acute and strategic challenge"* to democracies which needs *"a swift and decisive action at both European and national level on securing free and fair European and national elections"* [5]. But the fight against fake news proves particularly challenging given the complexity of the phenomenon and the risks that hard-core measures pose to the freedom of expression as they can inappropriately affect otherwise legitimate content, especially if taken down automatically through content filtering [6]. At the same time, it is also recognized that fake news dissemination does interfere with citizens' right to receive accurate and adequate information which is necessary for public debates and well-informed opinions and decisions [6].

In this context, the objective of this paper will be to examine how the newly revised EU data protection legislation can help to fight some of the root causes of fake news, while supporting the exercise of other fundamental rights such as the right to free expression, non-discrimination, effective remedy and the right to vote. While privacy and freedom of expression have been often considered opposing fundamental rights, which must be balanced in the context of one's reputation and private life, their mutual reinforcement is particularly relevant today as cornerstones of our democratic societies. As noted by the UN Special Rapporteur on the promotion and protection of the right to freedom of opinion and expression, *"Privacy and freedom of expression are interlinked and mutually dependent; an infringement upon one can be both the cause and consequence of an infringement upon the other"* [7]. The paper will aim to explore this interdependence and analyze the General Data Protection Regulation (GDPR) [8] and the draft e-Privacy Regulation [9] as legal instruments which could be applied against fake news, including during times of election, while also paying attention to the fair balance that must be ensured between the fundamental rights to privacy and freedom of expression.

First, the paper will examine how GDPR and the draft e-Privacy Regulation can be employed to address the business model of the global platforms based on data harvesting practices, profiling, micro-targeting and often unfair treatment of internet users which largely coincide with the root causes and the key drivers of the fake news' manipulative impact on users. Secondly, it will analyze when fake news dissemination can be considered personal data processing and to what extent data subjects can use their rights to deletion and correction when false or misleading information has been disseminated about them. The journalistic exemption under Article 85 of the GDPR will be also examined in order to reconcile the right to data protection with the journalistic freedom in a manner which can stimulate more quality journalism.

## 2  Addressing the Root Causes of "Fake News" Within the Global Platforms

As the European Data Protection Supervisor has pointed out, *"fake news is a symptom of concentrated, unaccountable digital markets, constant tracking and reckless handling of personal data"* [10]. In a similar vein, the UK Information Commissioner's Office's report on the investigation of the Cambridge Analytica scandal concluded that electoral manipulations have been possible thanks to the abuses of personal data committed by Facebook and its counterparts. As the report notes, *"we may never know whether individuals were unknowingly influenced to vote a certain way in either the UK EU referendum or in the US election campaigns. But we do know that personal privacy rights have been compromised by a number of players and that the digital electoral ecosystem needs reform"* [3].

Data protection legislation can thus help to address some of the shortcomings in the global platforms' business model structured around misuses of personal data which have also acted as the key driver for fake news' dissemination and a multiplier of their manipulative impact on internet users. These malpractices include notably the ubiquitous online surveillance, profiling, micro-targeting and the unfair algorithmic decisions which often take place in violation of data protection laws. The objectives of these malpractices to addict, "nudge" and guide the users' behavior naturally promote spreadable and sensational content by disregarding the veracity or authenticity of the information. The more viral the "news"/ad or effective to influence the profile of the user, the more attention is grabbed, the more profiling data is generated and it is the same profiling data and clicks, which enhance global platforms' power, knowledge and technology and generate profits [11].

It is thus suggested that proper enforcement of the GDPR and the quick adoption of the draft e-Privacy Regulation can significantly curtail the impact of fake news and address the global platforms' fundamental business model, which is part and parcel of the fake news phenomenon. The following sections will examine the key problems related to the business model of the platforms and how GDPR and the draft e-Privacy regulation can address them by imposing specific obligations on the global platforms and other data controllers.

### 2.1  Surveillance

One of the most rampant privacy interferences is the ubiquitous data collection and online surveillance of citizens, which takes place today in the digital space [2]. Both the Court of Justice of the EU (CJEU) [12] and the European Court of Human Rights (ECtHR) [13] have recognized the significant negative effects of surveillance for the rights to privacy and freedom of expression. Surveillance may not only have a "chilling effect" on citizens' freedom to hold opinions and exchange information, but it may also produce other negative consequences, if people's private information is not properly used or kept confidential, or if it is used with the intention to harass or discredit speakers, cause them harm or manipulate intentionally the audience e.g. by fake news.

**New Obligations for Controllers.** The GDPR has the potential, if properly enforced, to curtail significantly the current online surveillance with a number of restrictions and enlarged scope of application. Of key importance is its extra-territorial application to online platforms and other controllers that are not based in EU, but that offer services or goods to EU citizens or monitor their behavior, Article 3(2) GDPR. The protected personal data is also widened to cover any "personally identifiable information" through which a natural person can be directly or indirectly identified based on identifiers such as IP address, location etc. Article 4(1) GDPR. If not used for research or statistical purposes or made publicly available by the data subject, the processing of "sensitive" data is also allowed only if the data subject has given explicit consent or under some other limited exceptions, Article 9 GDPR. This should restrict the ever more intrusive online surveillance which allows controllers to infer such "sensitive" data about one's political opinions, beliefs, sexual orientation or health based on other indictors e.g. search engine lists, shopping behavior, Facebook's likes etc. [14]. Always when the processing activity is based on consent, the user should be able to withdraw it easily at any time which obliges the controller to stop the processing if there is no other legal ground to rely on. The conditions for consent are also strengthened as the consent will be valid only if it has been freely given, specific, informed, affirmative and unambiguous, Article 7 GDPR. This has already put into question many of the platforms' terms of use whereby the consent is bundled for many purposes into a single act or the user doesn't have a real choice, but is left with "take it or leave it". The recent 50 million fine imposed on Google by the French data protection authority (CNIL) signals how these new requirements will be applied in practice [15].

The draft e-Privacy Regulation also introduces important restrictions that are expected to reduce significantly the scale of online surveillance and regulate the use of tracking technologies to collect observed data e.g. cookies, web beacons, device fingerprinting etc. which can track across different devices. In particular, controllers will be obliged to make "Do Not Track" the default settings and use tracking only if the user has explicitly consented. 'Wi-Fi-tracking' or 'Bluetooth-tracking' are also included within the scope and the regime for cookies simplified, but subjected to greater control by users. Controllers will be also not able to rely on legitimate interests as a legal ground for processing in relation to the electronic communications which will require much more often consent to be sought from users, including for tracking or machine-to-machine communications applicable in the context of Internet of Things and geolocation tracking, Recital 12 draft e-Privacy Regulation.

## 2.2 Big Data Profiling

Big data technologies allow the surveilled information from different sources to be aggregated, compared and analyzed by algorithms which give insights to the global platforms, political parties and other actors why someone who has visited certain websites or liked a number of "Facebook" posts will vote or not for a particular candidate or support or not a particular action. Such predicative profiling performed by the global platforms is based on myriads of assumed personal traits and interests [16] and has been often used to "nudge" users towards particular economic or political decisions and guide their behavior [10]. The Cambridge Analytica scandal is a text book example how intricate psychological profiling can be applied to design tailored messages to influence people's beliefs or opinions and to launch viral fake news campaigns that could effectively swing public opinion or voters' electoral decisions [3]. As Mittelstadt [17] has argued, these new predictive profiling techniques disrupt the long-standing link between the individual, identity and privacy and allow for predictions and decisions to be taken at a group rather than individual level with much greater scale and impact.

**New Obligations for Controllers.** The GDPR has the potential to address this problem as it covers for the first time the profiling in Article 4 (4) GDPR, which tech companies and other actors have been doing at a large scale. Extensive or intrusive profiling would not be possible on the basis of the legitimate interests on which most tech companies normally rely as their interests will be overridden by the data subjects' right to privacy [18]. Even without sensitive data, extensive profiling will thus require controllers to seek explicit consent from the data subject [18]. The GDPR also keeps Big data analytics under rein as it maintains the "principle of purpose limitation" which requires further processing to be done only if *compatible* with the purpose for which the data has been originally collected, Article 5(1)(b) GDPR. Controllers should do a context-specific compatibility assessment on the basis of certain criteria, which as a "rule of thumb" must treat data subjects fairly and respect their reasonable expectations how their data will be processed [19], Article 6(4) GDPR. Article 29 Working Party (WP29) specifically considers incompatible the re-use of personal data where big data analytics are used for gaining information about individuals and for making decisions affecting them which must be done only where users have given their consent [19]. Sharing personal data with third parties within the big data ecosystem is also dependent on transparency and lawful processing given that users need to be informed how and by whom their data is to be processed and confidentiality guaranteed by all controllers, Article 5(1)(a) and (f) GDPR. The algorithms used for automated decision-making and profiling must also become more transparent as the controllers are obliged to provide users with information if they *"are subject to automated decision-making, including profiling, and, at least in those cases, meaningful information about the logic involved, as well as the significance and the envisaged consequences of such processing for the data subject"*, Article 13(2)(f) and Article 14(2)(g) GDPR.

## 2.3  Micro-targeting

The predictive modeling and intricate big data profiles are used to micro-target the internet users with tailored personalized messages and advertisements from commercial, political or other non-commercial actors that use the advertising services of the platforms as intermediaries often in an opaque for the user manner [20, 21]. The micro-targeting may consist in a more personal message to a segment of people sharing certain traits or even potentially determine the prices for products or services. It may consist also in how social media platforms determine which content appears on individual news feeds and in what order.

In the age of "personalized" online services some scholars point to a number of benefits of the microtargeting such as opportunities for engagement of new audiences, dissemination of more relevant and diversified content to individual users and voters, effectiveness and cost-savings [21]. But micro-targeting has also potential to discriminate, exacerbate polarization or social inequalities, dispatch public discourse and manipulate individuals by using their preferences and vulnerabilities, as evidenced by the effects of political micro-targeting or fake news on users. These micro-targeting activities may have little effect on some individuals, but may affect much more others. In this context, the European Data Protection Supervisor has highlighted *"the culture of manipulation in the online environment"*, be it as a result of the global platforms' business strategies or because of the actions of third actors seeking to abuse the platforms to disrupt or subvert markets, public discourse or the integrity of democratic processes [10]. As noted by a number of human rights NGOs, if illegal surveillance and profiling of citizens are stopped, micro-targeted disinformation campaigns would lose much of their alleged effectiveness and threat potential [11].

**New Obligations for Controllers.** While Recital 47 GDPR allows in principle direct marketing and micro-targeting on the basis of controllers' legitimate interests, the draft e-Privacy Regulation requires marketing through electronic means (sms, instant messages, notifications, e-mails, phone calls etc.) to be done only with individual's consent, Article 16. Online advertising and political and other non-commercial micro-targeting will be also covered in the future (Recital 32 and Article 4 (3) f), which will change substantially how advertisements are posted online. When marketing communications are sent, they should always indicate that the message is marketing, who is sending it and the right of the individuals to stop receiving similar communications. Masking of the identity and use of false identities, false return addresses or numbers will be also forbidden, Recital 34.

The e-Privacy Regulation will, furthermore, significantly increase the confidentiality of the online messaging services (such as Messenger, WhatsApp, Viber etc. mentioned in Recital 33) which will prevent exploiting the content of the messages for other purposes and curtail the usage of these communication channels for spreading fake news. All these changes should better protect the users from micro-targeting and provide more transparency about the sender's identity and the purpose which will oblige in practice the platforms to fulfill their commitments under the EU self-regulatory code of practice on disinformation [22]. Combined with the general obligation for transparency mentioned above, voters and users receiving ads/news should be informed if they are profiled and the logic of it and pointed to the possibility to object at any time to direct marketing, which includes profiling, Article 21(2) GDPR.

## 2.4   Unfair Treatment, Algorithmic Biases and Echo-Chambers

Machine-learning algorithms are already used by platforms to prioritize, obscure or block expression online or to take it down post factum, following reasonable, but also sometimes abusive reporting by other users or bots. On Facebook's News Feed, some content is highlighted, while other content is hidden or blocked [23]. Given that global platforms act as gatekeepers and key enablers for the exercise of people's right to free expression, they must also take due regard to ensure that internet users are treated fairly by the algorithms when they post or receive information throughout their infrastructure and when they are micro-targeted, as described above.

**New Obligations for Controllers.** The GDPR can help in this respect, in particular through the principle of fairness which is of growing importance in the context of the algorithmic society where services become "personalized" based on users' past behavior and algorithms often take discriminatory or biased decisions. Fairness is thus heavily weighted by issues of discrimination, bias and values such as equality, justice and due process especially where the algorithms make binding decisions [24]. The GDPR obliges, in particular controllers to take appropriate safeguards to regularly test the algorithms for biases and discriminatory results and to use appropriate mathematical or statistical procedures, Recital 71 GDPR. Factors which result in inaccuracies in personal data must be corrected and the risk of errors minimized. Fairness should also be taken into account when considering the manipulative impact and persuasiveness of practices and processing activities to avoid unfair consumer practices or compromise the integrity of key democratic process such as media pluralism, public discourse and fair elections. Holding the algorithms accountable and transparent about their decisions is also indispensable to ensure compliance of the global platforms with their accountability obligations under Article 5(2) GDPR and to prove that their processing is fair vis-a-vis the internet users.

Global platforms and other actors must also assess the risks for individuals' fundamental rights and interests as part of the data protection impact assessment (DPIA), in particular when systematically monitoring users or using AI and other new technologies, scoring or evaluating citizens or processing sensitive data at large scale, Article 25 GDPR. This should cover risks not only to the right to privacy, but also to the right to freedom of expression and information, freedom of thought, equality and non-discrimination, dignity, due process and effective remedy, the right to vote in elections etc. As part of the DPIA, the controllers must assess also the wider impact of the processing activities on social and ethical values [25], including whether the processing would cause any harms, biases, polarize opinions, create or exacerbate existing injustices or imbalances. This may also require addressing the filter bubbles to avoid biases and polarizations or at least ensure greater transparency in the personalization and provide users with the opportunity to customize their own preferences e.g. what information to be prioritized, from what sources in their search results or news feeds.

The new obligations for "privacy by design and by default" under Art.25 GDPR require also that any inferences with users' privacy and any potential negative impact on their rights and interests are minimized and appropriate safeguards envisaged, including by providing citizens with greater control over how their data is processed. Particularly important is also the obligation not to subject individuals to solely automated decision-making, including profiling, when it can produce legal or similarly significant effects unless this is necessary for the performance of a contract, legal obligation or the user has given explicit consent, Article 22(2) GDPR. Even when such solely automated decision-making is lawful, controllers are obliged to implement suitable safeguards under Article 22(3) GDPR, at least the right to obtain human intervention, to express his or her point of view and to contest the decision. In line with the principle of fairness and accountability, this paper concurs with the scholars who suggest that GDPR also provides individuals with a right to an explanation about the algorithmic decision reached about them. The right to an explanation of solely automated decisions has generated a lively academic debate [26–28] as it is only mentioned in Recital 71, but not in the core provision of Article 22(3) GDPR. It is also suggested that "similarly significant effects" could also concern discriminatory, biased or deliberately inaccurate or misleading information shown to internet users which can significantly influence their opinions or decisions on key issues such as vote in elections. It should also arguably apply to unreasonable removal or significant muting of content as such action may be equivalent to censorship, if the content has been otherwise lawful and protected by the freedom of expression. Thus, the data protection legislation could minimize the effects of false and harmful content being spread online, while supporting users' rights for effective remedy, non-discrimination, freedom of expression and information and the right to vote in elections.

## 3   Accuracy of Personal Data and Empowering Citizens to Fight Fake News About Them

Beyond addressing the root causes of fake news within the global platforms, GDPR may in certain circumstances impose also obligations to ensure accuracy of the information when it concerns identified or identifiable individual as interpreted by the Court of Justice of the EU (CJEU). In *Bodil Lindqvist* [29], the Court has basically concluded that any operation of loading personal data on internet must be considered a data processing activity by automated means falling within the scope of the data protection law. As far as the content of the information is concerned, in its more recent *Nowak* judgement [30], the Court held that personal data includes not only factual data (e.g. names, address), but also "opinion and assessment", provided that it is linked to a particular individual by *"reason of its content, purpose or effect"*. This conclusion is not questioned by the fact that the opinion/assessment is considered personal data also of the author of the opinions/comments [30]. WP29 [14] has also argued that the definition of personal data does not depend on verifiability and the nature of information is of no significance: it can be true or inaccurate, objective and subjective, including opinions and assessments. It is thus evident from the legal definition of personal data that statements posted online such as "All migrants are criminals" would be personal data of the individual who makes that statement, but not personal data of all migrants. The situation would be different though with the statement "All migrants in my building are criminals" which would be personal data of the author and the migrants living in that building as they could be indirectly identified. In any case, the purpose of the processing of this information through the platforms will be always to exercise one's right to free expression and individuals will be able to benefit from the so called household exemption from the GDPR, if they process the personal data in the course of a purely personal or household activity under Recital 18 GDPR (for example, when using social networking, which is often how posting or sharing of fake news happen in internet).

Irrespective of the household exemption for private users, GDPR does apply to the controllers or processors that provide the means for processing personal data for such personal or household activities, Recital 18 GDPR. The CJEU has confirmed this in its famous *Google Spain* judgement [31] where the search engine was considered a data controller that was furthermore not allowed to benefit from the journalistic exemption under Article 85 GDPR (for this exemption see more in Sect. 4 below). This broad interpretation of the concept of controller means that all participants in the digital ecosystem, including social media, website administrators and other global platforms, are obliged to fully comply with the GDPR and all the principles and obligations it imposes on controllers, including the obligation to ensure that the processed personal data is accurate and, where necessary, kept up to date, Article 5(1)(d) GDPR. This paper suggests, therefore, that albeit with different purposes and scope, the fight against fake news is aligned also with the obligations of the global platforms and other controllers under the GDPR which, inter alia, require them to take *"every reasonable step [...] to ensure that personal data that are inaccurate, having regard to the purposes for which they are processed, are erased or rectified without delay"*. To comply with this obligation, it is possible that the global platforms may be considered joint controllers in relation to the advertisements posted on their network under Article 26 GDPR [32] and may have to exercise some sort of editorial control over the accuracy and integrity of ads similar to traditional media as also evident from the Facebook's ads policy [33]. It is also suggested that the removal of fake accounts of users and bots is also supported by the obligations of the platforms to guarantee the accuracy of the personal data of their users which implicitly include the obligation to prevent fake accounts within their networks.

On the other hand, it is important to clearly highlight the role played by the global platforms as enablers for people's right to freely receive and impart information in the digital environment [34] and not expect from them to police and be responsible for the accuracy of the content of the messages posted and shared by private users who exercise their freedom of expression. While the recent judgement of the CJEU in *Buivids* [35] suggests that private users who make posts online to 'indefinite number of people' are also data controllers (potentially joint controllers together with the global platforms), this paper supports the opinion of AG Szpunar [36] who argues that an *ex ante* control of the global platforms over these users' posts is neither possible nor desirable given the limited *'responsibilities, powers and capabilities'* of the global platforms vis-à-vis the content placed by private users. Still, obligations to ensure accuracy of the content could be imposed *ex post* and this is notably done with the data subjects' rights that can be exercised directly against the platforms, in particular the right to be forgotten and the right to correction. These two data subjects' rights will be examined below as powerful tools for citizens to fight fake news about them.

## 3.1 The Right to Be Forgotten

Established in the landmark Google Spain judgement [31], the "right to be forgotten" is now reproduced in Article 17 of the GDPR, which allows citizens to request deletion of their data in certain cases. Given the tension between the right to be forgotten and the freedom of expression, para. 3 envisages specifically that this right is not applicable to the extent the data processing is necessary for exercising the right of freedom of expression and information. In this respect, WP29 has issued guidelines [37], specifically emphasizing that "any impact on freedom of expression and access to information should be very limited [..] and a balancing exercise would need to be performed between the opposing rights and interests, in particular, on the one hand, the interests of the data subject along with his or her right to privacy, and on the other hand, the commercial interests of Google and more importantly the public's interest in accessing information". Results should not be de-listed if the interest of the public in having access to that information prevails which requires a delicate balancing assessment on a case-by-case basis, using a set of 13 criteria, none of which is, however, determinant. It is important to note that two criteria concern notably if the data is "accurate" and "up-to-date" which means that outright false information should receive less protection and may be subject to deletion more often than accurate data. It is thus argued that the new obligations for the platforms to implement the right to be forgotten may be rather useful for people affected by fake news to ask the platforms to remove inaccurate content about them without the need to go through lengthy court proceedings.

As evidenced from the WP29 guidance [37], the right to be forgotten still requires a very delicate balance that Google itself finds sometimes rather challenging [38] given the risk of inappropriate restrictions on the freedom of expression, characterized by Balkin [39] as a form of "new school speech regulation" and recognized by Ausloos [40] and other scholars as a new risk of 'subtle censorship'. Difficulties arise given the distinction between "facts" and "opinions" which are not subject to verification [41], the legally protected "exaggeration and provocation" [42], the satire and parody as artistic forms of expressions [43] as well as the protection of ideas that are not only favorably received or inoffensive, but also those that "offend, shock or disturb" [44]. All these examples, even if containing false or misleading information, are recognized by the European Commission [45] as falling outside the scope of fake news and protected by the settled ECtHR case-law on the freedom of expression, if not constituting illegal content such as hate speech, incitement to violence, defamation etc. As Rasmus Nielsen underlines, "much of this misinformation might be uncomfortable and undesirable, but it is not necessarily illegal, nor necessarily a threat to democracy, and it is not easily identified in an objective way. Because it is not simply a matter of true or false – it can also be wild exaggeration or highly opinionated opinions" [46].

Thus, when carrying out the assessment, platforms must also carefully consider another criterion from the WP29 guidance [37], in particular whether the information "reflects an individual's personal opinion or does it appear to be verified fact". Any objectively non-verifiable opinions and information should be therefore protected and kept which is even more important when these opinions concern public figures or individuals playing other role in public life or represent criticism in the political domain. Interestingly enough, a key milestone from the ECtHR's case-law on the freedom of expression is missing from the WP29 guidance, notably whether the information would contribute to a debate of public interest [47, 48] which must be arguably also duly considered by the platforms and kept as a form of protected speech. Given that the social networks and global platforms act as "gatekeepers" and "enablers" for users to exercise their freedom of expression and information, they must also ensure that existing legal standards for free speech are respected in the digital space to avoid any unreasonable censorship and interference with internet users' freedom of expression and their right to receive and impart information, especially when the information is in public interest. Another very important criterion to be considered is therefore whether the original content of the information has been published "in the context of journalistic purposes" which presumably includes the public interest of sharing the news.

It can be concluded that the right to be forgotten may provide individuals affected by fake news with an out-of-court remedy, but its application will be very context-specific and will need to go through a careful review by the platforms to ensure that citizens' right to free expression is not unreasonably encroached.

### 3.2   The Right to Correction

Where the "right to be forgotten" cannot be applied as going against the freedom of expression and information, it may still be possible for people who consider that false or misleading information have been spread online about them to ask for correction. Article 16 of the GDPR states that, taking into account the purposes of the processing, the data subject shall have the right without undue delay to have inaccurate or incomplete personal data corrected or completed, including by means of providing a "*supplementary statement*". WP29 [14] explicitly attributes the right to correction not only to verifiable information, but also to opinions and assessments. It is thus argued that Facebook, Twitter, Google etc. should enable affected citizens to make a statement to be displayed visibly just next to the contested information in their platforms. Such supplementary statements resemble the right to reply in traditional media laws and could provide the general public with both perspectives to take an informed position about the truthfulness or inaccuracy of the information/opinions at issue, thus stimulating more diverse points of view and critical thinking.

## 4   The Journalistic Exemption from the GDPR as an Incentive to Encourage Quality Journalism

GDPR can also provide incentives for more quality journalism, in particular by subjecting media and journalists deliberately disseminating fake news to the full application of the GDPR and not allowing them to rely on the privileged media exemption under Article 85. This article envisages specific derogations when personal data is processed for journalistic purposes so as to reconcile the fundamental right to freedom of expression with data protection. The derogations may concern practically all controllers' obligations under the GDPR (except liability and available remedies) and Member States are left with a wide margin of discretion how lenient or strict regime for journalists and media to apply in their national laws. Recital 153 of the GDPR emphasizes also the need to interpret notions relating to the freedom of expression, such as journalism, broadly. This should be read in line with the case-law of the CJEU [49] which has held that 'journalistic activities' are those whose "object is the disclosure to the public of information, opinions or ideas, irrespective of the medium which is used to transmit them. They are not limited to media undertakings and may be undertaken for profit-making purposes". The journalistic exemption should therefore apply not only to traditional media and journalists, but also to non-professional journalists such as bloggers or non-media organisations which process the personal data in view of publications of public interests [50]. Still, the CJEU [31] has ruled that global platforms such as Google are not covered by the exemption as they are not processing the data for journalistic purposes - a conclusion which has been criticized by some scholars and which may need to be reconsidered if such status is accorded to them in sectoral media legislation.

Given the wide scope of the exemption for journalistic purposes, it is suggested that it should be used to encourage quality journalism and exclude in principle media and journalists which are deliberately disseminating fake news – an assessment to be made in accordance with established media standards and code of ethics which impose strict obligations for reliability of the information and good faith on behalf of the journalists. The UK Data Protection Act [51] seems to provide a good example how this can be done in practice. It envisages a simple exemption from almost all provisions of the GDPR, but only if compliance with them would be incompatible with the freedom of expression and insofar the data processing concerns a publication of public interest that must be prepared and published in compliance with journalistic ethics. In France, Belgium and Italy, the possibility to rely on the journalistic exemption from the GDPR is also dependent on compliance with journalistic ethical codes [52]. Such conditional exemption is in line with the consistent case-law of the ECtHR that gives strong protection to the media freedom of expression, but imposes at the same time important obligations on journalists, including the duty to act in good faith in order to disseminate reliable and accurate information in accordance with ethical standards. The journalistic exemption under GDPR can thus become an incentive for media and journalists to comply with ethical standards and disseminate accurate and reliable information, while sanctions imposed by national data protection authorities could be, on the contrary, the "stick" for those who without the necessary diligence and good faith create and disseminate fake news that affect individuals whose personal data has been processed in violation of the journalistic ethical standards and the GDPR.

Given the importance of this exemption for the media freedom, it is suggested that the European Data Protection Board should provide guidance to the Member States on the necessary derogations from the GDPR and closely follow the adoption of the implementing national laws. A more coordinated European approach should be also followed to integrate data protection into media's code of practices and ethics which can eventually contribute to increased media professionalism and reduce the propagation of false or defamatory information by European news outlets and websites. De lege ferenda, it is furthermore suggested to harmonize the media exemption at EU level in order to ensure a level playing field and stronger guarantees for quality journalism, while excluding media and journalists who do not respect ethical standards and deliberately disseminate inaccurate information.

# 5 Conclusion

This paper has argued that rigorous enforcement of the GDPR and the e-Privacy Regulation (once adopted) will address some of the root causes of fake news and reduce the extent to which personal data has been so far misused in the digital space, including for manipulation or deception by spreading false and misleading information to influence people's decisions or opinions. If the illegal surveillance, profiling and use of personal data is stopped, fake news will be significantly deprived from their manipulative effect on users and will not be any more such a serious threat to democracy and electoral integrity. The objective of the GDPR to ensure accuracy of the personal information processed within the global platforms and to empower citizens with greater control over their data may also provide effective ways to fight fake news, which however must be carefully implemented to avoid unreasonable interference with the freedom of expression and information. Finally, this paper also suggests that Member States could effectively use the journalistic exemption under Article 85 of GDPR to encourage quality journalism by setting conditions for media and journalists to rely on it such as the dissemination of only reliable and accurate information in compliance with ethical codes.

While the EU data protection legislation is certainly not a magical solution to all problems in the digital space and many more complementary measures should be undertaken to address the problem of fake news, it can still play a significant role for the protection of the freedom of expression and information. The importance of these fundamental rights will be ever more growing in the age of digital surveillance and rising illiberal movements in Europe and essential to ensure vibrant and stable democracies. As Balkin [39] puts it well, both privacy and freedom of expression ultimately concern power—how to prevent abuses and hold it accountable. And this statement is equally valid not only for the states, but also for the power of the global platforms who have become today not just dominant market players, but an essential utility without which no economic, political or social life is reasonably possible in the digital age [53].

# References

1. World Press Freedom Index (2018). https://rsf.org/en/rsf-index-2018-hatred-journalism-threatens-democracies
2. Zuboff, S.: Big other: surveillance capitalism and the prospects of an information civilization. J. Inf. Technol. 30, 75–89 (2015). https://ssrn.com/abstract=2594754
3. UK Information Commissioner's Office's (ICO): Report to the Parliament on Investigation into the Use of Data Analytics in Political Campaigns (2018)
4. Communication from the European Commission: Tackling Online Disinformation: a European Approach, COM/2018/236
5. Conclusions of the European Council from 13–14 December 2018
6. Special Rapporteurs on Freedom of Opinion and Expression of the UN, OSCE, OAS and ACHPR: Joint Declaration on Freedom of Expression and "Fake News", Disinformation and Propaganda FOM.GAL/3/17, 3 March 2017

7. United Nations Human Rights Council, Report of the Special Rapporteur on the promotion and protection of the right to freedom of opinion and expression, Frank La Rue, A/HRC/23/40, 17 April 2013
8. Regulation (EU) 2016/679 of the European Parliament and of the Council of 27 April 2016 on the protection of natural persons with regard to the processing of personal data and on the free movement of such data, and repealing Directive 95/46/EC (GDPR) OJ L 119, p. 1–88, 4 May 2016
9. Proposal from the European Commission for a Regulation of the European Parliament and the Council concerning the respect for private life and the protection of personal data in electronic communications and repealing Directive 2002/58/EC (e-Privacy Regulation) COM/2017/010 final - 2017/03 (COD)
10. European Data Protection Supervisor: Opinion 3/2018 on online manipulation and personal data, 19 March 2018
11. Civil Liberties Union for Europe, Access Now and EDRi: Informing the "misinformation debate, 18 October 2018. https://edri.org/files/online_disinformation.pdf
12. CJEU, C-293/12 and C-594/12 Digital Rights Ireland and Seitlinger and Others. ECLI:EU: C:2014:238
13. ECtHR, Big Brother Watch and Others v UK (App. No. 58170/13, 62322/14 and 24960/15)
14. Article 29 Data Protection Working Party: Opinion 4/2007 on the Concept of Personal Data, 01248/07/EN WP 136
15. Vinocur, N.: Google Fine Launches New Era of Privacy Enforcement. In: Politico.eu, 21 January 2019. https://www.politico.eu/article/google-fine-privacy-enforcement-france-gdpr/
16. Wachter, S.: Affinity Profiling and Discrimination by Association in Online Behavioural Advertising, 15 May 2019. https://ssrn.com/abstract=3388639
17. Mittelstadt, B.: From individual to group privacy in big data analytics. Philos. Technol. **30** (4), 475–494 (2017). https://doi.org/10.1007/s13347-017-0253-7
18. Article 29 Data Protection Working Party, Opinion 06/2014 on the Notion of Legitimate Interests of the Data Controller under Article 7 of Directive 95/46/EC, 844/14/EN WP 217, 09/04/2014. It stipulates that the data subjects' rights override the controller's legitimate interest in case of extensive profiling and consent is necessary as a legal basis
19. Article 29 Data Protection Working Party: Opinion 03/2013 on Purpose Limitation, 00569/13/EN WP 203
20. Rubenstein, I.: Voter privacy in the age of big data. Wis. Law Rev. **861** (2014). https://ssrn.com/abstract=2447956. http://dx.doi.org/10.2139/ssrn.2447956
21. Borgesius, Z.F., et al.: Online political microtargeting: promises and threats for democracy. Utrecht Law Rev. **14**(1), 82–96 (2018). https://ssrn.com/abstract=3128787
22. EU Code of Practice on Disinformation (2018)
23. Citron, D., Richards, N.: Four principles for digital expression (you won't believe #3!). In: University of Maryland Legal Studies Research Paper No. 15: 95 (2018) and Washington University Law Review 1353 (2018). https://ssrn.com/abstract=3155384
24. Dwork, C.: It's not privacy, and it's not fair. Stanf. Law Rev. Online **66**, 35 (2013). https://scholarship.law.berkeley.edu/cgi/viewcontent.cgi?article=3626&context=facpubs
25. Mantelero, A.: AI and big data: a blueprint for a human rights, social and ethical impact assessment. Comput. Law Secur. Rev. **34**(4), 754–772 (2018). https://ssrn.com/abstract=3225749
26. Wachter, S., Mittelstadt, B., Floridi, L.: Why a right to explanation of automated decision-making does not exist in the general data protection regulation. Int. Data Priv. Law **7**, 76, 78 (2017)
27. Selbst, A., Powles, J.: Meaningful information and the right to explanation. Int. Data Priv. Law **7**(4), 233–245 (2017). https://ssrn.com/abstract=3039125

28. Malgieri, G., Comande, G.: Why a right to legibility of automated decision-making exists in the general data protection regulation. Int. Data Priv. Law **7**(4), 233–245 (2017). https://academic.oup.com/idpl/article/7/4/243/4626991
29. CJEU, Case C-101/01 Bodil Lindqvist, ECLI:EU:C:2003:596
30. CJEU, C 434/16 Peter Nowak v Data Protection Commissioner, ECLI identifier: ECLI:EU:C:2017:994
31. CJEU, C- 131/12 Google Spain SL and Google Inc. v Agencia Española de Protección de Datos (AEPD) and Mario Costeja González. ECLI:EU:C:2013:424
32. In its recent case-law e.g. C-210/16 Facebook Fanpage, ECLI:EU:C:2018:388, the CJEU seems inclined to consider two entities processing data as joint controllers even if the they have rather different roles in defining the purposes and means for processing the data
33. Facebook's Ads policy. https://www.facebook.com/policies/ads/. Accessed 10 July 2019. It imposes restrictions on placing false and misleading content of the ads, specific rules for political and social issue ads as well as a review process of the ads
34. E.g. Times Newspapers Limited (Nos. 1 and 2) v. the United Kingdom (App. no. 3002/03 and no. 23676/03) the ECtHR underlined that, in the light of its accessibility and its capacity to store and communicate vast amounts of information, the Internet plays an important role in enhancing the public's access to news and facilitating the dissemination of information
35. CJEU, C–345/17 Buivids ECLI:EU:C:2019:122
36. CJEU, Advocate-General Szpunar Opinion on C-136/17 G.C. et al. v CNIL. ECLI:EU:C:2019:14
37. Article 29 Data Protection Working Party: Guidelines on the Implementation of the Court of Justice of the European Union Judgement on "Google Spain", C-131/12, 14/EN WP 225
38. Google's Privacy Policy, Frequently Asked Questions: How are you implementing the recent Court of Justice of the European Union (CJEU) decision on the right to be forgotten?. https://policies.google.com/faq?hl=en&gl=bg. Accessed 10 July 2019
39. Balkin, J.: Free speech in the algorithmic society: big data, private governance, and new school speech regulation. In: UC Davis Law Review. Yale Law School, Public Law Research Paper No. 615 (2018 Forthcoming). https://ssrn.com/abstract=3038939
40. Ausloos, J.: The 'Right to Be Forgotten' - worth remembering? Comput. Law Secur. Rev. **28** (2), 143–152 (2012). https://ssrn.com/abstract=1970392
41. ECtHR, Jerusalem v. Austria, 27 February 2001 (App. No. 26958/95)
42. ECtHR, Feldek v Slovakia hudoc (2001)-VIII
43. ECtHR, Eon v. France (App. No. 26118/10)
44. ECtHR, Handyside v. United Kingdom, (App. No. 5493/72) (1976)
45. European Commission and the High Representative of the EU for Foreign Affairs and Security Policy: Joint Communication on Action Plan against Disinformation, JOIN(2018) 36 final
46. Report from the High-Level Hearing organized by the European Commission on Preserving Democracy in a Digital Age, 22 February 2018. https://ec.europa.eu/epsc/events/high-level-hearing-preserving-democracy-digital-age_en
47. ECtHR, Von Hanover v Germany hudoc (2004)-VI; 43 EHRR 1
48. ECtHR, MGN Ltd. v UK hudoc (2011) 143
49. CJEU, C-73/07 Tietosuojavaltuutettu v Satakunnan Markkinapörssi Oy and Satamedia Oy.; ECLI:EU:C:2008:727
50. UK Information Commissioner's Office (ICO): Data Protection and Journalism: A Guide for the Media (2014)
51. Section 5 of Schedule 2 of the UK Data Protection Act 2018
52. Twobirds. https://www.twobirds.com/en/in-focus/general-data-protection-regulation/gdpr-tracker/personal-data-and-freedom-of-expression. Accessed 10 July 2019
53. Rahman, K.S.: Regulating informational infrastructure: internet platforms as the new public utilities. Georgetown Law Technol. Rev. **2**, 2 (2018). https://ssrn.com/abstract=3220737

# Author Index

Printed in the United States
By Bookmasters